ONE NEW MAN BIBLE
COMPANION

Commentary and Articles

Rev. William J. Morford

ONE NEW MAN BIBLE COMPANION
Commentary & Articles

Cover and Interior Page design by True Potential, Inc.

ISBN: 978-1-943852-54-3 (paperback)

Library of Congress Control Number: 2017941770

True Potential, Inc.
PO Box 904, Travelers Rest, SC 29690
www.truepotentialmedia.com
Printed in the United States of America.

FOREWORD

The "Body of Christ," known today as the Church, desperately needs a transforming work of the Spirit of Truth in our midst—the truth of God's inspired Word that's free from distorted doctrine and 'religious philosophy.'

Under God's gracious direction, Bill Morford has done a great service to the Saints with the writing of this companion book. The *One New Man Bible*, with its more than 4,000 footnotes, along with this supplement, is a tremendous help for clearing up much miss-interpretation, miss-understanding, miss-aligned applications and conclusions of biblical texts. Biblical terms that have been miss-understood by much of the Community of Believers are now made clear and understandable. It offers us more accurate knowledge of God's inspired message to humanity.

Within these pages you will find a treasure of knowledge and understanding of the whole Bible and, hopefully, a renewed love for the Truth of God's Word. It is one thing to read about truth, but quite another to understand it correctly for a righteous walk of faith. Consider this material to be a "magnifying glass" that exposes distortions imposed by religious tradition, compromise, and a limited defining of biblical terms. It is also a 'light' shining into our hearts to bring us fuller knowledge of Truth; it is our knowing the Truth that sets us free and our experiencing Truth that makes us and keeps us free.

We 'Preachers' and 'Ministers' must remember that New Testament Greek is largely a translation of Hebrew text and that our Savior spoke and taught in Hebrew. Bill has brought us back to the Hebrew roots of Scripture with its rich meaning, along with its Hebraic idioms not usually understood in both Hebrew and Greek grammar and 'English thinking.' We must also remember that the New Covenant is the Old Covenant Renewed. They are two corresponding parts of the "Whole Covenant" of God and both are binding upon the Child of God. This is made clear with Morford's One New Man translation and this "Companion."

As you ponder and savor this knowledge, apply it back to Scripture and discover a plethora of scriptural wealth that will advance your spiritual growth and walk in Christ. May you flourish with the rich treasures of God's inspired

Word, so it will become a living reality in your life by the operation of the Spirit of Life in Christ Jesus our LORD—our Adonai Yeshua HaMashia<u>h</u>. Enjoy It; I have!

Humbly Submitted,
Thomas A. McRae
Director of Intercessors for Revival

TABLE OF CONTENTS

INTRODUCTION

This book is a combination of commentary and explanatory articles to accompany the *One New Man Bible*. The *One New Man Bible* is an accurate translation of the Masoretic Hebrew text of the New Testament, an accurate translation of the 4th Edition UBS Greek New Testament text. For both the Hebrew and Greek texts, *One New Man Bible* translates words that many other translations either do not translate or do not translate correctly. Some are words that lexicons and Bible dictionaries miss. Rabbi Eliezer Ben-Yehuda, a conservative Jewish rabbi, was eager to help in this project because he said English-speaking Christians needed a more accurate Bible.

The goal in devoting so many years to this project is Truth over Tradition, since many Hebrew and Greek words are often translated by tradition. The *One New Man Bible* strives to translate all correctly, valuing truth rather than tradition. Several examples of the literal translation are given here.

Genesis 7:1. *And the LORD* said to Noah, "Come into the box, you and your entire house!"* Some say Go into, but God is already there and is also with Noah, so He says Come! The Hebrew text has "box" not "ark."

Genesis 12:1. *Now the LORD* had said to Abram, **"Get yourself out of here!"*** He does not just say Go. Two verses before this, the LORD* said to go to Canaan, but Abram stopped in Haran.

Genesis 15:6. *And he believed in the LORD*, and He counted it to him for acts of loving kindness.* Acts of loving kindness is the appropriate translation of Ts'dakah, but it is nearly always translated Righteousness, which is misleading. Ts'dakah means going beyond God's minimum standard, which is righteousness. (See Ts'dakah under <u>H</u>esed in the Glossary of the *One New Man Bible*.)

Genesis 37:3. *Now Israel loved Joseph more than all his children, because he was the son of his old age and he made him a long tunic.* "Coat of many colors" is from the Latin.

Leviticus 23:24. *"In the seventh month, on the first day of the month, you will have a Sabbath, a memorial announced with a blowing of horns a holy convocation."* This solemn day is called the Feast of Trumpets, but it is not a feast and there are no trumpets. Trumpet is from the Latin text. Shofars are blown to call the people to repentance in preparation for Yom Kippur. (See "Seasons of the LORD*" in Glossary.)

Matthew 4:12. *And when He heard that John was arrested He returned to Galilee. 13. And after He left Nazareth, He went and stayed in Capernaum, by the lake in the region of Zebulun and Naphtali: 14. in order that what was spoken through the prophet Isaiah would be fulfilled saying,*

> *15. "Land of Zebulun and land of Naphtali,*
> *way of the lake, beyond the Jordan,*
> *Galilee of the heathens,*

Others say Galilee of the Gentiles instead of Heathens, but Gentile is the Latin word for heathen, so in this Bible, Gentium is translated, not just using the Latin word. Gentium means "of the Heathens."

Matthew 11:30. *...for My yoke is pleasant and My burden is insignificant.* Others say His yoke is easy, but the literal is pleasant. Easy is the translation of the Latin text. Y'shua never said it would be easy, but His assignments, though often difficult, are to be pleasant: We are to enjoy ministry, loving what we do.

John 14:2. *In My Father's house are many dwelling places: and if it were not so, would I tell you that I am going to prepare a place for you?* The traditional Mansion is the Latin word, not translated, that means dwelling or place. Y'shua says He is going to prepare a place for each of us on His heavenly team. We will have work to do, not mansions to relax in. (See Mansions in Heaven in Myths.)

There are other words that are either not translated or use the Latin translation. Here are two: Red Sea is from the Latin and is the Greek name of the Hebrew name Reed Sea. The Hebrew word Anokhi is not translated, but it is very significant. Anokhi means "I AM determined to do this, so the *One New Man Bible* uses bold type **I AM** for Anokhi and has an article titled Anokhi in its Glossary to explain further.

INTRODUCTION

There are many other examples. This is Truth, not Tradition.

The Index in the back of this book is the easiest way to find the various subjects covered here because subjects are in different chapters. This is meant for you to browse through, and the subjects are divided into chapters, such as Myths, which is quite varied. Enjoy!

GOD, THE FATHER

Redeems, Crowns You with Loving Kindness and Compassion

Who **REDEEMS** *your life from destruction! Who* **CROWNS YOU WITH LOVING KINDNESS AND COMPASSION!** (Psalm 103:4)

The Kinsman-Redeemer not only redeems you, He encircles, crowning you with loving kindness and compassion. He truly cares about you and feels the same pain you feel.

Forgives, Heals

Who **FORGIVES** *all your iniquities! Who* **HEALS** *all your diseases!* (Psalm 103:3)

It is His love for us that leads Him to forgive us. That He forgives ALL your iniquities has great significance because the translated Hebrew word Iniquities means intentional sin that is forgiven once it has been repented. The word 'you' is singular, so this promise is for each individual. His love also leads to His healing power, in this case the word diseases means any incidence of any illness.

Pardons Iniquity, Passes over the Transgression, Does Not Retain His Anger Forever, Delights in Loving Kindness

Who is a God like You, Who **PARDONS INIQUITY** *and* **PASSES OVER THE TRANSGRESSION** *of the remnant of His heritage?!* **HE DOES NOT RETAIN HIS ANGER FOREVER,** *because* **HE DELIGHTS IN LOVING KINDNESS.** (Micah 7:18)

The iniquity that is pardoned is intentional sin. That is powerful! The transgression that is passed over is willful sin that is committed with the intention of angering God. How powerful His love must be in order for Him to be so forgiving. The remnant of His heritage is made up of those who have been faithful and **humble**. This comes from teachings about the remnant as seen in 1 Kings 19:18. Rabbi David Kimkhi, 12th and 13th century scholar wrote that the Hebrew Scriptures frequently use Humble to "denote the faithful minority in Israel who remained staunch throughout the national trials and did not yield to the pressure of the nations among whom they were scattered." There are about two dozen verses with this reference, but they are hidden in most English translations because the Hebrew word for humble, anav, is translated into different English words such as poor, meek, or lowly, in addition to humble.

Some of the verses where anav refers to the remnant are: *He will guide the* **humble** *in judgment and He will teach the* **humble** *His Way.* (Psalm 25:9) *But the* **humble** *will inherit the earth* (Matthew 5:5) *and will delight themselves in the abundance of Shalom.* (Psalm 37:11) *You caused judgment to be heard from heaven; the earth was awed and was still, 10. when God rose to judgment, to save all the* **humble** *of the earth. Selah.* (Psalm 76:9,10) *Surely He scorns the scorners, but He gives grace to the* **humble**. (Proverbs 3:34) *The* **humble** *also will increase their joy in the LORD*, and the* **humble** *among men will rejoice enthusiastically in the Holy One of Israel.* (Isaiah 29:19) *The Spirit of Adonai, the LORD*, is upon me, because the LORD* has anointed me to preach Good News to the* **humble**. (Matthew 5:3) *He has sent me to bind up the broken-hearted, to proclaim liberty to the captives, and opening of eyes* (Isaiah 42:7) *for those who are bound,* (Isaiah 61:1) *Seek the LORD*, all you* **humble** *of the earth who have done His ordinance! Seek righteousness!* **Seek humility!** *It may be you will be hidden on the Day of the LORD's* anger* (Zephaniah 2:3).

Whenever you see Humble, know that you can substitute Repentant.

Often Anav is translated as meek, but meek has a different connotation today; meek now relates to low self-worth, a great lack of confidence. To be humble is to be without pride—but at the same time—to have confidence, to know who you are in the Lord. Moses was the most humble of his day, but he was not afraid to argue with God.

God's Love, Mercy, and Grace are shown dramatically in the transforming power of our Heavenly Father.

Saul Persecutes the Congregation
Acts 8:1b. *And there was in that day a great persecution against the congregation in Jerusalem, and all except the apostles were scattered throughout the regions of Judea and Samaria. 2. And devout men buried Stephen and they made great lamenting over him. 3. And Saul was damaging the congregation by entering their houses, dragging away and giving men and women over to prison.*

Y'shua Summons Saul
Acts 9:1. *And Saul, still breathing threat and murder among the disciples of the Lord, when he went to the High Priest, 2. asked from him letters to the synagogues in Damascus, to the end that if he would find any who were of the Way, both men and women, he would lead them bound to Jerusalem. 3. And it happened while he was going as he drew near to Damascus, a light from heaven suddenly shone around him 4. and as he fell to the ground he heard a voice saying to him, "Saul. Saul! Why are you persecuting Me?" 5. And he said, "Who are You, Lord?" And He said, "I AM Y'shua Whom you are persecuting: 6. but you must now rise and enter the city and it will be told to you what is necessary for you to do." 7. And the men traveling with him had stood speechless, hearing the voice on the one hand but on the other hand not seeing anyone. 8. Then Saul got up from the ground, but when he opened his eyes he was not seeing anything: and taking him by the hand they were leading him to Damascus. 9. And he was without sight three days and he was neither eating nor drinking.*

Acts 9:10. *And there was a certain disciple in Damascus named Ananias, and the Lord said to him in a vision, "Ananias." And he said, "Here I am, Lord." 11. Then the Lord said to him, "When you get up you must be going to the street called Straight and you must at once seek in the house of Judas someone named Saul of Tarsus: for behold he is praying 12. and he saw in a vision a man named Ananias who had entered and after he laid his hands on him then he would regain his sight." 13. But Ananias answered, "Lord, I have heard from many about this man who did evil to Your saints in Jerusalem: 14. and here he has authority from the high priests to bind all those who call on Your name." 15. Then the Lord said to him, "You must be going, because this one is a chosen vessel for Me, to carry My name before heathens and even kings and children of Israel: 16. for I shall show him how much it is necessary for him to suffer on behalf of My name." 17. Then Ananias left and entered the house and when he placed his hands on him said,*

"Saul, brother, the Lord has sent me, Y'shua the One Who set upon you on the way while you were coming, so that you would regain your sight and you would be filled with the Holy Spirit." 18. And immediately there fell away from his eyes something like scales, and he regained sight and then when he got up he immersed 19. and when he took food he regained strength.

Saul Preaches at Damascus
And he was with the disciples in Damascus some days 20. and right away he preached Y'shua in the synagogues, that He was the Son of God. 21. And all those who heard were amazed and were saying, "Is this not the one who devastated those who called on this name in Jerusalem, and has he not come here for this, so that after he bound them he could lead them to the high priests?" 22. And Saul was becoming stronger and threw the Jewish people living in Damascus into dismay by proving that Y'shua was the Messiah.

Saul Escapes from the Jewish Mob
Acts 9:23. *And when many days had passed, the Jewish leaders plotted to kill him: 24. but their plot was known by Saul. And they were even watching the gates both day and night so they could kill him: 25. so his disciples, having taken him by night, let him down, having lowered him through the wall in a hamper.*

Saul in Jerusalem
Acts 9:26. *And when he arrived in Jerusalem he was trying to join the disciples, but they were all afraid of him, not believing that he was a disciple. 27. But then Barnabas took hold of him and led him to the apostles and he related to them how on the road he saw the Lord and that He spoke to him and how in Damascus he spoke openly in the name of Y'shua. 28. And he went in and out among them at Jerusalem, speaking openly in the name of the Lord, 29. and he was speaking and debating with the Hellenists, and they were trying to kill him. 30. But when the brothers found out they led him down to Caesarea and they sent him out to Tarsus.*

Saul Grows into His Apostolic Role
Acts 9:31. *Then in fact the congregation throughout the whole of Judea and Galilee and Samaria was having peace, being built up and going in the reverence of the Lord and it was being filled with people in the comfort of the Holy Spirit.*

Saul then went on to be the strongest and most prolific apostle who wrote much of the New Testament, having been transformed by **God's Mercy, Love, and Grace**. He acquired personal knowledge of Him, in place of religious knowledge, something we all need to do. Paul was determined to seek loving kindness, judgment, and acts of loving kindness, and to imitate our loving God.

Death is Destroyed by the Living God in the Person of Y'shua:

Isaiah 25:6. *And on this mountain the LORD* of Hosts will make a feast of fat things for all people, a feast of wines on the lees, of fat things full of marrow, of wines on well refined lees. 7. And on this mountain He will destroy the face of the covering cast over all peoples, and the veil that is spread over all nations. 8. **He will destroy death forever and Adonai, the LORD*, will wipe away tears from all faces.***

The fat things are fat from olive oil, so these are delicacies, like date cakes. The wine is aged.

The covering and the veil prevented the heathens from seeing and committing to the Most High God. (See Genesis 48:19; Romans 11:25.)

Hosea 13:12. *The iniquity of Ephraim is bound up, his sin is hidden. 13. Sorrows of a travailing woman will come upon him, he is an unwise son, for he should not stay long in the place of the breaking forth of children. 14. I, (Y'shua), **shall ransom them from the power of sheol. I shall redeem them from death! O death, where are your plagues? O grave, where is your destruction?** Repentance will be hidden from My eyes.*

That last statement is God's answer for the backsliders of the Book of Hosea, answering the questions of verse 14. The answers for those who walk in repentance with the God of Abraham, Isaac, and Jacob are Yes and Amen! To those same questions, as Paul makes clear in 1 Corinthians 15:50–58.

1 Corinthians 15:50. *But I say this, brothers, that flesh and blood are not able to inherit the Kingdom of God, nor does corruption inherit incorruption. 51. Behold I am telling you a mystery: we will not all be asleep in death, but we will all be transformed, 52. in a moment, in a twinkling of an eye, at the last shofar: for a shofar will sound and the dead will be raised incorruptible and we will be transformed. (Isaiah 26:19; Daniel 12:13; Revelation 20:5) 53. For it is necessary to*

clothe this corruptible with the incorruptible and to clothe this mortal with the immortal. 54. And when this mortal will be clothed immortal and this corruptible will be clothed incorruptible then the written word will happen,

> *"Death was swallowed up in victory."*
> *55. Where, O Death, is your victory?*
> *Where, O Death, is your sting?"*

56. But sin is the sting of death, and the power of sin is taken from the Torah (Teaching): 57. but thanks to God, to the One Who gives us victory through our Lord Y'shua Messiah. 58. Thus, my beloved brothers, you must continually be steadfast, immovable, abounding in the work of the Lord always, since you have known that your labor is not without result in the Lord.

This adds up to **Eternal Life, with the Destruction of Death** for the repentant.

El Shaddai, commonly translated **God Almighty**, speaks of the awesome power of our God. Nothing is too difficult for Him, too hard for Him. His arm is never too short. El Shaddai is introduced in Genesis 17:1.

Genesis 17:1. A*nd when Abram was ninety-nine years old, the LORD* appeared to Abram, and said to him, "**I AM Almighty God!** Walk before Me and be innocent. 2. And I will give My covenant between Me and you and will multiply you exceedingly." 3. And Abram fell on his face and God talked with him saying, 4. "As for Me, behold, My covenant is with you, and you will be a father of many nations."*

The root word of Shaddai is Shadad, meaning to "deal violently with." Some references incorrectly relate to Shad, the female breast, but there is no relationship between Shaddai and Shad. The doubling of the letter D in Shaddai ties Shaddai to Shadad. Shadad is written Sh-D-D in Hebrew, where the vowels are placed beneath the letters.

Genesis 18:14. ***Is anything too hard for the LORD*?*** (Jeremiah 32:17; Matthew 19:26; Luke 1:37) *At the time appointed I shall return to you, about this time next year, and Sarah will have a son."*

Jeremiah 32:16. *Now when I had delivered the deed of the purchase to Baruch the son of Neriah, I prayed to the LORD* saying, 17. Ah Adonai, LORD*! Behold, You have made the heavens and the earth by your great power and outstretched arm,* **there is nothing too hard for You.**

Luke 1:36. *And behold your kin Elizabeth has also conceived a son in her old age and this is her sixth month from her being called barren: 37. because* **with God nothing is impossible.**" (Genesis 18:14; Jeremiah 32:17,27; Job 42:2) *38. And Miriam said, "Behold the servant of the Lord: may it be according to your word." Then the angel left from her.*

Our God is an awesome God! Nothing is too difficult or too hard for Him! He is almighty!

Throne of Glory is the throne of the One and Only Living God! His throne is described several times in Scripture.

1 Samuel 2:8. *He raises up the poor out of the dust and lifts up the beggar from the dunghill, to set them among princes and to make them inherit the* **Throne of Glory***, for the pillars of the earth are the LORD's* and He has set the world upon them.*

Jeremiah 14:21. **Do not abhor us!** *For Your name's sake,* **Do not disgrace the Throne of Your Glory! Remember! Do not break Your covenant with us!**

Matthew 19:28. *And Y'shua said to them, "Truly I say to you that you who follow Me, in the restoration of all things when the Son of Man would sit upon the* **Throne of His Glory***, then you will be seated upon twelve thrones judging the twelve tribes of Israel.*

Matthew 25:31. *"And when the Son of Man would come in His glory and all the angels with Him, (Deuteronomy 33:2) then He will sit upon the* **Throne of His Glory***: 32. and all the multitudes will be gathered in front of Him, and He will separate them from one another, as the shepherd separates the sheep from the goats, 33. then indeed He will place the sheep on His right hand, but the goats on His left. 34. Then the King will say to those on His right hand, 'Come, the blessed of My Father, you must now inherit what has been prepared for you in the kingdom from the foundation of the world.*

The Heavenly Throne is made of Glory! There is only One **Throne of Glory**. There is only One Throne for the Only God.

Isaiah 6:1. *In the year that king Uzziah died I saw the Lord sitting on a **Throne**, high and lifted up, and His train filled the palace.*

There is only one throne, only One God. Y'shua said, "The Father and I are One!"

John 10:27. *My sheep hear My voice and I know them and they are following Me, 28. and I am giving them eternal life, and they would not ever die and no one is able to seize them from My hand. 29. My Father Who has given them to Me is greater than all, and no one is able to seize them from the hand of the Father. 30. **We, the Father and I, are One.***"

What Does God Require? Moses tells us in very direct terms, so there is no excuse of not knowing.

Deuteronomy10:12. *"And now, Israel, what does the LORD* your God ask of you, but to **revere the LORD* your God, to walk in all His Ways**, to **love Him**, and to **serve the LORD* your God with all your heart and with your entire being**, 13. to **keep the commandments of the LORD* and His statutes**, which I command you this day for your good?* (Micah 6:8) *14. Behold, the heaven and the heaven of heavens are the LORD's*; your God, the earth also, with all that is in it. 15. Only the LORD* had a delight in your fathers to love them and He chose their seed after them, above all people, as at this day. 16. Circumcise therefore the foreskin of your heart, and no longer be stiff necked. 17. For the LORD* your God is God of gods and Lord of lords, a great, a mighty, and an awesome God, Who does not show favoritism or take a bribe, 18. executing judgment for the fatherless and widow, and loving the stranger, in giving him food and clothing. 19. Therefore you will love the stranger, for you were strangers in the land of Egypt. 20. You will revere the LORD* your God. You will serve Him and you will cleave to Him and swear by His name. 21. He is your praise and He is your God, Who has done these great and awesome things for you, which your eyes have seen. 22. Your fathers went down to Egypt with seventy people and now the LORD* your God has made you as the stars of heaven for multitude."*

HOLY SPIRIT

The Holy Spirit is introduced to us in Genesis 1:2 as hovering over the face of the Earth. The Holy Spirit is hovering as a concerned, loving parent watching over a child, an indication of the mothering instinct that is the nature of the Holy Spirit.

Is the Holy Spirit Feminine? If so, why do most references in Scripture use masculine pronouns, and one uses a neuter pronoun? The reason has everything to do with which language is used for a translation. The Spirit is masculine in Latin, the language used for the first English translations. That happenstance has given English speakers a masculine Holy Spirit. Greek was used later, but only changed one pronoun in Acts 8:16 where the Holy Spirit is referred to as "It." The Hebrew language that Y'shua used whenever He preached or taught holds that Ruah is feminine. Yes! Ruah Hakodesh, the Hebrew term, is feminine! Jewish teachings even refer to the Holy Spirit as the feminine side, the nurturing Spirit, of our Heavenly Father. For that reason this book uses the feminine pronouns in the following verses.

John 14:17. *the Spirit of Truth, Whom the world is not able to accept, because it does not see and does not know Her: you know Her, because She remains beside you and will be inside you.*

John 16:12. *I still have much to say to you, but you are not now able to bear it: 13. but when that One would come, the Spirit of Truth, She will guide you in all truth: for She will not speak from Herself, but whatever She will hear She will speak and report the things that are coming to you.*

Acts 8:14. *And when the apostles in Jerusalem heard that the Samaritans welcomed the Word of God, they sent Peter and John to them, 15. who, when they went down from Jerusalem, prayed on their behalf to the end that they would take the Holy Spirit: 16. for not yet was She fallen upon any of them, but they were only being immersed in the name of the Lord Y'shua.*

Romans 8:16. *The Spirit Herself bears witness with our spirit that we are children of God. 17. And if children, then we are heirs: indeed heirs of God, and fellow heirs of Messiah, provided that we suffer together to the end so that we would also be glorified together.*

Romans 8:26. *And likewise also the Spirit helps together with us in our weakness: for we do not know what we should pray according to what is needed, but the Spirit Herself intercedes in unutterable groanings:*

1 Corinthians 12:11. *but the one and the same Spirit operates all these things, distributing Her own gifts to each, just as She wishes.*

This does not mean to look for a different person, but that we should recognize the feminine attributes of God Himself, the nurturing Spirit that took over, agreeing with Moses' arguments not to destroy the people in the desert. Then look at His continual forgiving of the people of Israel after repeated sins of idolatry, like our continual sinning today with improper teachings abounding and our seeking the trappings of wealth more than relationship with Him.

Seven-Fold Holy Spirit

*John to the seven churches that are in Asia: Grace to you and peace from the One Who is, and Who Was, and the One Who Is Coming and from the **SEVEN SPIRITS** which are before His throne.* (Revelation 1:4)

And you must write to the messenger of the congregation in Sardis:

*The One Who has the **SEVEN SPIRITS** of God and the seven stars says these things: I know your deeds and that you have a reputation, that of life, but you are dead.* (Revelation 3:1)

*And lightnings and voices and thunders were going out from the throne, and in front of the throne seven lamps of fire were burning, which are the **SEVEN SPIRITS** of God...* (Revelation 4:5)

*... And I also saw in the midst of the throne the four living creatures and in the midst of the elders a Lamb standing as having been slain, having seven horns and seven eyes which are the **SEVEN SPIRITS** of God that were sent into all the earth.* (Revelation 5:6)

Why did the LORD* have Zechariah and John use the number seven in reference to the Holy Spirit? We know seven is the number of completion (perfection), which is certainly appropriate for the Spirit of God.

The seven-fold character of the Holy Spirit is spelled out in Isaiah 11:2 and can be enumerated as below.

1. The Spirit of Wisdom
2. Understanding
3. The Spirit of Counsel
4. Might
5. The Spirit of Knowledge
6. Reverence
7. Awe

And there will come forth a shoot out of the trunk of Jesse, and a Branch will grow out of his roots: 2. and the Spirit of the LORD will rest upon Him, the Spirit of **1 WISDOM** and **2 UNDERSTANDING**, the Spirit of **3 COUNSEL** and **4 MIGHT**, the Spirit of **5 KNOWLEDGE** and of the **6 REVERENCE** and **7 AWE** of the LORD*.* (Isaiah 11:1,2)

Examine each characteristic of the seven-fold Holy Spirit:

1. Wisdom
Not from man's intellect, but straight from the Throne Room:
*Happy is the man who finds **wisdom** and the man who gets understanding. 14. For its merchandise is better than the merchandise of silver and its increase than fine gold. 15. It is more precious than pearls and all the things you compared to it. 16. Length of days is in its right hand; in its left hand riches and honor. 17. Its ways are ways of pleasantness and all its paths are peace. 18. It is a tree of life to those who lay hold on it and happy is everyone who retains it. 19. The LORD* by **wisdom** has founded the earth; by understanding He has established the heavens.* (Proverbs 3:13–19)

*He has made the earth by His power. He has established the world by His **wisdom** and has stretched out the heavens at His discretion.* (Jeremiah 10:12)

*Who is wise and learned among you? He must constantly show by good conduct his works of **wisdom** in humility. 14. But if you have bitter jealousy and strife in your heart, do not boast against and do not tell lies against the truth. 15. This **wisdom** is **not wisdom** coming down from above, but is earthly, worldly, proceeding from an evil spirit. 16. For where there is jealousy and strife, from that place is disorder and every worthless, wicked deed. 17. But the **wisdom** from above is indeed first pure, then peaceable, kind, obedient, full of mercy and of good fruits, unwavering, without hypocrisy. 18. And the fruit of acts of loving kindness is sown in peace by those who make peace.* (Jacob 3:13–18. See also Jeremiah 51:15; Psalm 104:24; Proverbs 8:1–36,9:1.)

God's Wisdom is not our rationalizing, but His Spirit bringing us His Wisdom. His ways are not our ways, so we should not rely on our own reasoning (common sense)—but, in prayer, rely on His Spirit. As Paul wrote:

O Timothy, you must now guard the deposit, turning away for yourself from the profane chatter and contradictions of what is falsely called knowledge... (1 Timothy 6:20)

2. Understanding
*Your hands have made me and fashioned me: give me **understanding**, so I can learn Your commandments.* (Psalm 119:73)

This is the same as the gift of discernment in 1 Corinthians 12:10. The gift of understanding is the gift of discernment. In Proverbs 8:14b God says *I am **Understanding**.*

3. Counsel
You will guide me with Your counsel and afterward take me to glory. (Psalm 73:24)

***Counsel** and sound Wisdom are mine:* (Proverbs 8:14a)

Also this comes forth from the LORD of Hosts, doing wonders in **Counsel**, making sound Wisdom great.* (Isaiah 28:29)

*There is no wisdom and no understanding and **no counsel** against the LORD*.* (Proverbs 21:30)

Surely God is telling us to stop storing up our knowledge of men, even godly men. And He tells each one of us to rely more and more on the Holy Spirit to bring us God's Wisdom, Understanding, and Advice. This means spending hours in His Word, in prayer, in fasting, and in total obedience. Sensitivity to the counsel of the Holy Spirit cannot be gained by studying this book or any other book written by man. It can be acquired only by careful obedience in doing the will of the Father.

Not everyone who says to Me, 'Lord. Lord!' will enter the kingdom of the heavens, but the one who does the will of My Father, the One in the heavens. Matthew 7:21. (See also verses 22–29.)

4. Might
*Listen, you who are far off, to what I have done! And, you who are near, acknowledge My **Might**! Selah.* (Isaiah 33:13)

God's Power is extended to us by His Spirit.

This is the same Power that enabled His Word to create the earth and about which Y'shua spoke:

...whoever would say to this mountain, 'You must immediately be removed and you must immediately be cast into the sea,' and would not doubt in his heart but would believe that what he is saying is happening, it shall be to him. (Mark 11:23)

Since there is no one like You, LORD, Your name is Great and Your name is Great in **MIGHT**.* (Jeremiah 10:6)

The **Spirit of Might**, therefore, is now available to us to move mountains, to heal, to do spiritual warfare.

These four aspects of the Holy Spirit are to be received by us: **Wisdom, Understanding** (Discernment), **Counsel**, and **Might**. They are gifts from God, but they must be taken by faith. The remaining three aspects of the Sevenfold Spirit require something from us.

5. Knowledge

Teach me good judgment and **KNOWLEDGE**, *for I have believed Your commandments. 67. Before I was afflicted I went astray, but now I have kept Your word.* (Psalm 119:64–66)

My son, if you will take my words and hide my commandments with you, 2. so that you incline your ear to wisdom, applying your heart to understanding, 3. and if you cry after intelligence and lift up your voice for understanding, 4. if you seek it as silver and search for it as for hidden treasures, 5. then you will understand the reverence of the LORD* and find the **KNOWLEDGE** *of God.* (Proverbs 2:1–5)

And all your children will be taught by the LORD*, and the peace of your children will be great. (Isaiah 54:13)

(Y'shua speaking) *It has been written in the Prophets, 'And all will be taught by God:'* (Isaiah 54:13) *everyone who has heard and learned from the Father comes to Me.* (John 6:45)

At that time Y'shua said, "I praise You, Father, Master of Heaven and Earth, because You hid these things from the wise and intelligent and You revealed them to babies: (Matthew 11:25)

Just as Y'shua chose disciples who worked with their hands, and did not choose scribes, we must come to Him with open hearts. We cannot strengthen our **knowledge** of God with our intellectual exercises alone, but by being open and letting His Spirit teach us. Y'shua said:

My teaching is not Mine, but of the One Who sent Me: (John 7:16)

Then His Spirit can teach us all things. If we fail to put His Word in ourselves, then His Spirit will have nothing with which to work and will not be able to teach us. If we hunger and thirst after His righteousness, spending extended time every day in the Word, then the Holy Spirit will have the raw materials with which to work. Only then can She teach us.

In Y'shua's day education was mandatory for Jewish boys. Jewish girls could be excused if their help was needed at home. School consisted of learning Scripture; each synagogue having its own school. The children started memorizing Scripture by the age of five, beginning with the Book of Leviticus, the book of holiness. By the age of twelve, they had committed the entire Torah (the first five Books of the Bible) to memory. Scrolls were very expensive, so only the wealthy had personal copies of the Torah, Prophets, and Writings—the Hebrew Scriptures. However, many had memorized all Hebrew Scripture.

Reading the sermons of Peter, Stephen, and Paul in the Book of Acts should convince us how well grounded the disciples were. In gaining **knowledge**, our first responsibility is to put the Word in us. Only then can the Spirit teach us all things. **Knowledge**, then, might be thought of as the interface characteristic of the Holy Spirit, with action going both ways. But we need to study so the Holy Spirit can teach us the deep meanings of Scripture.

6. Reverence

REVERENCE *for the LORD* is the beginning of wisdom: a good understanding have all those who do His commandments. His praise endures forever.* (Psalm 111:10)

*The God of Israel said, the Rock of Israel spoke to me, He who rules over men must be just, ruling in **REVERENCE** of God. 4. And he will be like the light of the morning, when the sun rises, a morning without clouds, like the tender grass springing out of the earth by shining clear after rain.* (2 Samuel 23:3,4)

Y'shua is ruling in obedience. David speaks here of Messiah, and we know that Y'shua is our ultimate example of obedience to God's perfect will in every step He walked and every word He spoke. He is also the paragon of **reverence**. Of these two qualities, **reverence** and obedience, obedience seems to be the more troublesome. We can be disobedient, even by trying to do good things, if we don't first seek Him. How many of us could respond day in and day out as Y'shua did? At the pool called Bethesda were a great number (possibly hundreds) of infirm, blind, lame, withered, all awaiting the stirring of the water. All of them were believers in the Living God, and each was there hoping for God to bring healing. For many of us, the fleshly impulse in that situation would be to lay hands on each one, to pray for healing. Y'shua, however, singled out just one man and asked him one brief question, *"Do you desire to become whole?"* The answer to that question was in the man's heart, although not in his open response, which was that he had no one to cast him into the pool. Y'shua's healing statement was, *"Rise, take up your pallet and walk."* (John 5:2–9) There is no record of Y'shua's having spoken to or having healed anyone else there. Also, just as it is possible to be **reverent** without obedience, we can be obedient without being wholly **reverent**.

7. Awe

Do not be in AWE, Abram! I AM your Shield! *Your reward will be exceedingly great.* (Genesis 15:1)

Numbers, chapters 22 through 24, tell of Balaam being asked by Balak to curse Israel. Balaam would not go with Balak's representatives without God's approval. But Balaam would not take "No" for an answer, so he went in God's permissive will. After he arrived in Moab, he spoke only what God gave him. *But Balaam answered and said to Balak, "Did I not I tell you, saying, All that the LORD* speaks, that I must do?"* (Numbers 23:26)

And Balaam said to Balak, "Did I not also tell your messengers whom you sent to me saying, 13. 'If Balak would give me his house full of silver and gold, I cannot go beyond the commandment of the LORD*, to do good or bad of my own mind, but what the LORD* says, that will I speak?'" (Numbers 24:12,13)

Balaam was careful to be obedient, but earlier had talked to God like a child pleading for permission to do something after a parent says "No." *And God said to Balaam, "You will not go with them! You will not curse the people, for they are blessed."* (Numbers 22:12)

God was certainly clear: *"You will not go."* But Balaam, like a child, did not respect this answer, having to plead for permission to go. Right at the beginning of his meeting with Balak, Balaam said, *"Come, I shall advise you..."* Balaam was obedient to the extent that he prophesied a true word to Balak, but since his advice apparently led to the harlotry of Numbers 25:1, he paid for his treachery with his life (Numbers 31:8). When Israel killed the kings of Midian, Balaam was added to the list. The story clearly warns us that we have to be both **reverent** and in **awe** of the Living God. Balaam did not hold God in Awe.

The Hebrew word Yar-e has, by tradition, been translated Fear, but that tradition is because the first English translations were made from Latin, with the Latin text using Timeo, which does mean fear. Those who **revere** God and serve Him are not to fear or even be **Awed** by their spiritual, physical, or emotional enemies.

Fear is not an option for believers. **Do not even be awed** by your obstacles. Have faith that He is on your side and will fight for you.

There is no place in the Hebrew Scriptures telling believers to Fear God. Fear would be a hindrance to our relationship with Him, the most Loving Father ever. Paḥad is the Hebrew word for fear, and it is used as Fear of God only for heathens and backsliders, never for godly people.

The Seven-fold Holy Spirit presents the Holy Spirit as the Great Communicator, and as the agent through Whom God makes His Power available to men. Since Elohim spoke to create things, we know that God can do anything He wants and does not need people. Throughout history, though, we see the Lord working through people, or even a donkey (Numbers 22:21–31), and people do not do wondrous works unless the Holy Spirit has come upon them. Anyone who desires the Holy Spirit to work through him (or her) must reach a state of total commitment to God. Y'shua did not move in ministry (power) until after His immersion in the Holy Spirit. He said, *"We, the Father and I, are One."* (John 10:20) God can, at His pleasure, work through unbelievers as He did with Cyrus (Ezra 1:1,2), but those who are seeking to move in the power of the Holy Spirit need to follow the example of Y'shua. The Holy Spirit functions as the Eyes and Ears (carrying our supplications) of the Lord. The Holy Spirit knows no bounds on earth or in the heavens, but roams even more freely than the wind, which, unlike Her, is limited to the earth's atmosphere. The Holy Spirit is the Great Communicator, bringing us wisdom, understanding, and revealing the truths hidden in God's Word. She brings the prophetic according to Joel 2:28 *And I will pour out My Spirit on all flesh and your sons and your daughters will prophesy.* Her purpose is to encourage and comfort and to bring power. How blessed we are to have God's Spirit upon and within us. To receive these blessings of the Spirit-filled life, we must be rooted in the Word, then totally committed to God—nothing less than 100% commitment. Our commitment is expressed in **reverential and obedient awe** of the Lord.

The Seven-fold Holy Spirit gives us the Gifts of the Spirit:

And there are varieties of gifts, but the same Spirit: 5. and there are varieties of ministry, but the same Lord: 6. and there are varieties of activities, but the same God, the One Who works all things in all people. 7. And to each is given the manifestation of the Spirit toward that which is profitable for all. 8. For indeed through the Spirit to one is given a word of wisdom, and to another a word of knowledge according to the same Spirit, 9. to another faith by the same Spirit, and to another gifts of healings by the one Spirit, 10. and to another activities that call forth miracles, and to another prophecy, and to another discernings of spirits (John 16:8), *to another to speak in different kinds of tongues, and to another interpretation of tongues: 11. But the one and the same Spirit operates all these things, distributing Her own gifts to each, just as She wishes.* (1 Corinthians 12:4–11)

These verses from 1 Corinthians not only show us what the gifts are, but that they are given to us for good use, for "God's purposes." They are not given to us for entertainment, or so we may enjoy Holy Ghost goose bumps. They are given to bring healing, comfort, deliverance, and all of God's provisions and power to the Body of Messiah.

MESSIAH

The Messiah is the One for Whom we are looking, expecting Him to come soon, very soon. English speakers call Him Jesus, but English was not even a language when the Bible was written thousands of years ago. His name then was Y'shua or Yeshua, depending on the transliteration chart you use. So when Scripture speaks of the Name above, every Name referred to was Y'shua.

Philippians 2:9. *On this account then God raised Him to the highest rank and He freely gave Him the name above every name, 10. so that at the name "Y'shua!" every knee of the heavenlies and the earthly and those below the earth would bow 11. and every tongue would confess that Y'shua Messiah is Lord in the glory of God our Father.*

Y'shua is used many times in the Hebrew Scriptures to refer to our Heavenly Father.

Messiah is prophesied in several passages, but Isaiah describes His birth in great detail. The article Exodus 14:13 in this chapter.

> Isaiah 7:13. *Then Isaiah said, Listen now, O house of David, Is it a small thing for you to weary men, but will you weary my God also? 14. Therefore the Lord Himself will give you a sign. Behold, the pregnant young woman will bear a son and she will call His name Emanuel. 15. He will eat butter and honey, when he knows to refuse the bad and choose the good.*

The sign from the LORD in verse 14 will be an extraordinary event, brought through an extraordinary young woman who will give birth to an extraordinary person known as "God With Us." The word translated "young woman" is Almah, meaning a marriageable young woman, a virgin. Although Almah does not mean virgin in biblical Hebrew, an Almah who got pregnant would have been stoned.

Deuteronomy 22:13. *"If any man takes a wife and goes in to her and hates her, 14. and speaks against her and brings up a bad name over her and says, I took this woman and when I came to her, I found her not a virgin. 15. Then the father and mother of the girl will take and bring forth the tokens of the girl's virginity to the elders of the city in the gate 16. and the girl's father will say to the elders, I gave my daughter to this man to wife, and he hates her 17. and, see, he has given occasions of speech against her saying, I did not find your daughter a virgin, and yet these are the tokens of my daughter's virginity. And they will spread the cloth before the elders of the city. 18. And the elders of that city will take that man and punish him. 19. And they will fine him a hundred shekels of silver and give them to the father of the girl, because he has brought up a bad name upon a virgin of Israel, and she will be his wife. He may not put her away all his days."*

Deuteronomy 22:20. *"But if this thing is true, and the tokens of virginity are not found for the girl, 21. then they will bring out the girl to the entrance of her father's house and the men of her city will stone her with stones so she dies, because she has wrought folly in Israel, to play the harlot in her father's house. So you will put away bad from your midst."*

In Modern Hebrew Almah means virgin, but there can be no doubt that in first century Israel an Almah was a virgin. So this virgin birth was the extraordinary event prophesied by Isaiah 7:14. There is also no question the birth was of Emanu-El, God With Us, also known as Y'shua.

Messianic Prophecies were introduced by Moses in Deuteronomy:

Deuteronomy 18:15. *The LORD* your God will raise up for you a **prophet (Y'shua) like me** from among you, of your brothers. You will listen to Him 16. according to all that you desired of the LORD* your God in Horeb in the day of the assembly saying, 'Let me not again hear the voice of the LORD* my God, neither let me see this great fire any more, so I do not die.'*

Deuteronomy 18:17. *"And the LORD* said to me, 'They have well-spoken that which they have spoken. 18. I shall raise up a **prophet** like you for them from among their brothers and will put My words in His mouth and He will speak to them all that I command Him. (Acts 3:22) 19. And it will be, whoever will not hearken to My words which He will speak in My name, I shall require it of him.*

This next is about a visit to Earth by Y'shua.

Judges 13:16. *And the angel of the LORD* said to Manoah, Though you detain Me, I shall not eat of your bread and if you will offer a burnt offering, you must offer it to the LORD*. For Manoah did not know that He was an angel of the LORD*. 17. And Manoah said to the angel of the LORD*, What is your name, so when your sayings come to pass we can honor you? 18. And the angel of the LORD* said to him, Why do you ask this about my name, seeing it is* **Miracle**?

Y'shua appears as an angel, with His Name as **Miracle**. In another hidden prophecy, He appears to Jacob, who wrestles with Him.

Genesis 32:25. *And Jacob was left alone, and a* **Man** *wrestled with him there until the breaking of the day. 26. And when the* **Man** *saw that He did not prevail against him, He touched the socket of his hip, and the socket of Jacob's thigh was out of joint as he wrestled with Him. 27. And He said, "Let Me go, for the day is breaking." And Jacob said, "I shall not let You go until You bless me." 28. And the* **Man** *said to him, "What is your name?" And he said, "Jacob." 29. And He said, "Your name will no longer be called Jacob, but Israel, for as a prince you have power with God and with men, and you have prevailed." 30. And Jacob asked and said, "Tell me, I pray You, Your name." And He said, "Why do you ask after* **My Name**?*" And He blessed him there. 31. And Jacob called the name of the place* **Peniel**, *for "I have seen God face to face and my life is preserved." 32. And as he passed over Peniel the sun rose upon him, and he was limping on account of his hip.*

The word translated **Man** is **Ish**, frequently translated **Husband** in the Hebrew Scriptures, very appropriate for our **Bridegroom**.

Yaakov's two names are related: Yaakov means "Follow Close After, to heed (God's will)," and Israel means "Prevailing with God."

Anointing on Messiah He spoke in Luke 4:18 when He read in a synagogue:

Isaiah 61:1. *The Spirit of Adonai, the LORD*, is upon me, because the LORD* has anointed me to preach Good News to the humble.* (Matthew 5:3) *He has sent me to* **bind up the broken-hearted, to proclaim liberty to the captives, and opening of eyes for those who are bound, 2. to proclaim the acceptable year of the LORD*, and the day of vengeance of our God; to comfort all who mourn, 3. to appoint to those who mourn in Zion, to give to them beauty instead of ashes, the oil of joy instead of mourning, the garment (prayer**

shawl) of praise instead of the spirit of infirmity, so they could be called
oaks of righteousness, the planting of the LORD*, so He would be glorified.

Humble is a Hebrew idiom for repentant, so the **Good News** is for the repentant. (See Good News in Glossary.)

To **Bind up the broken-hearted**, with binding, is a Hebrew idiom meaning to forbid. It gives this double meaning: first, to treat the wound, bring comfort to the hurting; second, to forbid the wound to fester, whether talking about a physical injury or an emotional trauma.

To proclaim **Liberty to the Captive** is to speak to the spiritual, making whole those who have generational curses and/or other spiritual burdens, including rejection, addictions, fears, and any other spiritual and emotional injuries.

Opening of eyes is the Hebrew word P'kah-Koah relating to opening eyes and ears, spiritually and physically of all those bound.

The Acceptable Year of the Lord is the year of His anointing, which Y'shua announced at the service in Nazareth. After this was read in the synagogue, Y'shua sat down, saying ,"Today this Scripture has been fulfilled in your ears."

Beauty, P'ar, uses the headdress of a bridegroom to speak of **beauty** accompanied by **Joy**, adding more joy to the **Joy** being given to the mourners. That makes the superlative for **JOY**.

The outer garment, the **Prayer Shawl**, is the covering of **Praise instead of the spirit of infirmity**.

Spirit of Infirmity, Kehah, meaning to be pale or dim, is an expression of being weak, sickly, puny. Those who are sickly or weak are being replanted as **OAKS**, with superhuman strength. They are now born again **Oaks of Righteousness**, the Planting of the Lord.

This glorifies Him.

When this was read in the synagogue in Nazareth, the reaction of the congregation was recorded in Luke:

Luke 4:16. *Then He came into Nazareth, which was where He grew up, and He entered the synagogue according to His custom on the day of Sabbaths and He stood up to read. 17. And a scroll of the prophet Isaiah was handed to Him and when He opened the scroll He found the place where it was written,*

18. "The Spirit of the Lord is upon Me
because He has anointed Me
to preach Good News to the repentant,
He has sent Me to preach release to captives
and recovery of sight to the blind,
to send release to the oppressed,
19. to preach the acceptable year of the Lord."

20. Then rolling up the scroll, after He gave it back to the attendant, He sat down. And the eyes of all in the synagogue were looking attentively at Him. 21. And He began to say to them **"Today this Scripture has been fulfilled in your ears."** *22. And everyone was speaking well of Him and was amazed by the grace in those words that came out from His mouth, and they were saying, "Is this not a son of Joseph?" 23. Then He said to them, "Certainly you will tell Me this parable, 'Physician, You must now heal Yourself:' what we heard happened in Capernaum You must now do here in Your home town." 24. Then He said, "Truly I say to you that no prophet is welcome in his home town. 25. And in truth I say to you, there were many widows in Israel in the days of Elijah, when the sky was locked for three years and six months, as there was a great famine on all the Earth, 26. but Elijah was sent to not one of them except to a widow woman in Zarephath of Sidon. (1 Kings 17:9) 27. And there were many lepers in Israel in the time of Elisha the prophet, but not one of them was cleansed except Naaman the Syrian." (2 Kings 5:1–14) 28. And when they heard these things everyone in the synagogue was filled with rage 29. and* **when they stood up they drove Him outside the city to the brow of the hill o***n which their city had been built so that they could throw Him down: 30.* **but then He went through the middle of them and left***.*

Isaiah wrote that passage about 700 years before Y'shua read this in Nazareth.

Now look at a few times the Name Y'shua refers to our Heavenly Father.

Exodus 14:13. And Moses said to the people, *"**Do not be in awe!** Stand still! See the **Deliverance/Salvation of the LORD***, which He will show you today, for the Egyptians whom you have seen today, you will see them again no more forever.*

> **Deliverance/Salvation is Y'shuat**, with the suffix T because the next word begins with a vowel.

Exodus 15:2. *YAH is my strong song and melody for He has become my **Salvation**. This is my God and I shall praise Him; the God of my father and I will exalt Him!*

> **Salvation is Y'shuah.**

Psalm 68:20. *Blessed be Adonai, Who daily bears burdens for us, the God of our **Deliverance/Salvation**. Selah.*

> **Deliverance/Salvation is Y'shuatenu**, Our Deliverance. The suffix, tenu is the pronoun Our.

Psalm 68:21. *He that is our God is the God of **Deliverance/Salvation**, and to the LORD*, my Lord, belong the issues from death.*

> **Deliverance/Salvation is Moshaot.** The prefix M means this was God's plan from the beginning. This Name is plural, same as Elohim.

Isaiah 43:11. ***I AM, I AM** the LORD*. Besides Me there is no **Deliverer/Savior**.*

> **Deliverer/Savior is Moshia**, Y'shua with an M prefix, noting the power and that Y'shua was planned from the foundation of the world.

(Read God Incarnate, Coming of Messiah, Son of David/Son of Joseph, Donkey, Division of Abijah, Testimony of Y'shua, Y'shua, and Genealogy of Y'shua in Glossary.)

When Y'shua was born and throughout His life, the world recognized Joseph as His father, but Y'shua was and is the Son of God! Joseph was not His father, but Miriam was His mother. (See Elizabeth in Teachings.) Elizabeth and

Miriam were cousins. If their fathers were brothers, Miriam was an Aaronite, the perfect bride for the Father of Y'shua.

Hidden Prophecy of Messiah found in Psalm 85.

Psalm 85:3. *You have **forgiven (carried)** the iniquity of Your people, You have covered all their sin. Selah.*

The word translated Forgiven is **Nasah**, which means **Carried**. He, Y'shua, literally **Carried** our iniquities, deliberate sins. Y'shua took them on Himself, prophesied here a thousand years before the fact!

2 Corinthians 5:16. *Thus from now on we know no one according to the flesh: if then we had known Messiah according to the flesh, nevertheless now we no longer know. 17. So if someone is in Messiah, he is a new creation: the old things passed away, behold he has become new. 18. And all things are from God, the One Who reconciled us to Himself through Messiah and Who gave us the ministry of reconciliation, 19. because God was reconciling the universe to Himself by means of Messiah, since He does not reckon their transgressions to them, and because He placed in us the message of reconciliation. 20. Therefore we are ambassadors on behalf of Messiah as God exhorts through us: we beg, in the name of Messiah, that you must immediately be reconciled to God. 21. **He made <u>the One Who did not know sin to be sin</u> on our behalf, so that we ourselves would know the righteousness of God by means of Him.***

Joseph Not Father of Y'shua is shown right away as Matthew announces the birth of Y'shua.

Matthew 1:12. *After the Babylonian captivity Jeconiah begat Shealtiel, and Shealtiel begat Zerubbabel, 13. and Zerubbabel begat Abiud, and Abiud begat Eliakim, and Eliakim begat Azor, 14. and Azor begat Sadok, and Sadok begat Achim, and Achim begat Elihud, 15. and Elihud begat Eliazar, and Eliazar begat Matthan, and Matthan begat Jacob, 16. and Jacob begat **Joseph, the husband of Miriam, of whom was born Y'shua**, the One called **Messiah**.*

Joseph did not father Y'shua, so Matthew could not continue saying "begat." (For insight to this name, see Son of David/Son of Joseph in Glossary. See Genealogy of Y'shua in Glossary.)

Miriam is the Hebrew name of Y'shua's mother, with Mary the English spelling of the Latin Maria. The Greek spelling is Mariam. (See Section II in Glossary for more on names.) The word Whom in Greek is feminine, referring specifically to Miriam. Some say this makes the lineage that of Miriam, but it really is only saying that she gave birth to Y'shua. (See both Book Order and Genealogy of Y'shua in Glossary.)

Melchizedek is Y'shua!

Psalm 110:4. *The LORD* has sworn and He will not be sorry, You are a priest forever after the order of **Melchizedek**.*

Hebrews 5:6. *Just as in another He then says,*

> *"You are a priest forever*
> *according to the order of **Melchizedek**,"*

*7. Who in the days of His flesh, in prayers and also supplications with loud crying and by having brought tears to the very One able to rescue Him from death and then He was heard because of His godliness, 8. although He was a Son, He learned obedience from that which He suffered, 9. and when He was finished He became the source of eternal salvation for all those who were obedient to Him. 10. Then He was designated by God, High Priest according to the order of **Melchizedek**.*

Hebrews 7:1. *For this "**Melchizedek**, King of Salem, priest of the Most High God, the one who met Abraham when he returned from the slaughter of the kings and had blessed him, 2. with whom Abraham also divided a tithe from everything," first on the one hand translated "**King of Righteousness**" but then also "**King of Salem**" which is King of Peace, (Genesis 14:17–20) 3. without a father, without a mother, without genealogy, having neither beginning of days nor end of life, but Who was made like the **Son of God**, remains a priest forever.*

Hebrews 7:4. *But you see how great he was to whom Abraham the Patriarch gave a tithe of the spoils. 5. Now indeed those of the sons of Levi, the priesthood, have a command, that they take a tithe from the people according to the Torah (Teaching), these are their brothers, who also come from the seed of Abraham: 6. but the one who does not have descent has received a tithe from Abraham and he blessed the one who had the promises. 7. And without any dispute the inferior is blessed by the greater one. 8. So then indeed mortal men take a tithe, but there with*

Melchizedek *it is testified that he lives forever.* (Psalm 110:4) *9. And so it could be said that Levi, the one who takes a tithe, has paid a tithe through Abraham: 10. for Levi was still in the loin of his father when **Melchizedek** met him.*

Hebrews 7:11. *So if perfection was obtained through the Levitical priesthood, for the people have received Torah (Teaching) through it, why then is there a need for a priest to be raised in the order of Melchizedek and not in the order of Aaron? 12. For when the priesthood is changed, then from necessity there is a change of Torah (Teaching). 13. For over Whom it says these things, He belonged to another tribe, from which no one had officiated at the altar: 14. for it is clear that our Lord has descended from Judah, for which tribe Moses spoke nothing about priests. 15. And yet it is even more clear, if another priest rises according to the likeness of Melchizedek, 16. He was not according to the tradition of fleshly command but according to the power of endless life. 17. For it is testified that*

> *"You are a priest forever*
> *according to the order of **Melchizedek**."*

18. *For certainly a preceding commandment becomes set aside because of its weakness and uselessness — 19. for legalism perfected nothing — but a better hope is introduced through which we draw near to God.*

The author of the Book of Hebrews assumed that Y'shua was the son of Joseph, but even the demons recognized Him as the Son of God, meaning He did not inherit the tribe (Judah) of Joseph, but the tribe of God.

Matthew 8:29. *And behold they cried out saying, "What do You have to do with us, **Son of God**?*

The apostles also recognized Y'shua as the **Son of God**:

Matthew 14:32. *Then when they got up in the boat the wind stopped. 33. And those in the boat paid homage to Him saying, "Truly You are the **Son of God**."*

The centurion at His crucifixion recognized Him:

Matthew 27:54. *And after the centurion, and those who were keeping watch over Y'shua with him, saw the earthquake and the things that happened, they became very greatly fearful, saying, "Truly He was the **Son of God**."*

John the Immerser recognized Y'shua as the **Son of God**:

John 1:32. *And John testified, saying that "I had seen the Spirit descending from heaven as a dove and it was staying on Him. 33. And I would not have known Him, but the One Who sent me to immerse in water, that One said to me 'Upon whomever you would see the Spirit descending and remaining upon Him, He is the One Who immerses in the Holy Spirit.' 34. And I saw and I had borne witness that this One is the **Son of God**."*

Y'shua is **Melchizedek**. **Melchizedek** is the One and Only **Son of God**!

APPRECIATING GOD

God of Relationship. This God we serve desires real relationship with each one of His children. This is a relationship that stretches our imaginations to reach the levels to which He is calling each one of us. This is not an exhaustive list, but it gives pause to think as you find more as you read Scripture. Rather than just talk about it, read the following verses:

Isaiah 9:5. *For unto us a child is born, unto us a Son is given, and the government is upon His shoulder, and His name will be called **Wonder, Counselor, Mighty God, Eternal Father, Prince of Peace**. 6. Of the increase of His government and Shalom there will be no end, upon the throne of David and upon His kingdom, to order it, and to establish it with judgment and with acts of loving kindness from now even forevermore.* (John 12:34) *The zeal of the LORD* of Hosts will perform this.*

Isaiah 9:5 establishes the **Son** as both **Mighty God** and **Eternal Father**, boldly stating the deity of Y'shua from a time long before His birth. Wonder means Miracle, so it is Wonder as in Signs and Wonders. Wonder is a noun, not the adjective Wonderful.

Isaiah 63:16. *Doubtless You are our **Father**, although Abraham was ignorant of us, and Israel does not acknowledge us. You, the LORD*, are our **Father**, our **Redeemer**. Your name is from everlasting.*

The LORD* is our **Father**, the most loving father of all time.

Isaiah 64:7. *But now, LORD*, You are our **Father**.*

Malachi 2:10. *Have not all of us one **Father**?!*

All the above verses reinforce His being our **Father**, our **Heavenly Father**.

Jeremiah 3:4. *Will you not from this time cry to Me, **My Father**!*

Jeremiah 3:19. *But **I AM** said, How will I put you among the children and give you a pleasant land, a goodly heritage of the hosts of nations? And I said, You will call Me, **My Father**,*

Psalm 89:27. *He will cry to Me, You are my **Father**, my **God** and the **Rock of my Deliverance**.*

His desire is for each of us to call Him **Father**!

1 Chronicles 17:12. *He will build a House for Me and I shall establish his throne forever. 13. I shall be his **Father**, and he will be My son (Hebrews 1:5) and I shall not take My loving kindness away from him, as I took it from the one, Saul, who was before you.*

Isaiah 54:5. *For your Maker is your **Husband**! His name is the **LORD*** of Hosts and your **Redeemer the Holy One of Israel**. He will be called **The God of the Whole Earth**.*

Hosea 2:18. *And it will be at that Day, says the LORD*, you will call Me Ishi, **My Husband**, and will no longer call Me Baali, My Husband.* Ishi and Baali both mean my husband, but Baali also means "my master" in Hebrew. Ishi is the equal status in which Adam and Eve were created.

Isaiah 54:5 and Hosea 2:18 bring a relationship that is more difficult for most of us to imagine, speaking of the most intimate of all relationships. That relationship is also alluded to in Psalm 91:4, referring to our finding refuge under His wings. The wing of a prayer shawl relates to marriage, as in Ruth 3:9. (See Prayer Shawl in Glossary.)

Matthew 12:48. *And He said to the one speaking to Him, "Who is My mother and who are My brothers?" 49. Then stretching out His hand to His disciples He said, "Behold My mother and My brothers. 50. For whoever would do the will of My Father, the One in the heavens, this one is My brother and sister and mother."* (Psalm 22:23; Hebrews 2:12)

Mark 3:33. *And answering them He said, "Who are My mother and My brothers?" 34. And looking around He said to those who were sitting all around Him, "Behold My mother and My brothers. 35. For whoever would do the will of God, this one is My brother and sister and mother."* (Psalm 22:23; Hebrews 2:17)

Isaiah 53:4. *Surely He has borne our sicknesses, our pains; He carried them, yet we esteemed Him stricken, smitten of God and afflicted.* (1 Peter 2:24) *5. But He was wounded because of our transgressions, bruised because of our iniquities: the chastisement of our peace was upon Him, and we have been healed by His wounds.* (Matthew 8:17; Luke 24:46; 1 Peter 2:24) Transgressions are committed with the intention of angering God; Iniquities are committed intentionally; and Sins are committed in error, unintentionally.

Isaiah 53:5 has an unusual twist because the word translated Wounds or Stripes is listed in Modern Hebrew dictionaries with a different meaning. The word is Havurah. The confusion comes because another root, H-v-r, relates to fellowship, so at least one modern English translation used by Orthodox Jewish congregations in the U.S. translate this as fellowship, that we have been healed by fellowship with Him. That is true because we serve the God of relationship and our relationship with Him is foundational to godly living and to receiving His blessings. Havurah (Hebrew collective singular) literally means Sore, but Stripe(s) or Wound(s) are appropriate translations. In Isaiah's time all his readers understood that as stripes or wounds, but now we see more depth in those words. Havurah is one of very few words in Modern Hebrew that differs significantly from its ancient meaning. Still, remember that relationship with Him is what this is all about, a subliminal message in Isaiah 53:5.

Consider all the relationships our Heavenly Father desires to have with us: Father, wanting us to call Him Father. Husband, wanting us to call Him by the intimate, equal name of Ishi! Then He has Brother, Sister, even Mother! The more understanding we have of these relationships, the closer we come to appreciating His love for each one of us. Some will only do this slowly, one step at a time, while others will get a revelation, a "suddenly" that will catapult them into His presence. The important point here is to accept the words of this article, knowing that God Himself responds when you call Him "Father" or "my Husband!"

Holiness is a state of being. We are called to be Holy. Leviticus 11:44. *For I AM the LORD* your God! You will therefore sanctify yourselves and you will be **holy**, for I AM **holy**.* To sanctify one's self means: 1. Repent 2. Be clean in thought and body 3. Mikveh, immersing seven times, dunking thoroughly while recognizing that you are coming out, like a newborn baby from the amniotic fluid, into a new life.

The Power of God is shown when He has the children of Israel turn back toward Egypt on their way out to the wilderness. They actually turn back to draw the army of Egypt to the Reed Sea.

> Exodus 14.1. *And the LORD* spoke to Moses saying, 2. "Speak to the children of Israel, to **turn back** and camp before Pi Ha<u>h</u>irot, between Migdol and the sea, over against Baal-Zephon: camp by the sea before it. 3. For Pharaoh will say of the children of Israel, 'They are entangled in the land, the wilderness has shut them in.' 4. And I shall strengthen Pharaoh's heart so he will follow after them, and I shall be honored by Pharaoh and by his entire army, so the Egyptians will know that I AM the LORD*." And they did so.*

In what must have baffled those leaving Egypt, this great mass of people turned back toward Egypt to draw the Egyptian army closer, encouraging the Egyptians to pursue the Israelites, luring the whole Egyptian army to its destruction.

When you may be in some perilous situation, you can be sure God has a plan and purpose, that He is assuredly able to bring you out.

Declares the End from the Beginning and it does come to pass.

> Isaiah 46:8. *Remember this and show yourselves to be men! Bring it again to mind, O you transgressors. 9. Remember the former things of old! For **I AM** God, and there is no other! God, and there is none like Me, 10. **declaring the end from the beginning**, and from ancient times the things that are not done, saying, My counsel will stand, and I shall do all My pleasure, 11. a ravenous bird from the east, the man who executes My counsel from a far country! Yes, I have spoken it, I shall also bring it to pass! <u>I have purposed it, I shall also do it</u>.*

> Isaiah 48:3. *I have **declared the former things from the beginning**: they went forth out of My mouth and I made them heard, then I did them suddenly and*

they came to pass. 4. Because I know that you are obstinate and your neck is an iron sinew, and your brow bronze, 5. I have even from the beginning declared it to you. Before it came to pass I announced it to you, lest you should say, My idol has done them, and my graven image and my molten image has commanded them.

Our compassionate God warns us of coming trouble and encourages with promises of times, restoration.

COVENANT
EVERYTHING I HAVE IS YOURS

Renewing Covenant is what we do each time we take communion, as done by Y'shua in Luke 22:20. Jeremiah 31:30–33. *This is the ReNewed Covenant in My blood which is being poured out on your behalf.* Y'shua is referring to the custom that we still have of renewing the covenant relationship frequently. Now most Christians call this Communion. When taking communion, each of us is saying to God, "Everything I have is Yours." Then He says that back to us. (See Passover under Seasons in Glossary.)

Paul in Romans 9:4 and Ephesians 2:12 refers to covenants, plural. The root of the Hebrew word usually translated New has the meaning of Renew, so this is really a renewal of the previous covenants plus the addition of a new blessing made possible by a deeper relationship through His blood. The underlined words are the new points given in this covenant. As those under this covenant read and study Scripture, God will put the tenets into their spirits and reveal hidden meanings. This will facilitate a change in our behavior, bringing true knowledge of Him. What a blessing that He no longer remembers our sin. Satan does keep a record and wants to remind you of past sins, but do not let Satan put you in that trap. God's record says that that sin never happened, so believe Him. (See "Sin, Forgiveness of" in Glossary. See Covenant in Glossary.)

Right Thinking is shown many times by Paul, but this statement in 1 Timothy is most notable, an attitude that needs to be shared by all who seek **Covenant Relationship** with the Most High God, the King of the Universe.

1 Timothy 1:12. *I have received undeserved kindness from Messiah Y'shua, the One Who made me strong in our Lord, because He considered me faithful when He placed me in ministry 13. although I was formerly a blasphemer and persecu-*

44

tor and arrogant, but I received mercy, because, not knowing, I acted in unbelief: *14. and the grace of our Lord overflowed with faith and love in Messiah Y'shua.* **15. The statement is faithful and worthy of all approval, that Messiah Y'shua came into the world to save sinners, of whom I am foremost.** *16. But I received mercy because of this, so that Messiah Y'shua would show all patience with me first, for an example for those who were going to believe in Him for eternal life.* **17. Now to the Eternal King, Immortal, Invisible, the Only God, be honor and glory forever and ever. Amen.**

HEBREW TEXT

The Hebrew text used for *One New Man Bible* was the Masoretic Text, named for the Masoretes who faithfully copied the text. The name Masorete comes from the word Masorah, meaning Tradition. The Masoretes counted the use of each letter on each line and the words on each line, with a mistake causing the manuscript to be destroyed. The Qumran Scrolls have shown the Masoretic text to be quite accurate, more so than any other Hebrew text.

Timeline for Samuel, Saul, David, and the Missing Ark. The Ark of the Covenant was missing from the Tabernacle, having been taken to a battle without consulting the LORD*. When the Ark travelled, it was to be covered since it was to be seen by the Aaronite priests only. Numbers 4:5. *and when the camp sets forward, Aaron and his sons will come and they will take down the covering veil and cover the Ark of Testimony with it, 6. and will put on it the covering of badgers' skins and will spread over it a cloth wholly of blue, and will put in its poles.* Not even the Kohathite priests who carried the Ark were to see the Ark, only the Aaronite priests were given that privilege. Numbers 4:19. *But do thus to them, so they may live and not die when they approach the most holy things: Aaron and his sons will go in and appoint them, each one, to his service and to his burden, 20. but they will not go in to see when the holy things are being covered, lest they die!* When the children of Israel crossed the Jordan River, coming into the Promised Land for the first time, the Ark was not only covered, but the people were not permitted to come within 3,000 cubits of the Ark—well over three quarters of a mile! (Joshua 3:3,4)

Going against the commandment to cover the Ark, the first and only time the Ark was taken to a battle is described in 1 Samuel 4:3. *And when the people came into the camp, the elders of Israel said, Why has the LORD* struck us today before the Philistines? Let us bring the Ark of the Covenant of the LORD* out of Shiloh to us, so when it comes among us it can save us out of the hand of our* *enemies.* The result of this disobedience was the defeat of the Israelites and the capture of the Ark by the Philistines. Since the Philistines were not supposed to have the Ark, their problems with it are described in 1 Samuel chapter 5. God permitted the Ark to return to Israel uncovered on a cart pulled by two milk cows. The Israelites put the Ark in the house of Abinidab where it remained for twenty years. Those twenty years are significant because they include the full judgeship of Samuel, the reign of Saul, and the first seven and half years of David's reign.

1 Samuel 3:2 tells of Samuel's first hearing the voice of the LORD*. *And it was at that time when Eli was lying down in his place and his eyes began to grow dim, he could not see. 3. And the lamp of God had not yet gone out and Samuel was lying down in the Temple of the LORD*, where the Ark of God was.* For Samuel to be in the Holy Place, he had to be at least thirty years old, so he had been with Eli for a long time. The last verse is the only time the Tabernacle was called the Temple in Scripture.

1 Samuel 13:1. *In the first year of Saul's reign, after he became king, and he reigned two years over Israel..* There is a statement in Acts 13:21 that Saul reigned for forty years, but obviously that is not possible. The forty years must have been changed by an early copier, which did happen in early copies of the New Testament. (See Greek New Testament Texts in Glossary.) Paul, who was speaking, and Luke, who wrote the Book of Acts, had memorized the Hebrew Scriptures, so Paul could not have spoken nor could Luke have written forty years. While many say Luke was a gentile, he actually was a Hebrew. The Gospel of Luke has more Hebraic expressions than any other book of the New Testament. (See Luke in Myths.)

2 Samuel 5:3. *So all the elders of Israel came to the king to Hebron and king David cut a covenant with them in Hebron before the LORD*, and they anointed David king over Israel. 4. David was thirty years old when he began to reign, he reigned forty years. 5. In Hebron he reigned over Judah seven years and six months and in Jerusalem he reigned thirty-three years over all Israel and Judah.*

David being thirty years old when he began to reign means he could not have been less then twenty-seven when he fought Goliath. *And Saul said to David, You are not able to go against this Philistine to fight with him for you are a young man, and he has been a man of war from his youth.*

1 Samuel 17:33. The Hebrew word Na'ar refers to a man from eighteen or nineteen to late twenties, used several times in Scripture regarding soldiers who had to be at least twenty years old. Na'ar was translated into Latin as Puer, meaning child. Since early English translations were made from Latin, then some English translations use child.

The key to the times of Samuel, Saul, and David is the twenty years that the Ark of the Covenant spent in the house of Abinidab. That works out to about ten years for Samuel's judging Israel, two for Saul, and seven and a half for David. Those numbers add up to nineteen and half, leaving six months to be distributed to the reign of one or more of the three men.

Hebrew Scriptures are referred to hundreds of times in the New Testament. Every time a New Testament author refers to Scripture, he is referring to the Hebrew Scriptures. Y'shua said in Luke 8:21 *And He said to them,* **"My mother and My brothers are these who hear and DO the Word of God."** The only Word of God at that time was in the Hebrew Scriptures.

Matthew 5:17. *"Do not think that I came to do away with, or to bring an incorrect interpretation to, the Torah or the Prophets:* **I did not come to do away with but to bring (spiritual) abundance, for the Torah (Teaching) to be obeyed as it should be and God's promises to receive fulfillment. 18. For truly I say to you: until the sky and the Earth would pass away, not one yod or one vav could ever pass away from the Torah (Teaching), until everything would come to pass.** (Luke 16:17; Hebrews 10:28) *19. Therefore, whoever would break one of the least of these commandments, and would teach people this way, will be called least in the Kingdom of the Heavens: but whoever would do the commandments and would teach them, will be called great in the Kingdom of the Heavens.*

Hebrews 10:26. *Indeed when we are sinning deliberately after taking the knowledge of the truth, no further offering remains concerning sins, 27. but some fearful expectation of judgment with its blazing flames appears like a living being intent on devouring God's adversaries. 28.* **Anyone who has set aside the Torah (Teaching) of Moses dies without pity on testimony by two or three witnesses:** (Deuteronomy 17:6,19:15; Matthew 5:18) *29. how much more worthy of punishment do you suppose the one will be who trod down the Son of God and who looked upon the blood of the covenant, by Whom he was sanctified, as defiled, and has insulted the Spirit of Grace? 30. For we know the One Who said,*

Vengeance is Mine, I shall repay. (Deuteronomy 32:35)
And again,

The Lord will judge His people. (Deuteronomy 32:36; Psalm 135:14)
31. It is fearful to fall into the hand of the Living God.

Today the one who teaches the heresy of setting aside Torah is not to be stoned, but will not inherit eternal life. He will die the second death. (Revelation 20:14)

Paul clearly states in Acts 24:14 *But I confess this to you that regarding the Way, which they call a sect; this is how I worship God the Father, believing all these things according to the Torah (Teaching) and the things that were written in the Prophets, 15. since I have hope in God, which hope they also accept, that there is to be a resurrection of both righteous and unrighteous.* Paul stands firmly on the Hebrew Scriptures, and we all need to do likewise.

With hundreds of quotes from the Hebrew Bible in the New Testament, why are there preachers and schools teaching that now we need the New Testament only? It is obvious from the examples above that those who teach the Torah are no longer valid and will be in very real trouble when standing before the Judgment Seat. Jacob 3.1. *Not many of you will become teachers, my brothers, since you know that we will take greater judgment.* Just a glance at the examples above is ample proof of a big problem with that heretical attitude that rejects the Hebrew Scriptures.

Hebrew Collective Singular is used frequently in the Hebrew text. Sometimes the word is translated with the plural and sometimes it is not, but the singular is used to point out the Collective Singular. In Isaiah 53:5, the word translated Wounds is a Collective Singular. When you see a singular in the *One New Man Bible* that obviously should be plural, know that the singular is there to show the Hebrew idiom.

Verb Tenses: The Hebrew Perfect Tense expresses completed action. The Imperfect Tense in biblical Hebrew is more complicated because a vowel with a one-letter prefix often determines the tense. An example of the Imperfect is in Exodus 3:14, Ehyeh Asher Ehyeh, usually translated "I AM Who I AM, but it could be "I Will be Who I Will be." In Modern Hebrew this is the Future Tense. The Present Tense is the ongoing present. The Imperative mood in

Hebrew is used only in the second person, with no first person or third person like in the Greek. The Hebrew Imperative is always future tense because what is commanded has not yet been done.

GREEK TEXT

The Oldest Texts We Have of the New Testament are in Greek, but many scholars believe at least Matthew, Mark, and Luke were originally written in Hebrew, although not even a fragment of one of those manuscripts is known to exist. Also, it is possible that the Books of Hebrews, Jacob, Peter, and Jude could have been written in Hebrew since they were written to Hebrews, all of whom could read Hebrew, the language of the synagogue. There is not even a small fragment from any first century New Testament manuscript in Hebrew, Greek, Syriac, or any other first century language.

Hebrew New Testament Books. There have been claims that descendants of first century Hebrew New Testament Books have recently surfaced, but the copy of Matthew that I have seen, purporting to be a copy of the original, contains passages that were added to the Byzantine text in later centuries, so that cannot be a copy of a first century text. Scholars also say the Syriac texts, a language close to Aramaic and related to Hebrew, were translated from Greek, not originally written in Syriac or translated from Hebrew. The descendants of the oldest Syriac texts were probably translated from Greek at the end of the second century or the beginning of the third century. The most reliable Syriac texts are from the fifth century and later, with the best known being the Peshitta, translated from Greek early in the fifth century.

Harmony of the Gospels is often talked about and has been written about, beginning in the second century. The disciples and Y'shua went around without notes or scrolls, with no need for constant word for word messages, so similar messages have variants. Because of those variations, a number of copiers of the earliest manuscript of the New Testament made changes in order to harmonize, to bring the Gospels into complete agreement. Around the middle of the second century, Tatian made the ultimate harmony by combining all four Gospels into one document called Diatessaron, *Through the Four*. There certainly is a great deal of agreement among the Gospels, each one preserving the basic elements of our Christian faith. Many of the differences between Gospels are there because Y'shua taught similar messages in different settings. In His many travels through Israel, He spoke to different crowds, sometimes using parables and other teachings that He had used before. Two examples of this are from the Sermon on the Mount.

Matthew 5.1. *And when He saw the crowds He went up on the mountain, and after He sat down His disciples came to Him: 2. then opening His mouth He taught them...*

Luke 6:17. *Then, when He went down with them, He stood on a flat place, and a great crowd of His disciples, and a great multitude of people, from all of Judea and Jerusalem and the coast of Tyre and Sidon 18. came to hear Him...*

Obviously, these are different times, locations, and audiences.

The Lord's Prayer, which is part of the Sermon on the Mount, is not a part of a similar message in Luke chapter 6, but is given in Luke chapter 11. It may be tempting to try to harmonize these two prayers, but they were not meant to be harmonized. Matthew records Y'shua beginning the Lord's Prayer with "Our Father" while Luke records beginning with "Father." Beginning a prayer with either of those is fine, without any need to analyze.

Compare in the Beatitudes the first few blessings of Matthew versus the first few blessings of Luke:

Matthew 5:3. *Blessed are the repentant,*
because theirs is the Kingdom of the Heavens. (Isaiah 61:1)
4. Blessed are those who mourn,
because they will be comforted. (Isaiah 61:2,3)
5. Blessed are the humble
because they will inherit the Earth. (Psalm 37:11)

Luke 6:20. *Then when He lifted up His eyes to His disciples He was saying,*

"Blessed are the repentant,
because the Kingdom of God is yours. (Isaiah 61:1)
21. Blessed are those who hunger now, (John 6:53)

because you will be filled. (Numbers 25:11; Psalm 4:6; Hosea 10:12)
Blessed are those who cry now,
because you will laugh. (Isaiah 61:2,3)

The harmony of the Gospels is established in the themes, the entire Gospel message of the redeeming blood of Y'shua, which is woven through each Gospel. When you see differences as shown above, look for the background of each passage and look for the theme of each passage. There you will find real harmony in the message of His love for all of humanity.

Verb Tenses: Koine Greek verb tenses are much more rigid than biblical Hebrew. Present tense is the ongoing Present, continuing indefinitely; the Imperfect is continuing action in past time; the Perfect is completed action that is ongoing, as in Matthew 16:19. *I shall give you the keys of the Kingdom of the Heavens, and whatever you would bind upon the Earth will already have been bound in the heavens with ongoing effect, and whatever you would loose upon the Earth will already have been loosed in the heavens with ongoing effect.*

"To Bind" is a Hebrew idiom meaning to Forbid. "To Loose" is a Hebrew idiom meaning to Permit. Binding and loosing here refer specifically to the judicial applications for all the dietary, Sabbath, and other regulations, including civil law, and extend to the spiritual realm as well.

The Greek Aorist Tense is completed action, closed case, like an event, a ball game that is over and in the record books. The moods of Greek verbs are also very specific: Indicative is a definite statement; the Subjunctive means could, should or would; the Optative means something might be done; and the Imperative is an order—in the Aorist tense, the order is to be done NOW! In the present tense, the order is to be done CONTINUOUSLY, as in Matthew 4:17 From then on Y'shua began to preach and to say, *"You must continuously repent: for the Kingdom of the Heavens has come near."*

53

MYTHS

Abraham in many bibles is called a **friend of God**, but that is not anywhere in the Hebrew Scriptures. Isaiah 41:8. *But you, Israel, are My servant; Jacob whom I have chosen, the seed of **Abraham, who loves Me.*** Even some dictionaries and lexicons say that the Hebrew word **Ohavi** means "my friend," listing **Ohavi** as a noun. **Ohavi** is a verb, present tense, meaning "loves Me." In 2 Chronicles 20:7. *Are You not our God, Who drove out the inhabitants of this land before Your people Israel and gave it forever to the seed of **Abraham, who loves You?*** The Hebrew word in this verse is **Ohav'kha**, a verb meaning **"loves You"** but again with some dictionaries and lexicons citing **Ohav'kha** as a noun when it is a verb, present tense. If you see "My friend" or "Your friend," use whiteout and put in "loves Me" or "loves You."

Abstain From the Appearance of Evil is a myth because that is not a translation of the Greek New Testament or of the Vulgate. Both of those agree with the following:

> 1 Thessalonians 5:19. *You must habitually not ever quench the Spirit, 20. you must continually not ever despise prophecy, 21. but you must constantly prove all things; you must incessantly hold fast the good, 22. **you must faithfully keep yourselves away from every form of evil.***

Keeping away from every form of evil is very different from abstaining from the appearance of evil. Abstaining from the appearance of evil has two meanings: One is not to do anything that might even appear to be evil, even if it is innocent and permitted; the other is you can do something evil as long as it does not appear to be evil.

Keeping away from every form of evil means to be above reproach in whatever you do or say.

All the People of Judea were taken to Babylon by Nebuchadnezzar in the Captivity is a common misunderstanding.

Jeremiah 24:1. *The LORD* showed me and, behold, two baskets of figs were set before the Temple of the LORD*, after Nebuchadrezzar king of Babylon had carried away captive **Jeconiah** the son of Jehoiakim king of Judah and **the princes of Judah**, with the **carpenters and smiths** from Jerusalem, and had brought them to Babylon.*

All the leadership was taken and certain skilled artisans, but the bulk of the population was not taken. Shopkeepers, clerks, farmers, and others stayed behind.

Amen Means True or So Be It is a Myth because Amen is not a Hebrew word. Amen is an acrostic and is not from any Hebrew root word. The acrostic is: El Melekh Ne'eman, meaning, **God is a Faithful King**. (See Amen in Glossary.)

Anointing Breaks the Yoke is a Myth. The literal translation is: Isaiah 10:27. *And it will be in that day, his burden will be taken away from off your shoulder, and his yoke from off your neck, and the yoke will be destroyed because of your **robustness**.*

There is not one word in this verse that means Anointing. The Hebrew word Shamen is related to the word Shemen, which means olive oil, but Shamen when it does not refer to people means fat or fatness. When Shamen refers to people it speaks of someone like today's pro football guard or tackle, very big and very strong. Think of yourself as being that awesome against the burden or yoke you are fighting. These next three verses show how fearsome an enemy you can destroy.

Judges 3:29. *And they slew of Moab at that time about ten thousand men, every one **robust** and every one courageous, and not a man escaped.*

Ezekiel 34:16. *I shall seek that which was lost and bring back that which was driven away and will bind up that which was broken and will strengthen that which was sick, but I will destroy the **robust** and the strong. I will feed them with judgment.*

Psalm 78:29. *So they ate and were well filled, for He gave them their desire. 30. They were not estranged from their lust, but while their meat was still in their* *mouths, 31. the wrath of God came upon them and slew the most **robust** of them and struck down the chosen men of Israel.*

All these translated **Robust** are the Hebrew word Shamen. Isaiah says the burden will be taken from our shoulders, and the yoke on our neck will be destroyed because of our strength, because we are to be spiritually strong. Our strength comes from faith, the knowledge, and the certainty that God is in us and nothing is too hard for Him.

Ark of the Covenant is shown being carried in public for all the world to see, but the Ark had to be covered when it travelled (Numbers 4:4). *This will be the service of the sons of Kohath in the Tent of Meeting, about the most holy things, 5. and when the camp sets forward, Aaron and his sons will come and they will take down the covering veil and cover the Ark of Testimony with it, 6. and will put on it the covering of badgers' skins and will spread over it a cloth wholly of blue, and will put in its poles.*

There are many pictures of the Ark being carried, but not even the Levites who carried the Ark were permitted to look at it. Only Aaronite priests could see the uncovered Ark, and only on Yom Kippur or when the LORD* ordered the Tabernacle to move. There is no mention of covering when the Ark was in the house of Abinidab, and then the house of Obed Edom, or on its travels before being placed in the tent in the City of David. There is no way of knowing if the sons of Eli covered the Ark before taking it to the battle, or if it was covered when sent back to Israel by the Philistines. In 1 Samuel 14:16 Saul called for the Ark to come to the battle, but there is no way to know if the Ark was taken to the battle, because of the element of panic immediately following the call for the Ark.

1 Samuel 14:18. *And Saul said to Ahijah, Bring the Ark of God here. For the Ark of God was at that time with the children of Israel. 19. And it happened, while Saul talked to the priest, that the noise that was in the army of the Philistines went on and increased and Saul said to the priest, Withdraw your hand.*

Can Two Walk Together Unless They Agree is a Myth that comes from a Greek Septuagint manuscript.

Amos 3:3. ***Can two walk together unless they meet?!*** This is the translation from the Hebrew text. This is a rhetorical question as shown by the exclamation point after the question mark.

David was barely a teenager when he fought Goliath is a Myth, although he is shown in many illustrations as very young. That comes from the Latin text which calls David a child, a miss-translation of the Hebrew, which calls him a young man. David was at least twenty-seven, maybe twenty-eight, when he fought Goliath. The key to David's age is the two years of Saul's reign and the seven and a half years that David was king over Judah while he was in Hebron. David was thirty when he began his reign in Hebron, which came immediately after Saul's two-year reign. (See 1 Samuel 13:1. See Timeline in Hebrew Texts.)

Esther is Mordecai's niece is a Myth because they are actually cousins.

> Esther 2:5. *Now in the Shushan palace there was a certain Jew, whose name was **Mordecai**, the son of Jair the son of Shimei the son of Kish, a Benjamite, 6. who had been carried away from Jerusalem with the captivity which had been carried away with Jeconiah king of Judah, whom Nebuchadnezzar the king of Babylon had carried away. 7. And he brought up Hadassah, that is **Esther, his uncle's daughter**, for she had neither father nor mother and the maid was pleasing and beautiful, whom Mordecai, when her father and mother were dead, took for his own daughter.*

Every Word of an English Bible is God's Word is a Myth because English was not even a language when the Bible was written. The Biblical languages were not even used for the first English translations; Latin was the language used. Some Latin words are still in many English Bibles, like Gentile, the Latin word for heathen. Ark is the Latin word that translated the Hebrew for Tevah, meaning box and for Aron, meaning chest.

First Fruits Offerings are now to be in the form of money. This is a Myth because all First Fruits offerings are to be in crops—none in animals and none in any other form.

> Deuteronomy 8:7. *For the LORD* your God is bringing you into a good land, a land of brooks of water, of fountains and depths that spring out of valleys and*

*hills; 8. a land of **wheat, barley, vines, fig trees**, and **pomegranates**; a land of olive oil and honey; 9. a land in which you will eat bread without scarceness.*

The crops in bold are the ones to be offered, with the important distinction of being the **first** of each crop. This is the entirety of the First Fruits offering. (See First Fruits in Seasons of the LORD in Glossary.)

Flood, as "When the enemy comes in like a flood" is a Myth because the Hebrew, Greek and Latin all speak of this as a flowing river.

Isaiah 59:19. *So they will revere the name of the LORD* from the west and His glory from the rising of the sun. When the enemy comes in like a **River**, the Spirit of the LORD* will make him flee.*

This is a major river with a strong flow, sweeping everything in its path as a picture of an enemy army coming through like a German blitzkrieg of WW II, sweeping everything in its path, but then the LORD makes the enemy flee.

The word traditionally translated **Flood** is Nahar, which means **River**. The Hebrew word for **Flood** is Mabool. So this is not a flood with high water like that in which Noah floated, but it is a picture of a flowing, forceful river that carries everything in its path. How and when **Flood** came into the English translation of Isaiah 59:19 I do not know, but it was there in the King James Version, and tradition has kept it in some modern English translations.

Gentile is a Myth because it is the Latin word for Heathen. If you say you are a Gentile, you are saying that you are a heathen. (See Gentile in Glossary.)

High Priest's Robe with the bells and pomegranates was worn in the Holy of Holies, so having a rope tied around his ankle is a Myth. That robe was not even worn when he went in the Holy of Holies. The myth that he went into the Holy of Holies with a rope tied around his ankle is not true. Leviticus 16:2. *2. And the LORD* said to Moses, "Speak to Aaron your brother, so at all times he does not come into the Holy Place within the veil before the cover, which is on the Ark, so he does not die: for I shall appear in the cloud upon the cover. 3. Thus will Aaron come into the Holy Place with a young bull for a sin offering and a ram for a burnt offering. 4. He will put on the holy linen tunic and he will have the linen breeches upon his flesh and will be girded with a linen belt and he will be attired* *with the linen turban. These are holy garments, therefore he will immerse his flesh in water and so put them on.*

There was no use for a rope around his ankle because he would not be wearing the robe with the bells and pomegranates, and no one would know if he fell. If he had not prepared himself and went in with sin, he would have died when one of his feet touched the threshold of the Holy Place, the entrance of the Sanctuary. A priest or Levite without sin could grab his ankle and pull him out. There is no record of any priest dying because of sin on entering the Holy Place as all these commands were taken very seriously.

The making of the **Robe** is described in Exodus 39:

Exodus 39:22. *And he made the robe of the ephod of woven work, all of blue. 23. And there was a hole in the middle of the robe, as the hole of a coat of mail, with a band around about the hole, so it would not tear.*

This garment was made like a poncho, only narrower. It was open on the sides and had no sleeves, so it was like a narrow prayer shawl. Notice the band around the hole for the head so the garment does not tear. God thinks of everything, does He not?

Horses Were Hamstrung is a Myth, although some translations of the Hebrew Scriptures say they were hamstrung. Joshua 11:6. *And the LORD* said to Joshua,* **Do not be in awe because of them!** *For tomorrow about this time* **I AM** *will deliver them up, all slain before Israel: you will make geldings of their horses and burn their chariots with fire.* God specifically told Joshua to geld the horses. David also gelded horses, recorded in 2 Samuel 8:4 and 1 Chronicles 18:3. *And David smote Hadarezer king from Zobah to Hamath, as he went to establish his dominion by the river Euphrates. 4. And David took from him a thousand chariots and seven thousand horsemen and twenty thousand foot soldiers. David also castrated all the chariot horses, but reserved of them a hundred for chariots.* The literal translation is castrated, making geldings of the war horses. To hamstring a horse would be terribly cruel and leave it crippled, so it could not be used at all to pull a wagon or to ride. Making the horse a gelding made it unsuitable for war as a chariot horse, but very useful for riding or pulling a wagon. The word hamstring is from the Latin text, kept in various translations by tradition.

Isaiah 6:1. *In the year that king Uzziah died I saw the Lord sitting on a throne, high and lifted up,* (Revelation 4:2,9,7:10) *and His train filled the **palace**. 2. Above Him stood the seraphim: each one had six wings, with two he covered his face, with two he covered his feet, and with two he flew. 3. And one cried to another and said, Holy! Holy! Holy is the LORD* of Hosts!* (Revelation 4:8) *The whole earth is full of His glory! 4. And the posts of the door moved at the voice of the one who cried, and the house was filled with smoke.*

The word translated **palace** is haikhal, which can be translated either **Temple** or **Palace**. If the throne is in the heavenly **Temple**, it would have to be in the Holy Place, the first room, but God sits on the Ark cover in the Holy of Holies. There is no throne or throne room in the first Temple, the second Temple, or in Ezekiel's Third Temple, so **the throne must be in His Palace**, which is only named this one time.

Jacob Supplanted Esau. Jacob has been much maligned because of Esau's referring to Jacob as having supplanted him. That is the Myth because the Hebrew text does not say Jacob supplanted Esau. How come some new translations still have supplant? That is tradition from the Latin text, with the translators not going by the Hebrew. The correct translation of the Hebrew is literally "Jacob outwitted Esau." Genesis 27:36. *And he said, "Is he not rightly named Jacob? For **he has outwitted me** these two times: he took away my birthright and, behold, now he has taken away my blessing."* The Hebrew word translated **Outwitted** is Yak'veni, from the same root as the word Jacob. (See Yak'veni under Words.)

Jehovah Nissi is The LORD My Banner is a Myth because Nissi means **My Miracle**.

Exodus 17:14. *And the LORD* said to Moses, "Write this in a book for a memorial and repeat it in the ears of Joshua, for I shall utterly blot out the remembrance of Amalek from under heaven." 15. And Moses built an altar and called the name of it **Adonai-Nissi, The LORD* is My Miracle**. 16. For he said, "Because the LORD* has sworn that Yah will have war with Amalek from generation to generation."*

This is the word Nes, the same as on the dreidel, "Nes Gadol Haya Sham," A Great Miracle Happened There.

Joseph is thought of as innocent when he was sold into slavery, but he himself did contribute to his problem when he brought very evil reports of his brothers to Jacob. Joseph exaggerated the things being done by his brothers in order to curry favor with his father. The exaggerations made a strong impression on Jacob, so Jacob made a special mantle for Joseph that showed a higher rank than any of his brothers. It was not of different colors or just a different color, but the size, from wrist to wrist and down to the ground, indicated that Joseph had a higher rank than any of his brothers. Theirs were wrist to wrist but only went to the knees. The robe of many colors came from the Latin text, not the Hebrew. The Hebrew expression is k'tonet hapayim, meaning Long Tunic. That reward for slandering his brothers led to his being sold into slavery, but even worse, slandering his brothers opened the door for the slander by Potiphar's wife. Of course, all of this was part of God's plan from the beginning because God declares the end from the beginning. Isaiah 46:10 *declaring the end from the beginning, and from ancient times the things that are not done, saying, My counsel will stand, and I shall do all My pleasure.*

Judaism is commonly seen in Galatians 1:14 when Paul was referring to his working in Galatians 1:13 and 14, but concerns the Greek word, Ioudaismos, which is commonly translated Judaism. Ioudaismos does not mean Judaism, but because it looks like our modern word it is sometimes translated incorrectly. Ioudaismos means "of or pertaining to Judea."

The modern use of the word Judaism came centuries later, so Galatians 1:13 and 14 actually reads:

For you have heard about my earlier conduct when in Judea, that I persecuted beyond measure the congregation of God and was destroying it, 14. and I was advancing in Judea over many contemporaries in my generation, since I was a zealot of the traditions of my ancestors to a much greater degree.

When Paul wrote that, he was talking about his being known in the country of Judea as he spoke in Acts 22:2 *Then he said, 3. "I am a man, Jewish, born in Tarsus of Cilicia, but having been brought up in this city beside the feet of Gamaliel, instructed according to the precision of our fathers' tradition, being zealous for God, just as you all are today: 4. who did persecute this Way until death, putting both men and women in chains and giving them over into jail, 5. in the same way also the High Priest and all the council of elders spoke well of me, from whom I even took a letter to the brothers in Damascus where I was going, so after they were bound, I would lead those of the Way at that place to Jerusalem so that they could be punished."*

Law is a Myth, as in "We are not under **Law**, but under Grace." Law is a totally misleading translation of the Greek word nomos. While nomos generally is translated Torah, in this context Paul is not referring to Torah, but another meaning of Nomos, **Legalism**. The translation of the Hebrew word Torah and the Greek word Nomos as Law has done great damage to the Church, giving Christians a very distorted view of God's teachings.

Romans 6:14. *For sin will not rule you: for you are not under **legalism** but grace.*

Mark 8:14. *And they forgot to take bread, except one loaf they had in the boat with them. 15. And He ordered them saying, "You must continually take care, you must continually beware of the **leaven of the Pharisees** and the leaven of Herod."*

The leaven of the Pharisees was **Legalism**, the leaven of Herod was Hellenism. (See both Legalism and Hellenism in Glossary.)

Lawyers in the New Testament are a Myth because they are a remnant from the early English translations. The Greek word translated lawyer is Nomikos, which in lexicons is translated "pertaining to interpretation of Mosaic Law, an interpreter or teacher of Mosaic Law." So the interpreter has been called Lawyer in various English translations. The problem is that an interpreter of Mosaic Law is not a Lawyer, but a Torah scholar. The *One New Man Bible* consistently translates Nomikos as Torah scholar.

Luke 11:46. *Then He said, "And woe to you Torah scholars, because you load people with difficult burdens, then you do not even lift one finger to help with the burdens.*

Titus 3:13. *You must now make every effort to send Zenas, the Torah scholar, and Apollos on their way, so that nothing would be lacking for them.*

Let God Arise is a Myth! God's Word never says to LET Him arise!

Psalm 68:2. ***God will arise! His enemies will be scattered!*** *Those who hate Him will flee before Him.*

Numbers 10:35. *And it was, when the Ark set forward that Moses said, "**Arise LORD*! Your enemies will be scattered** and those who hate You will flee before You."*

Our God is **not** wishy-washy, but He is very bold and straightforward. Most of the time when you see the statement "Let something happen," the correct translation is "That will happen."

Let My People Go! Is a Myth because God never told Moses to plead with Pharaoh, but told Moses to command Pharaoh, **Send My People Away!**

Exodus 7:16. *And you will say to him, 'The LORD* God of the Hebrews has sent me to you saying, **Send My people away!** So they can serve Me in the wilderness. And behold, till now you would not listen.*

Each time Moses and Aaron went to Pharaoh, the word of the Lord was **Send My People Away!** Not once did they plead with Pharaoh to Let My People go.

Liberty as in 2 Corinthians 3:17, frequently translated "...where the Spirit of the Lord is there is **Liberty**." This is a Myth because the word Liberty is a holdover from the early English translation from the Latin. Liberty, translated from the Latin Libertas, means a release to do anything, which is like freedom. But the Greek word eleutheria translated freedom to specifically refer to freedom **from** something—from sin, then from bondage, both physical slavery and spiritual bondage. The New Thayer Greek-English Lexicon has "...freedom from the corrupt desires, so that we do by the free impulse of the soul what the will of God requires."

The translation of 2 Corinthians 3:17 from the Greek New Testament is:

And the Lord is Spirit: and where the Spirit of the Lord is, there is freedom.

You can be sure the freedom is not permission to do whatever, but it is freedom from evil impulses.

Little Lower than Angels in Psalm 8:6 is a Myth. This is referring to our Messiah, Y'shua, Who was not lower than angels. That translation came from the Septuagint, not from the Hebrew, or even from the Latin Vulgate. The correct use is *For You have made Him **a little lower than God** and have crowned Him with glory and honor.*

Although commonly translated "lower than the angels," those verses are given here: from the Hebrew, the word is Elohim, meaning God.

Psalm 8:5b. *And the Son of Man, that You visit Him? 6. For You have made Him **a little lower than God** and have crowned Him with glory and honor. 7. You made Him to have dominion over the works of Your hands. You have put all things under His feet: 8. all sheep and oxen, yea, and the beasts of the field, 9. the fowl of the air and the fish of the sea, whatever passes through the paths of the seas.*

These verses are about Messiah, Y'shua. The word Angels is only in the Septuagint; both the Hebrew and the Vulgate have God. If your Bible has "lower than angels," make a note that "lower than God" is the correct translation, that Y'shua was never lower than angels.

Lucifer is a Myth because that is the Latin name of the fallen former Archangel.

Isaiah 14:12. *How you have fallen from heaven, **O Shining Son of the Dawn!** How you, who did weaken the nations, are cut down to the ground! 13. For you have said in your heart, I shall ascend into heaven, I shall exalt my throne above the stars of God. I shall sit also upon the mountain of the congregation, in the recesses of the north. 14. I shall ascend above the heights of the clouds. I shall be like the Most High. 15. Yet you will be brought down to hell, to the lowest depth of the pit.*

The Hebrew text does not give him a name, but describes him as **Shining Son of the Dawn**.

Luke is commonly thought of as not being Jewish, but that is a Myth. The Gospel of Luke has more Hebraisms than any other Book in the New Testament. In the Book of Acts, Luke uses an expression that was only used by rabbis. Reverend Arnold Gause, a Bible scholar with a PhD in Greek, theorizes that Luke was a rabbi who fell on hard times and became a bond servant to some very wealthy person who, recognizing Luke's powerful intellect, had him trained to be his personal physician. Somehow, Luke later obtained his freedom. In the first century, nearly every physician was a personal physician to some very wealthy individual.

Mansion in Heaven is a Myth because the Latin word Mansiones was not translated, but put in the Bible as Mansion. Mansiones does not mean Mansion, but it means a place, like a place in an organization or on a team. It also means dwelling, but not in a mansion. John 14:2 *In My Father's house are many dwelling places: and if it were not so, would I tell you that **I am going to prepare a place for you?** 3. And if I would go, then **I shall prepare a place for you.** I am coming again and I shall take you along with Me,* (Exodus 6:7) *so that where I AM you would also be.*

May the LORD* Bless You is a Myth because the Lord is not a God of Maybe, He is very positive. God's Word is very positive and very bold. This is from the Priestly Blessing, which has **"The LORD* will bless you and He will Keep you!"** (See Priestly Blessing in Glossary.)

Noah's Ark has been represented many times by a cute little boat with animals on deck, especially elephants and giraffes. This is not at all what the Ark looked like. It was box, a big box, with three interior decks and just one window high on the side. This box was about 450 feet long by 75 feet wide and 45 feet high. The box housed thousands of animals for over a year, along with eight humans. (See Ark in Glossary.)

Precept upon Precept is misleading. We have a common misunderstanding that the verses in Isaiah are talking about teaching or admonishment—the primary meanings of the word Precept in modern English. The Hebrew and Latin texts for Isaiah 28:9 are *To whom will he, the prophet, teach knowledge? And whom will he make to understand doctrine? Those who are weaned from the milk. Those who are drawn from the breasts.* (Hebrews 5:13) *10. For **command must be upon command, command upon command**; line upon line, line upon line; here a little, there a little, 11. for he will speak to this people with stammering lips and another tongue.* (1 Corinthians 14:21) *12. To whom he said, This is the rest with which you may cause the weary to rest, and this is the refreshing, yet they would not listen. 13. But the Word of the LORD* was to them **commandment upon commandment, commandment upon commandment**, line upon line, line upon line; here a little, there a little; so they could go and fall backward, be broken, snared, and taken.*

Precept in English means an admonishing or teaching, but Isaiah said **Commandment**. Therefore, we are called to heed all His **Commandments**.

Preparation Day is thought by many to be preparation for Passover—to prepare for the weekly **Sabbath**, not Passover. (See Preparation Day in Seasons of the LORD* in Glossary.)

Prosperity is a Myth despite the Prosperity Message that has prospered for decades. Look at the attitude that those who want to be more like Y'shua should have:

Luke 12:15. *And He said to them, "You must continually understand and guard yourselves from all covetousness, because someone's life is not abundant from his possessions."*

Luke 12:29. *So you must not be seeking what you could eat and what you could drink and you must stop being anxious: 30. for the heathens of the world are searching for all these things, but your Father knows that you continually have need of these things. 31. But you must habitually seek His kingdom, and these things will be added to you. 32. You, little flock, stop being afraid, because* **your Father took delight to give you the kingdom. 33. You must sell your possessions and you must now give to the poor: you must now make for yourselves purses that do not wear out, an inexhaustible treasure in the heavens, where no thief comes near and no moth ruins: 34. for where your treasure is, there also will your heart be."**

Luke 18:18. *Then some official asked Him saying, "Good teacher, what must I do so that I will inherit eternal life?" 19. And Y'shua said to him, "Why do you call Me good? No one is good except One, God. 20. You know the commandments: 'Do not commit adultery, do not murder, do not steal, do not bear false witness, honor your father and your mother.'" 21. And he said, "I have kept all these from my youth." 22. And when He heard, Y'shua said to him, "Yet one thing is lacking for you:* **you must immediately sell everything which you have and you must right away distribute the money to the poor and you will have treasure in the heavens, then come, you must continually follow Me."** *23. But when he heard these things he became very sad: for he was extremely wealthy.*

Ephesians 5:1. *Therefore you must continually be imitators of God as beloved children 2. and you must walk constantly in love, just as also the Messiah loved us and gave Himself over on our behalf, an offering and a sacrifice to God for a fragrant aroma. 3. But any immorality or impurity or covetousness must not be named among you, as is fitting for saints, 4. nor foul speaking or foolish talking or low jesting, which things do not belong, but rather thanksgiving. 5. For you know this very well, that anyone who practices immorality or uncleanness or covetousness, who is an idol worshipper, does not have any inheritance in the kingdom of the Messiah and God.*

Colossians 3:5. *Therefore you must right now put to death the earthly parts, which are immorality, uncleanness, passion, evil desires, and covetousness, which is idol worship, 6. because of which the wrath of God is coming upon the sons of the disobedient.*

In both Ephesians 5 and Colossians 3, Covetousness is specifically referred to as idol worship. The **Prosperity Message** by its very nature is covetousness, which is idol worship. Covetousness is the problem, not wealth. (Read the article Wealth in Glossary, knowing that our attitude should be like Paul's in the next paragraph.)

Philippians 4:10. *And I rejoice in the Lord greatly because now then you have revived so as to take thought on my behalf, upon which also you were thinking about me, but you were lacking opportunity to show it. 11. Not that I am talking on account of a great need, for I have learned to be content with what things I have. 12. And I know how to submit myself to want, and I know how to be abundant: in everything and in all things I have learned the secret, both how to be filled and how to be needy and how to be affluent and how to suffer want: 13. I have strength to overcome all things in the One Who strengthens me. 14. Yet you did well, because you were sharers with me in my trouble.*

Paul's message to Timothy puts Prosperity into Perspective:

1 Timothy 6:1. *You must regularly teach and encourage these things. 3. If someone teaches a different doctrine and does not go in sound doctrine with those of our Lord Y'shua Messiah and in teaching that promotes Godliness, 4. he has become puffed up, since he knows nothing, but has a morbid craving for controversies and disputes, out of which come envy, strife, blasphemies, evil suspicions, 5. because people have been ruined by constant irritation of the mind and have destroyed the truth for themselves, **thinking that godliness is a means of financial gain. 6. But Godliness with Contentment is a great gain:** 7. for we have brought nothing into the world, so that as a result we are not able to take anything out: 8. but if we have food and covering, we will content ourselves with these. 9. But those who want to be rich are falling into temptation and trials and many foolish and harmful desires, which sink people into ruin and destruction. 10. For **the love of**

money is a root of all the evils, *which because some strove for, they went astray from the faith and they pierced themselves with many sorrows.*

1 Timothy 6:17. *You must continually command those who are rich in the present age not to be proud and not to hope in riches in uncertainty, but in God, the One Who supplies richly everything for our enjoyment, 18. and that they are to do good works, to be rich in good works, to be generous, sharing, 19. and in this way to be storing up for themselves a good foundation for the coming age, so that they would really take hold of life.*

Samuel's Age—That He Was a Child When God Called to Him is a Myth because he had to be at least thirty years old to be in the Sanctuary.

1 Samuel 3:1. *And the young man Samuel ministered to the LORD* before Eli. And the word of the LORD* was rare in those days. There was no frequent vision.*

1 Samuel 3:2. *And it was at that time when Eli was lying down in his place and his eyes began to grow dim, he could not see. 3. And the lamp of God had not yet gone out and Samuel was lying down in the Temple of the LORD*, where the Ark of God was.*

1 Samuel 3:4. *The LORD* called Samuel and he answered, Here I am. 5. And he ran to Eli and said, Here I am, for you called me.*

And he said, I did not call. Lie down again. And he went and lay down.

1 Samuel 3:6. *And the LORD* called yet again, Samuel!*

And Samuel got up and went to Eli and said, Here I am, for you did call me.

And he answered, I did not call, my son. Lie down again.

1 Samuel 3:7. *Now Samuel did not yet know the LORD*, neither was the word of the LORD* yet revealed to him.*

1 Samuel 3:8. *And the LORD* called Samuel again the third time. And he got up and went to Eli and said, Here I am, for you did call me. And Eli understood that the LORD* had called the young man.*

1 Samuel 3:9. *Therefore Eli said to Samuel, Go, lie down and it will be, if He calls you, that you will say, Speak, LORD*, for Your servant is listening.*

So Samuel went and lay down in his place. 10. And the LORD* came and stood, and called as at other times, Samuel. Samuel!

Then Samuel answered, Speak, for Your servant is listening.

1 Samuel 3:11. *And the LORD* said to Samuel, Behold,* **I AM** *doing a thing in Israel at which both the ears of everyone who hears will tingle. 12. In that day I shall perform against Eli all things which I have spoken concerning his house, from beginning to end. 13. For I AM has told him that I shall judge his house forever for the iniquity which he knows because his sons made themselves vile, and he did not restrain them. 14. And therefore I have sworn to the house of Eli that the iniquity of Eli's house will not ever be purged with a sacrifice or an offering.*

1 Samuel 3:15. *And Samuel lay until the morning and opened the entrance of the House of the LORD*. And Samuel was in awe to tell Eli about the vision. 16. Then Eli called Samuel and said, Samuel, my son.*

And he answered, Here I am.

1 Samuel 3:17. *And he said, What is it that He said to you?* **Please, now, do not hide it from me!** *God do so to you and more also, if you hide anything from me of all the things that He said to you. 18. And Samuel told him every bit and hid nothing from him. And he said, It is the LORD*. Let Him do what seems good to Him.*

1 Samuel 3:19. *And Samuel grew and the LORD* was with him and He did not let any of his words fall to the ground. 20. And all Israel from Dan even to Beer-Sheba knew that Samuel was a faithful prophet of the LORD*. 21. And the LORD* appeared again in Shiloh for the LORD* revealed Himself to Samuel in Shiloh.*

Because Samuel was sleeping in the Sanctuary, his age had to be at the very least thirty years old.

Samuel's Age When Brought to Eli was not three years old. The verses speaking of his being weaned are 1 Samuel 1:22–24. The Hebrew Gamal means to wean and is used in 1 Samuel 1:22 and 23: in verse 24 the word is G'malto, referring to a child who is old enough to leave his mother, generally considered to be at least eleven. 1 Samuel 1:24. *And when she had weaned him, she took him up with her, with three bulls and one ephah of flour and a skin-bottle of wine, and brought him to the House of the LORD* in Shiloh, and the **lad was young**.* This word translated Lad is Na'ar, usually used for men in their late teens to late twenties. While we do not know his age, the use of na'ar indicates mid-teens as the very youngest possible age.

Sea of Galilee is a Myth because this is a large fresh water lake, the source of drinking water for much of Israel.

Spirit of Fear is a Myth because the correct translation of the Greek is **Timidity**. The word Fear is from the Latin Timeo.

2 Timothy 1:6. *For which reason I am reminding you to rekindle the gift of God which is in you through the laying on of my hands. 7. For God did not give us a **Spirit of Timidity** but of power and love and self-control.*

This is a very important exhortation for Timothy and all of today's believers to use the gifts of the Spirit to advance the Kingdom, as Y'shua ordered His disciples to preach the Kingdom. The only appearance of the expression "Spirit of Fear" in Scripture is in 2 Timothy 1:7. Timidity keeps believers from using their spiritual gifts to bring the Kingdom to earth. We are not to be intimidated, but to be bold!

Matthew 10:7. *And while you are going you must preach, saying that '**The Kingdom of the Heavens has come near.**' 8. You must continually heal sicknesses, raise the dead, cleanse lepers, cast out demons: you took freely, you must now give freely.*

Study To Show Approval is a Myth. The literal translation of 2 Timothy 2:15 *is You must now **Be Diligent** to present yourself approved to God, a workman who has no cause to be ashamed, teaching the doctrine of the Truth correctly and directly.* Even the Latin text has to **be diligent**. It is important not just for pastors to be diligent, but every one of us Christians must **be diligent** to show with every word we speak and everything we do that we have a close relationship with the Most High God, the King of the Universe. (See Be Diligent in Teachings.)

Tabernacle of David is a Myth because of the Latin word Tabernaculum used for Booth in Acts 15:16.

> *15.* And in this the words of the prophets agree just as it has been written,
> *16. 'After these things I shall return*
> *and will build up again the Booth of David that has fallen down*
> *and the things that have been destroyed, I shall build up its ruins and I shall restore it,*
> *17. to the end that the remnants of the (Jewish) people and all the heathens upon whom My name would have been invoked would seek out the Lord, says the Lord Who does all these things'* (Amos 9:11,12)
> *18. known from eternity*

The rest of verse 18 gives the purpose of raising the Booth of David:

> *so they can possess the remnant of Edom and of all the nations that are called by My name.*

Sukkah in the Hebrew and skene in the Greek text do not mean tabernacle, which comes from the Latin text, but booth, speaking of the personal booth of the Feast of Booths. The booth of David represents two things: the restoration of the Davidic kingdom, which will be the Messianic reign, and the sovereignty of David, the establishment of the kingship authority, which is the legitimacy of David's—and the Messiah's—reign. That also clearly states the legitimacy of the national sovereignty of the state of Israel.

Raising the Booth of David is tied to evangelism to the heathen peoples. The Amos verses are not word for word. (See Memorization of Scripture in Glossary.)

Ten Commandments were all that was written on the stone tablets carried by Moses. This is a Myth because the entire Torah was written on the two tablets. The Torah was given in Exodus 20 and again in Exodus 34. Each time the entire Torah was given, and each time the entire Torah was written on the two tablets. Exodus 24:4. *And Moses wrote all the words of the LORD* and rose up early in the morning and built an altar at the foot of the mountain and twelve pillars,* *according to the twelve tribes of Israel. The scroll Moses wrote was placed beside the Ark, as the LORD* instructed Moses in Deuteronomy 31:26. Take this scroll of the Torah and put it beside the Ark of the Covenant of the LORD* your God so it will be there as a witness against you.*

God wrote all the words of the Torah on the two tablets. Exodus 24:12. *And the LORD* said to Moses, "Come up to Me on the mountain and be there, and shall give you the tablets of stone, the **Torah** (Teaching), and the **commandments** which I have written so you can teach them."* God specifically says the Torah and the commandments He had written. The statements that summarize the Torah, God refers to as "Statements" not as commandments.

Exodus 34:1. *And the LORD* said to Moses, "Hew two tablets of stone like the first and **I shall write upon the tablets the words that were on the first tablets**, which you broke. 2. And be ready in the morning and come up in the morning to Mount Sinai and present yourself there to Me on the top of the mountain. 3. And no man is to come up with you. **Neither will any man be seen throughout the whole mountain, nor will the flocks or herds feed before that mountain!"** 4. And he hewed two stone tablets like the first and Moses rose up early in the morning and went up to Mount Sinai, as the LORD* had commanded him, and took in his hand the two tablets of stone.*

This time Moses cuts the tablets. God writes on the tablets the entire Torah for the second time. What is recorded here is God's summary, very different from what we call the Ten Commandments.

The first tablets had:

Exodus 20:2. *"**I AM** the LORD* your God Who has brought you out of the land of Egypt, out of the house of bondage. 3. You will have no other gods before Me. 4. You will not make any graven image for yourself, or any likeness of anything that is in heaven above, or that is in the earth beneath, or that is in the water under the earth. 5. You will not bow yourself down to them, or serve them, for **I AM** the LORD* your God, a jealous God, visiting the iniquity of the fathers upon the children to the third and fourth generation of those who hate Me, 6. and showing loving kindness to thousands of those who love Me and keep My commandments.*

Exodus 20:7. *"You will not take the name of the LORD* your God in vain, for the LORD* will not hold him guiltless who takes His name in vain.*

Exodus 20:8. *"Remember the Sabbath, to keep it holy. 9. You will labor six days and do all your work, 10. but the seventh day is the Sabbath of the LORD* your God, you will not do any work, you or your son or your daughter, your manservant or your maidservant or your cattle or your stranger who is within your gates. 11. For in six days the LORD* made heaven and earth, the sea, and all that is in them and He rested the seventh day, therefore the LORD* blessed the Sabbath and sanctified it.*

Exodus 20:12. *"Honor your father and your mother, so your days will be long upon the land which the LORD* your God is giving to you.*

Exodus 20:13. *"You will not murder. You will not commit adultery. You will not steal. You will not bear false witness against your neighbor.*

Exodus 20:14. *"You will not covet your neighbor's house, you will not covet your neighbor's wife, or his manservant, or his maidservant, or his ox, or his donkey, or anything that is your neighbor's."* (Romans 7:7,13:9)

This time God's summary is quite different from that in Chapter 20. These concern relationship:

Exodus 34:10. *And He said, "Behold, **I AM** cutting a covenant: before all your people, I shall do amazing things, such as have not been done in all the earth, nor in any nation: and all the people among whom you are will see the work of the LORD*, for it is an awe-inspiring thing that I AM doing with you. 11. Mark well what **I AM** commanding you this day! See for yourself! I am expelling before you the Amorite, the Canaanite, the Hittite, the Perizzite, the Hivite, and the Jebusite. 12. 1 Take heed for yourself, that you do not cut a covenant with the inhabitants of the land where you are going, lest it be for a snare among you, 13. 2 but you will destroy their altars, break their images and cut down their groves, 14. 3 for you will worship no other god: for the LORD*, Whose name is Jealous, is a jealous God. 15. Lest you cut a covenant with the inhabitants of the land and they go astray after their gods and sacrifice to their gods and invite you and you eat of his sacrifice. 16. And you take of their daughters for your sons, and their daughters go astray after their gods and make your sons go astray after their gods. 17. 4 You will make no molten gods for yourselves."*

Exodus 34:18. *5 "You will keep the Feast of Unleavened Bread. You will eat unleavened bread seven days as I commanded you, in the time of the month Aviv, for in the month Aviv you came out from Egypt."*

Exodus 34:19. *6 "All that opens the womb is Mine and every firstling among your livestock that is male, whether ox or sheep. 20. But the firstling of a donkey you will redeem with a lamb, and if you do not redeem it, then you will break its neck. All the firstborn of your sons you will redeem. And no one will appear before Me empty.*

Exodus 34:21. *7 "You will work six days, but on the seventh day you will rest: in plowing time and in harvest you will rest.*

Exodus 34:22. *8 "And you will observe the Feast of Weeks of the First Fruits of wheat harvest (Shavuot), and the Feast of Ingathering (Sukkot) at the year's end.*

Exodus 34:23. *9 "Three times a year all your males will appear before the Lord, the LORD* God of Israel. 24. For I shall cast out the nations before you and enlarge your borders. Neither will any man desire your land, when you go up to appear before the LORD* your God three times a year.*

Exodus 34:25. *10 "You will not offer the blood of My sacrifice with leaven. Neither will the sacrifice of the Feast of the Passover be left to the morning.*

Exodus 34:26. *11 "The first of the First Fruits of your land you will bring to the House of the LORD* your God. You will not boil a kid in its mother's milk."*

This summary is dramatically different from the first summary, so you can see that the same words carved on the stone tablets relate to the whole Torah, not just the two summaries. The illustrations of one tablet with numbers 1–5 and the other tablet with 6–10 are incorrect.

God makes this third summary quite similar to the first in Exodus 20:

Deuteronomy 5:6. *"I AM the LORD* your God, Who brought you out of the land of Egypt, from the house of bondage.*

Deuteronomy 5:7. *"You will have no other gods before Me.*

Deuteronomy 5:8. *"You will not make for yourself any carved or molded image, or any likeness of anything that is in the sky above, or that is in the earth below, or that is in the waters beneath the earth. 9. You will not bow down yourself to them, or serve them, for **I AM** the LORD* your God, a jealous God, visiting the iniquity of the fathers upon the children to the third and fourth generation of those who hate Me, 10. and showing loving kindness to thousands of those who love Me and keep My commandments.*

Deuteronomy 5:11. *"You will not take the name of the LORD* your God in vain, for the LORD* will not hold guiltless who takes His name in vain.*

Deuteronomy 5:12. *"Keep the Sabbath to sanctify it, as the LORD* your God has commanded you. 13. Six days you will labor and do all your work, 14. but the seventh day is the Sabbath of the LORD* your God, you will not do any work, you, your son, your daughter, your manservant, your maidservant, your ox, your donkey, any of your cattle, nor your stranger who is within your gates, so your manservant and your maidservant may rest as well as you. 15. And remember that you were a servant in the land of Egypt, and the LORD* your God brought you out from there through a mighty hand and by an outstretched arm. Therefore the LORD* your God commanded you to keep the Sabbath day.*

Deuteronomy 5:16. *"Honor your father and your mother, as the LORD* your God has commanded you, so your days may be prolonged and so it may go well with you in the land which the LORD* your God is giving to you.* (Ephesians 6:3)

Deuteronomy 5:17. *"You will not murder.*

"Neither will you commit adultery.

"Neither will you steal:

"Neither will you bear false witness against your neighbor.

Deuteronomy 5:18. *"Neither will you desire your neighbor's wife,*

Nor will you covet your neighbor's house, his field, or his manservant, or his maidservant, his ox, or his donkey, or anything that is your neighbor's."

These are close to the summary in Exodus 20, but not identical. The point is the LORD* wrote all the Torah on the tablets Moses carried, that our pictures of the tablets with five commandments on one and five on the other are man's imagination. Both Christian and Jewish leaders endorse The Ten Commandments, but that is a Myth.

The Giver in Romans 12, in a list of Ministry gifts, is a Myth.

> Romans 12:3. *For I say, through the grace that has been given to me, to everyone who is among you, not to think too highly of yourselves beyond which it is necessary to think, but to think to put a moderate estimate of yourself, in the same manner as God divided to each a measure of faith. 4. For just as we have many members in one body, but all the parts do not have the same function, 5. in this way, we, the many, are one body in Messiah, but each one part of one another. 6. And having different gifts according to the grace given to us, whether **1** Prophecy according to the proportion of his faith, 7. or **2** Ministry/Service in his service, or the one who **3** Teaches in the teaching, 8. or the one who **4** Encourages in encouragement: the one who **5 Shares**,* (Ephesians 4:28; Hebrews 12:16) *in sincerity without grudging, the **6** Protector or guardian giving aid in diligent eagerness, the one who is **7** Merciful in cheerfulness.*

> Number Five, the one who Shares, is the literal translation, a very meaningful difference from Giving because you do not have to be affluent to share what little you have. In fact, the one who has little and shares it willingly really touches the heart of God, as we see in Mark 12:41. *And after He sat down opposite the treasury He was watching how the crowd cast copper coin into the treasury. And many rich were casting much: 42. and when she came one poor widow cast two small copper coins, which is about a quarter of a cent. 43. Then after He summoned the disciples He said to them, "Truly I say to you that this poor widow cast more than all those when they cast into the treasury: 44. for they all cast from their abundance, but she cast from her need all that she had her whole life."* (See One Who Shares in Teachings.)

We Are Kings and Priests is a Myth because the word is Kingdom in Revelation 1:6, not Kings. Revelation 1:5b. *To the One Who loves us and has loosed us from our sins by His blood, 6. and **made us a kingdom, priests to His God and Father**, to Him be the glory and the power forever and ever. Amen.*

A Kingdom of Priests is what is coming! Revelation 1:6 speaks of the Millennial Reign, saying we will be a kingdom of priests. Some translations say we will be Kings and Priests, but that is not in either the Greek or Latin texts. Both have a Kingdom, Priests. There is one Kingdom, and all believers are Priests.

Wise Men Visiting the Infant Y'shua are a Myth because they were idol worshippers, in a class with fortune tellers. Calling them Wise is a gross injustice to those who are Wise.

Matthew 2:1. *And after Y'shua was born in Bethlehem of Judea in the days of Herod the king, behold astrologers from the east arrived in Jerusalem 2. saying, "Where is the One Who has been born King of the Jewish People? For we saw His star in the east and we came to pay homage to Him." 3. And when King Herod heard, he was disturbed and all Jerusalem with him, 4. and gathering all the high priests and scribes of the people he inquired from them where the Messiah was to be born. 5. And they said to him, "In Bethlehem of Judea: for thus it has been written through the prophet:*

6. 'And you Bethlehem,' country of Judea,
'you are' by no means 'least among the princes of Judea:
for out of you will come a ruler,
who will shepherd My people Israel.'"

2:7. *Then Herod, having secretly called the astrologers, ascertained from them the time of the revealing of the star, 8. and sending them into Bethlehem he said, "When you go you must inquire carefully concerning the child: as soon as you would find Him, you must report to me right away, then when I come I shall pay homage to Him."*

These men were sorcerers—Magoi in the Greek, Magi in the Latin. It is gross miss-statement to call them wise. Those into astrology are fortune tellers and are not in the things of the LORD. The king and many of the people in Jerusalem were upset because they were Hellenists, so their world would have been lost with the coming of Messiah. (See Hellenists in Glossary.)

Women in Ministry, Romans 16:1. *And I am introducing our sister Phoebe to you, since she is also a minister of the congregation in Cenchrea, 2. so that you would welcome her in the Lord as befitting the saints, and you would stand by her in* *whatever matter she would have need of you: for she has also become a patroness of many, even of me.*

The word translated Minister can also be translated Servant. Some translations refer to Phoebe as a servant, but no one would send a servant to Rome from Cencrae, which was at the western end of the narrow isthmus connecting northern Greece to southern Greece. That was an expensive trip, especially considering that 50% of Rome's 2,000,000 people were slaves. Paul also refers to Phoebe as a Patroness, which means someone set over others, even of himself he then says. That has to mean that Phoebe was in some way vested with authority by the Jerusalem Council. That plus the naming of ten women in Romans 16 shows that the early Church had many women in ministry, that the early Church did not have the prejudice against women in ministry that has bound many churches to this very day.

Worship the Lord in the Beauty of Holiness is a Myth because the correct translation of Hadrat is:

Psalm 29:2. *Give to the LORD* the glory due His name!* ***Worship the LORD* in the adornment of holiness!***

Psalm 96:9. ***O worship the LORD* in the adornment of holiness!*** *Stand in awe before Him, all the earth.*

1 Chronicles 16:29. *Give unto the LORD* the glory due His name! Bring an offering! Come before Him!* ***Worship the LORD* in the adornment of holiness!***

2 Chronicles 20:21. *And when he had consulted with the people, he appointed singers to the LORD*, who would* ***praise*** *in the adornment of holiness as they went out before the army and to say, Give thanks to the LORD*, for His loving kindness endures forever.*

The primary meaning of Hadrat is Adornment, so these four Scriptures should all read Adornment of Holiness. Many of you have experienced this when worshipping and praising the LORD*, having actually felt the Presence of the LORD*.

Yoke is Easy is a Myth because that is a translation of the Latin text and is not what Matthew wrote.

Matthew 11:28. *Come to Me all those who work and are burdened, and I shall give you rest. 29. You must immediately take My yoke upon you and you must now learn from Me, because I am gentle and humble in My heart, and you will find rest in your lives: 30. for My yoke is **pleasant** and My burden is insignificant."*

The **Yoke** of the LORD is **Pleasant**, but not always easy. (See Yoke in Glossary and see Trials in Glossary.)

Your Body is a Temple of the Holy Spirit! This is a Myth because the word translated Temple is Naos, which means Sanctuary. In the New Testament, every time the body is spoken about as a place of worship, the Greek word used is Naos. The Latin text has Temple. So many English translations had Temple that now Bible dictionaries have Temple as the meaning of Naos. Naos is used every time the Sanctuary is the appropriate place, as in Matthew 23:35. *so would come upon you all the righteous blood being shed upon the earth from the blood of the righteous Abel until the blood of Zechariah son of Barachiah, whom you murdered between the Sanctuary and the altar.* Often this is translated between the Temple and the altar, but the altar and the Sanctuary are both in the middle of the Temple, so it is impossible to be between the altar and Temple. The Greek word Naos is used here. (See Sanctuary in Glossary for more on this.)

WORDS

Araunah was the owner of the threshing floor, which David bought to offer a sacrifice in 2 Samuel 24.

> 2 Samuel 24:21. *And **Araunah** said, Why has my lord the king come to his servant? And David said, To buy your threshing floor, to build an altar to the LORD*, so the plague may be stayed from the people. 22. And **Araunah** said to David, Let my lord the king take and offer up what seems good to him. Behold, here are oxen for the burnt offering and threshing instruments and the harness of the oxen for wood. 23. And **Araunah** gave all these things to the king. And **Araunah** said to the king, The LORD* your God will accept you. 24. And the king said to **Araunah**, No, but I shall surely buy it of you at a price. Neither will I offer burnt offerings to the LORD* my God of that which does not cost me anything. So David bought the threshing floor and the oxen for fifty shekels of silver. 25. And David built an altar there to the LORD*, and offered burnt offerings and peace offerings. So the LORD* prepared the land and the plague was stayed from Israel.*

Araunah is spelled **Alef-vav-resh-nun-heh**.

> 1 Chronicles 21:18. *Then the angel of the LORD* commanded Gad to say to David that David should go up and set up an altar to the LORD* on the threshing floor of **Ornan the Jebusite**.*

This time it is spelled **Alef-resh-nun-nun and written Ornan**. This is the same person, spelled a little differently around 700 years later. The **vav and the heh are soft letters which can be left out of a word and it would not be miss-spelled, so the only real difference is the second nun**. This is definitely the same person, without that much difference in the Hebrew name. The name difference came from the Latin transliterations.

Disarmed?

Colossians 2:14. *Since God wiped away the record against us in the decrees which were set against us, and He took each decree away, out from our midst, by nailing the record to the cross with Him: 15. when God **disarmed** the principalities and the authorities He made them an example, exposing them publicly, when He triumphed over them through Him, Messiah.*

This says God **Disarmed** the principalities and authorities, the very highest ranking of our spiritual opponents. WOW! But it is really much, much more than that. The Greek word is **Apekduomai**. The meaning is to strip off clothes so this is a direct comparison to the Roman practice of bringing a conquered king, his top leaders, and his generals to Rome where they were marched in a victory parade through the streets of Rome, stripped naked for all the people to see their shame. That is what Paul is saying—God has done with our spiritual enemies! So remember your spiritual enemies have not just been overcome by Y'shua, but they have been humiliated!

Gehenna is the Greek spelling of the Hebrew term, Ge Hinnom, for Valley of Hinnom, the place outside Jerusalem where garbage, trash, dead animals, and even executed criminals were disposed. Fires burned continuously to get rid of the trash and the bodies. Worms lived in whatever had not been consumed by the fires. The smoke, fires, and worms were a constant reminder to the residents and visitors to Jerusalem of the description of Sheol, so Gehenna was used as a synonym for Sheol. From early in the history of Israel, this valley was used for human sacrifices, offerings of babies to the heathen god, Moloch. Joshua 15:8 is the earliest reference, then Joshua 18:16; Jeremiah 7:32,19:2,6 and 32:35; 2 Chronicles 28:3. 2 Kings 23:10 uses the full name of the valley, Valley of the Sons of Hinnom. Hinnom means wailing, lamentation.

Grafted into the domestic Jewish olive tree. Graft is a horticultural term for:

1. a bud, shoot, or scion of a plant inserted in a groove, slit, or the like in a stem or stock of another plant in which it continues to grow.
2. the plant resulting from such an operation; the united stock and scion.
3. the place where the scion is inserted.

The fruit produced on the grafted branch is the same variety as the tree from which it was cut. For this analogy by Paul, the fruit produced on this grafted branch will still be Christian, but with a very significant difference, which is the same reason fruit is grafted into another root stock; the fruit of this branch will now have the characteristics of its new root! With oranges, the graftings are to give more freeze resistance, drought resistance, or some other quality to the fruit that branch produces. In Paul's analogy, the new fruit will have the advantage of the Jewish Roots, including relationships with Abraham, Isaac, and Jacob, plus a direct connection with Torah and all the Hebrew Scriptures.

Romans 11:17. *But if some of the branches were broken off, and you, since you are a wild olive,* **were yourself grafted into them,** *then you would be a participant for yourself of the* **richness of the root of the olive tree.** *18. Stop boasting of the branches: but, if you do boast,* **you do not support the root, but the root supports you.** *19. Therefore you will say, "Branches were broken off so that I could be grafted in." 20. Just so: they were broken off by unbelief, but you have stood by faith. Do not be proud, but you must continually fear for yourself: 21. for if God did not spare the natural branches,* **neither** *will He in any way spare you. 22. You must now see the goodness and severity of God: on the one hand severity upon those who fell, but on the other hand goodness of God upon you, if you would remain in the goodness, otherwise you would be cut off. 23. And even these, if they would not remain in unbelief, they will be grafted in: for God is able to graft them in again. 24. For if you were cut off from the naturally wild olive tree and contrary to nature you were grafted into the cultivated olive tree, how much more will these natural branches be grafted into their own cultivated olive tree.*

Every "you" in this paragraph is singular, so each one of us is individually grafted into the cultivated Jewish olive tree. The Richness literally means to grow fat, rich in your individual, personal relationship with the Lord. The fruit from this tree, containing both new and old fruit, relates to One New Man.

Ephesians 2:14. *For He is our peace, the* **One Who has made both things into one and Who has loosed the dividing wall of the fence, cause of the enmity to His flesh,** *15. by His nullifying the tradition of the commandments by decrees, so that He could create the two,* **Jewish and non-Jewish,** *into* **One New Man,** *establishing peace 16. so He could reconcile both in one body to God through the cross, as God killed their enmity by means of Him, Y'shua. 17. And when He came He proclaimed the Good News of peace to you, to those far away, and peace to those near: 18. because through Him we both have the introduction to the Father by means of one Spirit. 19. Therefore then, you are no longer aliens and* *strangers, but you are fellow citizens of the saints and members of the household of God, 20. building upon the foundation of the apostles and prophets, Messiah Y'shua being His cornerstone, 21. in Whom the whole building being constructed is being fit together into a holy sanctuary in the Lord, 22. and in **Whom you are built together into a habitation of God by the Spirit**.*

Isaiah 44:5. **One will say, I am the LORD's*, and another will call himself by the name of Jacob**, *and another will subscribe with his hand to the LORD*, and* **surname himself by the name of Israel**.

Ezekiel 34:23. *And* **I will set up one Shepherd over them** *and He will feed them, My Servant David. He will feed them, and He will be their Shepherd. 24. And I AM, the LORD* will be their God, and My servant David a prince among them. I AM, the LORD*, has spoken.*

John 10:14. *I AM the Good Shepherd and I know My sheep and My sheep know Me, 15. just as the Father knows Me and I know the Father, and I lay down My life on behalf of the sheep. 16. But I also have sheep that are not from this sheep-fold: and it is necessary for Me to lead those and they will hear My voice, and* **they will become one flock, one Shepherd**.

The grafting is permanent, with no doubt this is God's choice for all of us. It is a requirement for us to embrace our **Jewish Roots**. The LORD desires One People, unity between Christians and Jews, but Christians have been the fiercest persecutors of Jews, persecuting them more than any other group. That calls for deep repentance by those who profess to be Christian.

Minister/Servant may seem odd, but there is a very good reason. Y'shua said in Mark 10:42. *And after He summoned them Y'shua said to them, "You know that those who are considered to lead the heathens are lording over them and that the great ones of them tyrannize them. 43. But it is not so among you, but whoever would wish to become great among you will be* **your servant**, *44. and whoever among you would wish to be first will be* **servant of all**: *45. for also the Son of Man did not come to be served but to serve and to give His life as a ransom in exchange for many."*

All of us in ministry need to keep in mind this order to be servant of all.

Miss the Mark is a Hebrew idiom meaning to sin.

1 Timothy 1:5. *But the goal of the command is love out of a clean heart and a good conscience and sincere faith, 6. from which, when some **Missed the Mark** they turned away to fruitless talk 7. wanting to be teachers of Torah (Teaching), although they understood neither what they were saying nor about what they were confidently insisting.*

The Greek word is Astokheo, meaning "to miss the mark." It is used three times in the New Testament: 1 Timothy 1:6, 6:21; 2 Timothy 2:18. Stokhos means Target. The Greek word for sin used most often is Amartano.

Omma is used in Matthew and Mark, speaking of the healing of eyes;

Matthew 20:29. *Then when they went from Jericho a huge crowd followed Him. 30. And behold when two blind people sitting by the way heard that Y'shua was passing by, they cried out saying, "You must immediately have mercy on us! Lord! Son of David! 31. Then the crowd rebuked them so that they would be quiet: but they cried out more saying, "You must now have mercy on us! Lord! Son of David!" 32. And after Y'shua stopped He called them and said, "What do you want Me to do for you?" 33. They said to Him, "Lord, that our eyes would open." 34. And Y'shua, having compassion, touched their eyes, and they immediately **regained their sight** and they followed Him.*

Mark 8:23. *Then taking the hand of the blind man, He led him outside the village and having spit in his **eyes**, after He placed His hands on him, He was asking him, "Do you see anything?" 24. And when he looked up he was saying, "I see men that are as trees I see walking." 25. Then He again laid hands upon his **eyes**, and he stared straight ahead and he was restored and he was looking at everything clearly. 26. And He sent him to his house saying, "And do not enter the village."*

The word translated eyes is **omma**, which means both natural and spiritual eyes, used only in these two passages. **Omma** is a poetic word and is used to indicate the eyes of the soul.

Mark recorded that Y'shua spit in the blind man's eyes. That was done because the spittle of a man who was the firstborn son of his father was believed to have healing power.

Release or Sabbath Rest is now called **Shemitah**, coming from Leviticus and Deuteronomy:

Leviticus 25:1. *And the LORD* spoke to Moses **on Mount** Sinai saying,*

"Speak to the children of Israel, and say to them,

*"When you come into the land which I AM giving to you, then **the land will keep a Sabbath to the LORD***: 3. You will **sow your field for six years**, and for **six years you will prune your vineyard and gather in its fruit**, 4. But **the seventh year will be a Sabbath of rest** for the land, a **Sabbath** for the LORD*: you will neither sow your field nor prune your vineyard. 5. That which grows of its own accord of your harvest you will not reap, neither gather the grapes of your undressed vine for it is a year of rest for the land. 6. And the **Sabbath** produce of the land will be food for you, for you and for your servant, for your maid, for your hired servant, and for your stranger who lives with you, 7. And for your cattle and for the wild animals that are in your land, all its increase will be for food."*

Deuteronomy 15:1. *At the end of seven years you will make a **Release**. 2. And this is the manner of the **Release**: Every creditor who lends to his neighbor will **Release** it. He will not ask for it of his neighbor, or of his brother because a release has been proclaimed to the LORD*. 3. You may demand it from a foreigner but your hand will **Release** that which is yours with your brother, 4. But there will be no poor among you, for the LORD* will greatly bless you in the land which the LORD* your God is giving you for an inheritance to possess it: 5. Only if you carefully listen to the voice of the LORD* your God, to guard to do all these commandments which I command you this day. 6. For the LORD* your God blesses you, as He promised you, and you will lend to many nations, but you will not borrow, and you will reign over many nations, but they will not reign over you.*

The **Sabbath Rest** is still used today, a very efficient farming practice, given by God to all the world.

Jubilee Year is given in Leviticus 25:

Leviticus 25:8. *"And you will number seven Sabbaths of years for yourself, seven times seven years: and the space of the seven Sabbaths of years will be forty-nine years for you. 9. Then you will **sound the shofar on the tenth of the seventh month, on the Day of Atonement** you will sound the horn throughout all your land. 10. And **you will sanctify the fiftieth year and proclaim liberty throughout the entire land to all its inhabitants**. It will be a jubilee for you and you will return his possession to each man, and you will return each man to* *his family. 11. That fiftieth year will be a jubilee to you. You will not sow or reap that which grows of itself in it, or gather the grapes of your undressed vine. 12. For it is the jubilee; it will be holy to you. You will eat the increase of it out of the field. 13. In the year of this jubilee you will return each man to his possession. 14. And if you sell anything to your neighbor, or buy anything of your neighbor's hand, **you will not oppress one another**. 15. According to the number of years after the jubilee you will buy from your neighbor, and according to the number of years of the fruits he will sell to you. 16. According to the multitude of years you will increase its price, and according to the fewness of years you will diminish its price: for according to the number of the years of the fruits he sells to you. 17. You will therefore not oppress one another, but you will revere your God, for I AM the LORD* your God. 18. So you will do My statutes and keep My judgments, and do them and you will live in the land in safety. 19. And the land will yield its fruit and you will eat your fill and live in it in safety. 20. And if you will say, What will we eat the seventh year? Behold, we will not sow or gather in our increase. 21. Then I shall command My blessing upon you in the sixth year and it will bring forth fruit for three years. 22. And you will sow the eighth year and eat of old fruit until the ninth year, until her fruits come in you will eat of the old store. 23. The land will not be sold forever, for the land is Mine, for you are strangers and sojourners with Me. 24. And in all the land of your possession you will grant a redemption for the land.*

Leviticus 25:25. *"If your brother is poor and has sold off some of his possession and if any of his kin come to redeem it, then he will redeem that which his brother sold. 26. And if the man has no one to redeem it and is himself able to redeem it, 27. then let him count the years of its sale and restore what is left over to the man to whom he sold it, so he may return to his possession. 28. But if he is not able to restore it to him, then that which is sold will remain in the hand of the one who has bought it until the year of jubilee, and in the jubilee it will go out, and he will return to his possession.*

Leviticus 25:29. *"And if a man sells a house in a walled city, then he may redeem it within a whole year after it is sold, within a full year he may redeem it. 30. And if it is not redeemed within the space of a full year, then the house that is in the walled city will be established forever to the one who bought it throughout his generations: it will not go out in the jubilee. 31. But the houses of the villages that do not have a wall around them will be counted as the fields of the country: they may be redeemed and they will go out in the jubilee. 32. But as for the cities of the Levites and the houses of the cities of their possession, the Levites may redeem at any time. 33. And if a man purchases from the Levites, then the house that was sold and the city of his possession, will go out in the year of jubilee, for the houses of the cities of the Levites are their possession among the children of Israel. 34. But the field of the open land of their cities may not be sold, for it is their perpetual possession.*

The first **Jubilee** Year was 50 years after the Jewish people entered the Land of Israel, which was in the Jewish year 2448, corresponding to 1272 BC. Hence, the first Jubilee was in the year 1222 BCE. The year 2016 was a Jubilee, which ended on October 12, 2016 at sundown. The **Jubilee and the Sabbath Years begin and end on Yom Kippur**. The calendar year begins on the Day of Memorial or Rosh Hashanah, falsely named Feast of Trumpets.

The impact of a **Jubilee** Year now is minimal since it no longer affects property transfers or release of bond servants. There are various takes on modern events related to **Jubilees**, but the reality is to simply acknowledge the calendar, with some forecasting doom and others forecasting blessing.

Sanctify Yourselves is a command given a number of times when people were preparing for a blessing from God.

Leviticus 11:44. *For I AM the LORD* your God! You will therefore **Sanctify Yourselves** and you will be holy, for I AM holy. Neither will you defile yourselves with any manner of creeping thing that creeps upon the earth. 45. For I AM the LORD* Who brings you up out of the land of Egypt, to be your God. You will therefore be holy, for I AM holy!* (1 Peter 1:16)

Each individual is required to **Sanctify Himself or Herself**. No one can **Sanctify** another person, you are on the spot. It is you and you alone who can **Sanctify** you. Each time you take Communion, you are renewing your covenant relationship with the Living God, a relationship that **Sanctifies** you. Each time you immerse (baptize), you are renewing that relationship. Each time you take communion and each time you pray seeking relationship with God, you are **Sanctifying Yourself**.

Sheshach is a code word used by Jeremiah.

Jeremiah 25:17. *Then I took the cup from the LORD's* hand and made all the nations to drink, to whom the LORD* had sent me: 18. Jerusalem and the* *cities of Judah and their kings and their princes, to make them a desolation, an astonishment, a hissing, and a curse, as it is this day; 19. Pharaoh king of Egypt and his servants and his princes and all his people; 20. and all the mixed people and all the kings of the land of Uz and all the kings of the land of the Philistines and Ashkelon and Gaza and Ekron and the remnant of Ashdod, 21. Edom and Moab and the children of Ammon 22. and all the kings of Tyre and all the kings of Sidon and the kings of the isle which is beyond the sea, 23. Dedan and Tema and Buz and all that are in the utmost corners 24. and all the kings of Arabia and all the kings of the mixed people that dwell in the desert 25. and all the kings of Zimri and all the kings of Elam and all the kings of the Medes 26. and all the kings of the north, far and near, one with another, and all the kingdoms of the world, which are upon the face of the earth: and the king of **Sheshach** will drink after them.*

All those kings are of known countries except for **Sheshach**, so what is that? **Sheshach** is **Babel**, Babylon in English, using a code called Atbash. When this was written, Nebuchadnezzar was king of Babylon, ruling over the known world, so Jeremiah used this code. Atbash exchanges the first letter of the Hebrew alphabet, Aleph, for the last letter, Tav and the second letter, Bet for the next to last letter, Shin; then the twelfth letter Lamed for the eleventh letter, Chaf. Thus the king of Sheshach is Nebuchadnezzar, which would only be recognized by knowledgeable Hebrews. Jeremiah got away with it.

Stewardship is a broad subject, involving everything we do and think.

The major areas are Financial, Physical, and Spiritual.

Financial Stewardship encompasses Tithing, Debt management, Vows, and Responsibilities for Family.

Tithing is a major part of our stewardship, which is addressed in a Glossary article.

Debt management is very important in today's era of easy credit. Borrowing to buy things we want keeps many locked in an endless routine from paycheck to paycheck, never able to save for future needs. When an emergency comes, the hole only gets deeper and more difficult to get out of. Do not borrow!

Vows are often to a church, but Y'shua says, *Again you heard that it was said to the ancients, 'You will not swear falsely,* (Numbers 30:3) *and you will keep your oaths to the Lord.'* (Deuteronomy 23:22) *34. But I say to you not to swear at all: neither by heaven, because it is the throne of God, 35. nor by the Earth, because it is His footstool, nor by Jerusalem, because it is a city of the great King, 36. nor by your head may you swear, because you are not able to make one hair white or black. 37. But your word must consistently be, Definitely yes! or Definitely no! and what goes beyond these is from the evil one.* (Matthew 5:33–37. See Leviticus 19:12; Numbers 30:2; Deuteronomy 23:21,22; Psalm 76:12; Ecclesiastes 5:4; Jacob 5:12.)

Responsibilities for Family are another reason for staying out of debt. It takes tough love not to spend the money for wants of family and wants of children. A big screen TV is not a necessity, nor are a fancy cell phone, designer clothes, or an impressive home or car. Children are under pressure to get video and computer games that waste both time and money, so parents have to be proactive to involve children in wholesome activities rather than pass them off to wasteful playthings. Society today makes spending to meet the expectations of others almost a commandment, but it is important to resist that temptation.

Physical stewardship requires taking care of your physical body, eating a healthy diet, getting adequate rest, following the rules of good hygiene, and exercising regularly.

God made our bodies to heal themselves, but we have abused our bodies by eating the wrong foods and eating too much. Eating Bible foods goes a long way in keeping the body healthy. Try living on a Daniel fast for really good health.

We often are not getting adequate rest because we are so busy earning, spending, and playing. Being over-tired weakens your immune system, making sickness more likely, which will make you slow down more than if you were disciplined enough to get adequate rest.

One of the basic rules of good hygiene is hand washing, which many ignore or just rush, so the hands are not really clean. Each year at the start of cold and flu season, there are warnings to wash hands frequently because that is the first step in preventing sickness.

Spiritual Stewardship is the most important of all these factors. Your body is a Sanctuary, not a Temple. As important as the Temple was, every Scripture relating to your body relates it to the Sanctuary with the Greek word Naos. While most Greek-English dictionaries say Naos means Temple, only Naos is used in Scriptures referring to the Sanctuary.

Matthew 23:35. *so would come upon you all the righteous blood being shed upon the earth from the blood of the righteous Abel until the blood of Zechariah son of Barachiah, whom you murdered between the Sanctuary and the altar.* Here Naos is translated Sanctuary, but most translations say Temple. The Sanctuary and the altar are both in the Temple, so it is impossible to be between the altar and Temple.

Luke 1:9. *...according to the custom of the service, appointed to burn incense when he entered the Sanctuary of the Lord,..* The incense was in the Sanctuary, so Luke used Naos.

Revelation 11:1. *And a reed like a rod was given to me, the angel saying, "You must rise and you must measure the Sanctuary of God and the altar and count those who worship at it."* (Ezekiel 40:3; Zechariah 2:5) *2. And you must exclude the court outside the Sanctuary and do not measure this outside, because it has been given to the heathens, and they will tread upon the holy city forty-two months.* The court outside the Sanctuary was the inner court of the Temple where sin was dealt with. Anyone with sin entering the Sanctuary died at the threshold. Y'shua referred to His body as a Sanctuary in John 2:19. Paul referred to our bodies as Sanctuaries in 1 Corinthians 3:16,6:19; 2 Corinthians 6:16.

1 Peter 4:1. *Therefore since Messiah suffered in the flesh, then you must now arm yourselves with the same thought, that the One Who suffered in His flesh has stopped sin 2. with mankind not to live any longer in desires but for the remaining time to live in the will of God in the flesh. 3. For sufficient time has passed for you to be doing what the heathens like to do, as they go in licentiousness, lusts, drunkenness, carousing, drinking bouts, and lawless idolatries. 4. In which they are astonished at your not running together with them in this flood of debauchery, so they revile you. 5. They will render an account to the One ready to judge the living and the dead. 6. For this reason the Good News was proclaimed to the dead, so that they could be judged in the flesh according to men but they could live in the spirit according to God. 7. But the end of all things has come near. Therefore*

*you must now be serious and exercise self-restraint to help you pray: 8. above all things having constant love among yourselves, because love hides a multitude of sins. (Proverbs 10:12) 9. So be hospitable to one another without complaining, 10. just as each took a gift for himself, ministering this as **good stewards** of a diversified grace of God.*

Verse 6 says the Good News was proclaimed to the dead, which is prophesied in John 5:25. *Most definitely I say to you that a time is coming and now is when the dead will hear the voice of the Son of God, and those who listen will live.*

As a Sanctuary it is important to be determined to lead a holy life and bring your entire family into holiness.

Time with God is the foundation of a spiritual life. Your heavenly Father is eager for each of His children to treasure time with Him, in the Word, in Worship, and in Prayer. That is good Stewardship.

ake Captivity Captive does not make much sense until you realize it is a Hebrew idiom meaning to turn the tables on your enemies in warfare, that is, to reverse the captivity of the people. It tells of the Israelites return to Israel or to drive out their oppressors. The expression is used three times in the Hebrew Scriptures and once in the Greek.

Judges 5:12. *Awake. Awake, Deborah! Awake. Awake! Utter a song! Arise, Barak and lead your **captivity captive**, you son of Abinoam.*

Deborah orders Barak to take on Sisera and win! He does just that, but Yael (Jael) is the heroine of the day because she is the one who kills Sisera.

The next passage with the expression has the LORD prophesying that He will bring back the captivity of His people.

Amos 9:13. *Behold, the days are coming, says the LORD*, that the plowman will overtake the reaper and the treader of grapes, him who sows seed and the mountains will drop sweet wine and all the hills will melt. 14. And **I shall bring back the captivity** of My people of Israel and they will build and inhabit the waste cities and they will plant vineyards and drink their wine, they will also make gardens and eat their fruit. 15. And I shall plant them on their land and* *they will no longer be pulled up out of their land which I have given them, say the LORD* your God.*

In Psalm 68 David credits God with having freed His people, which He ha done at least ten times by the time Psalm 68 was written.

Psalm 68:19. *You have ascended on high: You have led **captivity captive**: Yo have taken gifts among men, yea, even among the rebellious, so Yah, God, migh dwell among them.*

Paul uses the expression in the book of Ephesians.

Ephesians 4:7. *And the grace was given to each one of us according to the measur of the gift of the Messiah. 8. For this reason it says,*

> *"When He ascended into the high places*
> ***He turned the tables on your enemies in warfare.***
> *He gave gifts to mankind."*

Here Paul uses **"turned captivity captive"** in the Greek text, but the idiom i translated instead of letting it be seen.

Way, in speaking of the early followers of Y'shua, most Christians seem to apply the **Way** to Christians only, but the **Way** was used many times in the Hebrew Scriptures in referring to believers.

The first time that is said, it is the LORD Who says it! Genesis 18:17. *And the LORD* said, "Will I hide from Abraham that thing which I am about to do 18. seeing that Abraham will surely become a great and mighty nation and al the nations of the earth will be blessed in him? 19. For I know him, that he wil command his children and his household after him and they will keep the **Way** o the LORD*, to do acts of loving kindness and judgment, so the LORD* may bring upon Abraham that which He has spoken of him."*

The next time is in Genesis 24:27. *And he said, "Blessed be the LORD* God o, my master Abraham, who has not left my master destitute of His loving kindnes. and His truth. I am in the **Way** of the LORD*. The LORD* led me to the house of my master's brothers.*

To be in the **Way** means to take the yoke of the LORD. (See Yoke in Glossary.)

Way with a capital W is used more than sixty times in the Hebrew Scriptures, and twenty-one times in the New Testament—all in reference to serving the LORD.

Yak'veni means "Outwitted me" and is used in Genesis 27:36 *And he (Esau) said, "Is he not rightly named Jacob? For he has **outwitted me** these two times: he took away my birthright and, behold, now he has taken away my blessing."*

The word commonly translated Supplanted is the Latin word Subplantavit, which tradition still uses in many English translations. The word Supplant has led to some really blasphemous messages about Jacob, one of our Patriarchs who has extraordinary zeal for the LORD* and who still is one of God's favorites.

TEACHINGS

Ahead of Time is often God's way to prepare us for whatever.

> Isaiah 42:9. *Behold, the former things have come to pass and new things do declare. Before they spring forth I tell you of them.*

> Isaiah 48:3. *I have declared the former things from the beginning: they went forth out of My mouth and I made them heard, then I did them suddenly and they came to pass.*

> Jeremiah 11:18. *And the LORD* gave me knowledge of it and I knew it: then You showed me their doings.*

It is a great blessing to serve the God Who tells us of things beforehand, the **only** God in the universe: Who loves each of us equally. **Only** He knows the end from the beginning, and **only** He cares for His children enough so that He has plans for each of us. We just have to love Him, listen to Him, and obey Him.

Balaam's Treachery cost him his life. Although Balaam told the messengers from Balak that he would only prophesy what God told him to say, he had another way to curry favor with Balak. In Deuteronomy 24:12. *And Balaam said to Balak, "Did I not also tell your messengers whom you sent to me saying, 13. 'If Balak would give me his house full of silver and gold, I cannot go beyond the commandment of the LORD*, to do good or bad of my own mind, but what the LORD* says, that will I speak?' 14. And now, behold, I am going to my people.* **Come, I shall advise you** *what this people will do to your people in the latter days."*

94

Balak's advice was to send the women to seduce the Israeli men, to cause sin to bring about the downfall of Israel: in Numbers 32:15. *And Moses said to them, "**Have you saved all the women alive? 16. Behold, these caused the children of Israel, through the counsel of Balaam**, to commit trespass against the LORD* in the matter of Peor and there was a plague among the congregation of the LORD*.*

By this time Balaam had already gone to his reward. Numbers 31:7. *And they warred against the Midianites, as the LORD* commanded Moses, and they slew all the males. 8. And they slew the kings of Midian, besides the rest of them that were slain; Evi, Rekem, Zur, Hur, and Reba, five kings of Midian: **they also slew Balaam** the son of Beor with the sword.*

Be Diligent! Do as Paul instructed Timothy in 2 Timothy 2:15. *You must now **be diligent to present yourself approved to God**, a workman who has no cause to be ashamed, teaching the doctrine of the Truth correctly and directly.* Being diligent means being industrious, hard-working, meticulous, thorough, careful, persistent, working so that he presented himself to the world with all those attributes.

Some translations say "study to show yourself approved," but study is not a possible translation of the Greek word Spoudadzo, meaning "to hasten, to exert oneself, endeavor, to give diligence." Nor is study a possible translation of the Latin word Solicitus.

The instruction for each of us is to make every effort to do every assignment of the LORD* with all our heart, all our mind, all our strength. Everything we do should be unto the LORD* like we swear in Deuteronomy:

The Sh'ma
Deuteronomy 6:4. *Listen! Obey, O Israel! The LORD* is our God! The LORD* is One! 5. And you will love the LORD* your God with all your heart, with your very being, and with all your might. 6. And these words, which I am commanding you this day, will be in your heart 7. and you will teach them diligently to your children, and you will talk of them when you sit in your house, when you walk by the way, when you lie down, and when you rise up. 8. And you will bind them as a sign upon your hand (Proverbs 7:3), and they will be as frontlets between your eyes. 9. And you will write them on the doorposts of your house and on your gates.*

Be Sure Your Sin Find You Out! Numbers 32:23. *But if you will not do so, behold, you have sinned against the LORD*, and* **be sure your sin will find you out***.*

Not one thing can be done without God's knowledge! He even knows your thoughts, so you need to be obedient to His will every moment of every day. There is no way to evade the LORD. Ananias and Sapphira thought they could escape notice, but look at this:

Acts 5:1. *And a certain man named Ananias, with his wife Sapphirah, sold property 2. and kept back from the payment, while his wife was also fully aware, and then he brought part and placed it beside the feet of the apostles. 3. And Peter said, "Ananias, by what means did Satan fill your heart, for you to have lied to the Holy Spirit and to have kept back from the price of the property? 4. While it remained unsold was it not remaining yours until you sold it by your authority?* **Why did you place this deed in your heart? You did not lie to men but to God." 5.** *And when Ananias heard these words, as he fell down* **he breathed his last***, and great fear came upon all those who heard. 6. Then the young men got up, covered him and after they carried him out, buried him. 7. And it was about a three hour interval when his wife came in, not knowing what had happened. 8. And Peter declared to her, "You must tell me, if you sold the field for so much?" And she said, "Indeed, so much." 9. And Peter said to her,* **"Why was it agreed between you to test the Spirit of the Lord? Behold the feet of those who buried your husband are at the door and they will carry you out."** *10. And* **she fell at once at his feet and expired***: and when the young men came in they found her dead and after they carried her out, they buried her beside her husband, 11. and great fear was upon the whole congregation and upon all those who heard these things.*

Since God can let prophets know about someone's sin, there is no point to depend on secrecy because the Holy Spirit can, and often does, tell others about someone's sin. Therefore, the plan is to do well, to obey the spirit of the LORD's commandments. Even if not one other person learns of someone's sin, the same thing happens as happened to Ananias and Sapphirah: eternal death.

Remember God's warning to Cain:

Genesis 4:7. *Behold, if you do well, you will be accepted. And* **if you do not do well, sin sits waiting at the door, and its desire is to possess you, but you can rule over it.***"*

Blessed are the Merciful is the literal translation of Matthew 5:7. But merciful is a Hebrew idiom for forgiveness, so the real meaning of the verse and what this verse meant to all those who were listening is:

Matthew 5:7. *Blessed are those who* **forgive**, *because they will be* **forgiven**.

Matthew 6:14. *For if you would* **forgive** *all other people their transgressions, your heavenly Father will also* **forgive** *you: 15. but if you would not* **forgive** *all other people, neither will your Father* **forgive** *your sins.*

Unforgiveness is an unforgiveable sin and has ruined many a life, leaving the unforgiving person a bitter, hurting soul. Unforgiveness can tear someone up and is so easy to overcome. Forgiveness must be spoken and believed, coming from the heart. Just mouthing the words and continuing to seethe does not work, but true forgiveness brings release, releasing the offending person to God's judgment if the offense is one-sided. Unforgiveness has the unforgiving person judging the other. Judging is not for any of us to do.

Matthew 7:1. *Do not judge, so that you would not be judged: 2. for in which judgment you judge, you will be judged, and in the measure in which you measure, it will be measured to you. 3. Then why are you looking at the speck in your brother's eye, but you do not perceive the beam in your eye? 4. Or how will you say to your brother, 'You must let me cast the speck from your eye,' and there is this beam in your eye? 5. Hypocrite! First you must cast the beam from your eye, and then you will see clearly to cast out the speck from your brother's eye.*

Luke 6:37. *And* **if you do not judge, then you would not be judged**: *and if you do not condemn, then you would not be condemned.* **You must set free, then you will be set free**: 38. *you must give, then it will be given to you: they will give a good measure, pressed down, shaken, poured into your bosom: for, in which measure you measure, it will be measured to you in return.*

Therefore, unforgiveness will be paid back to the person in the same measure that it was placed upon the opponent. Release yourself if you have unforgiveness against anyone. (Read "Sin, Forgiveness of" in Glossary.)

Blessed are the Peacemakers is more powerful than the English translation. The Greek version is:

Matthew 5:9. *Blessed are the peacemakers, because they will be called 'children of God.'*

The Hebrew, which Y'shua was speaking, has:

Isaiah 32:17. *And the work of acts of loving kindness will be **Shalom** (peace), And the effect of acts of loving kindness, quietness and security forever.*

Psalm 37:37. *Mark the perfect man, and behold the upright, for the end of that man is **Shalom**.*

While the English says Peace, the Hebrew Shalom is so much more than that. The Peacemaker has everything in his life in order, not just an absence of conflict. (See Shalom in Glossary.)

All believers should walk in Shalom as Children of God.

Book of Life is first mentioned by Moses in Exodus 32:32. *Yet now, if You will forgive their sin, and if not, **erase me, please, out of Your scroll (book) which You have written**." 33. And the LORD* said to Moses, "Whoever has sinned against Me, I shall erase him from **My book**.*

Psalm 69:21. *Reproach has broken my heart and I am sick: and I looked for some to take pity, but there was no one, and for comforters, but I found no one. 22. They gave me also poison for My food, and in My thirst they gave me vinegar to drink. 23. Let their table become a snare before them: and that which should have been for their welfare, let it become a trap. 24. Let their eyes be darkened, so they do not see, and make their loins continually to shake. 25. Pour out Your indignation upon them and let Your wrathful anger take hold of them. 26. Let their habitation be desolate, let none dwell in their tents. 27. For they persecute him whom You have smitten and they tell of the grief of those whom You have wounded. 28. Add injustice to their iniquity! **Do not let them receive Your acts of loving kindness!** 29. They will be erased from the **Book of Life**, and they will **not** be written with the righteous.*

Revelation 17:8. *The beast you saw which was earlier and is not any longer then it is going to ascend from the abyss and go into destruction. Then those who dwell upon the earth, whose names are not written in the **Book of Life** from the foun-*

dation of the world, will be amazed, when they see the beast, because it was and it is not and it will be present.

Revelation 20:11. *Then I saw a great white throne and the One Who sits upon it, from Whose presence the earth and the sky fled and a place was not found for them. 12. Then I saw the dead, the great and the small, standing before the throne. And **scrolls** were opened, and **another scroll** was opened, which is of **life**, and the dead were judged according to their deeds, by what had been written in the scrolls. 13. Then the sea gave up the dead that were in it and Death and Hades gave up the dead, those in them, and each was judged according to his works.*

Revelation 21:22. *And I did not see a Sanctuary in it for the Lord God of Hosts and the Lamb are its Sanctuary. 23. And the city has no need of the sun or of the moon, that they would give light to the city, for the glory of God, and the light of the Lamb, did illuminate it. 24. And the multitudes will walk by its light, and the kings of the earth will bring their glory into it, 25. and its gates would **never** be shut all day, for there will not be night there, 26. and they will bring the glory and the honor of the nations into it. 27. And **no** unclean thing and **no** one doing a detestable thing or telling a lie could enter it, only those whose names have been written in the **Scroll of Life** of the Lamb.*

Matthew 5:8. *Blessed are the pure in heart, because they will see God.* This is the ultimate reward, to see God after Judgment.

The **Book of Life** is real.

Bride, Wife of Y'shua.

Revelation 19:7 *Let us rejoice and be glad*
and we will give Him the glory,
because the marriage festival of the Lamb has come
and His wife has prepared herself
8. and it was given to her that she would be clothed
in brilliant pure fine linen:
for the fine linen is the righteous deeds of the saints." (Isaiah 61:10)

The bride having to prepare herself means that individually and collectively each one of us must prepare for the supper. Each of us must do the things in Matthew 25:34. *Then the King will say to those on His right hand, 'Come, the blessed of My Father, you must now inherit what has been prepared for you in the kingdom from the foundation of the world. 35. For I was hungry and you gave Me to eat, I was thirsty and you gave Me to drink, I was a stranger and you took Me in, 36. and I was poorly clothed and you clothed Me, I was sick and you visited Me, I was in prison and you came to Me.' 37. Then the righteous will answer Him saying, 'Lord, when did we see You hungry and we fed You, or thirsty and we gave You something to drink? 38. And when did we see You a stranger and we took You in, or poorly clothed and we clothed You? 39. And when did we see You sick or in prison and we came to You?' 40. Then the King will say to them, 'Truly I say to you, in so much as you did anything for one of these, the least of My brothers, you did it for Me.'*

Matthew 7:21. *"Not everyone who says to Me, 'Lord. Lord!' will enter the Kingdom of the Heavens, but the one who does the will of My Father, the One in the heavens. 22. Many will say to Me in that Day, 'Lord. Lord! Did we not prophesy in Your name? And we cast out demons in Your name, and we did many miracles in Your name?' 23. And then I will declare to them that 'I never knew you: you working without Torah (Teaching) must continually depart from Me.'"*

The bride is the One New Man.

Ephesians 2:14. *For He is our peace, the One Who has made both things into one and Who has loosed the dividing wall of the fence, cause of the enmity to His flesh, 15. by His nullifying the tradition of the commandments by decrees, so that He could create the two (Jewish and non-Jewish) into* **One New Man**, *establishing peace 16. so He could reconcile both in one body to God through the cross, as God killed their enmity by means of Him, Y'shua. 17. And when He came He proclaimed the Good News of peace to you, to those far away, and peace to those near: 18. because through Him we both have the introduction to the Father by means of one Spirit. 19. Therefore then, you are no longer aliens and strangers, but you are fellow citizens of the saints and members of the household of God, 20. building upon the foundation of the apostles and prophets, Messiah Y'shua being His cornerstone, 21. in Whom the whole building being constructed is being fit together into a holy sanctuary in the Lord, 22. and in Whom you are built together into a habitation of God by the Spirit.*

There is no robe for the person who has not done righteous deeds. (See Mitsvah in Glossary.)

The **Bride** is the wife of the LORD*

Circumcision of the Heart is used by Paul in instructing baby Christians about the necessary doctrines.

Romans 2:17. *But if you would call yourself Jewish and would cause yourself to rest upon Torah (Teaching) and to take pride in God 18. then you know His will and since you are instructed in the Torah (Teaching), you are testing the things that differ (holy and profane) 19. and you have persuaded yourself to be a guide of the blind, a light for those in darkness, 20. an instructor of the foolish, a teacher of infants, since you have the essence of the knowledge and of the truth in the Torah (Teaching): 21. then, why do you, the one who teaches another, not teach yourself? The one who preaches not to steal, are you stealing? 22. The one who says not to commit adultery, do you commit adultery? The one who detests idols, do you rob temples? 23. You who boast in Torah (Teaching), you are dishonoring God by violating the Torah (Teaching): 24. for just as it has been written, "The name of God is being blasphemed among the heathens because of you." 25. For what does it profit if on the one hand you would practice Torah (Teaching) in circumcision: if on the other hand you would be breaking Torah (Teaching), your circumcision has become uncircumcision. 26. Therefore if the uncircumcised one would keep the things established in Torah (Teaching), will not his uncircumcision be credited to his account as circumcision? 27. And the physically uncircumcised, who are keeping the Torah (Teaching) will condemn you, although you have Scripture and circumcision, you are a violator of Torah (Teaching). 28. **For the Jewish person is not the one to be plainly recognized (by what he wears, his prayer shawl or kippah) and neither is circumcision just openly in the flesh, 29. but one is Jewish inwardly, and circumcised in his heart** in spirit not letter, whose praise is not from people but from God.*

Circumcised in heart was not a new teaching by Paul, but from Scripture that Paul knew well.

Deuteronomy 10:14. *Behold, the heaven and the heaven of heavens are the LORD's*; your God, the earth also, with all that is in it. 15. Only the LORD* had a delight in your fathers to love them and He chose their seed after them, above all people, as at this day. 16. **Circumcise therefore the foreskin of your heart**, and no longer be stiff necked.*

Deuteronomy 30:4. *If you are driven out to the outermost of heaven, the LORD your God will gather you from there and He will fetch you from there, 5. and th LORD* your God will bring you into the land which your fathers possessed an you will possess it. And He will do good for you and multiply you above your fa thers. 6. And the LORD* your God will* **circumcise your heart** <u>and the heart o your descendants</u>, *to love the LORD* your God with all your heart and with you whole being, so you may live.*

Jeremiah 4:4. **Circumcise yourselves to the LORD* and take away the fore skins of your heart,** *you men of Judah and inhabitants of Jerusalem, lest My fur come forth like fire and burn so no one can quench it, because of your bad doings*

Jeremiah 9:24. *Behold, the days are coming, says the LORD*, that I shall punish all those who are circumcised along with the uncircumcised, 25. Egypt and Juda and Edom and the children of Ammon and Moab and all who are in the utmos corners, who dwell in the wilderness, for all these nations are uncircumcised an the entire House of Israel is* **uncircumcised in the heart.**

Ezekiel 44:4. *Then he brought me the way of the north gate in front of the House and I looked and, behold, the Glory of the LORD* filled the House of the LORD and I fell upon my face. 5. And the LORD* said to me, Son of man, mark wel and look with your eyes and listen with your ears to all that I say to you concerning all the ordinances of the House of the LORD* and all its teachings. Mark well the entrance of the House, with every going forth from the Sanctuary. 6. And you wil say to the rebellious, to the House of Israel, Thus says Adonai, the LORD*, O you House of Israel, Enough of all your abominations! 7. In that you have brought in strangers,* **uncircumcised in heart** *and uncircumcised in flesh, to be in My Sanc tuary, to pollute it, My House, when you offer My bread, the fat and the blood, and they have broken My covenant because of all your abominations. 8. And you have not kept the charge of My holy things, but you have set keepers of My charge in My Sanctuary for yourselves.*

These verses reinforce the need to die to self, which is what happens when you circumcise your heart, giving yourself totally to the LORD* your God. Do not hold anything back.

Colossians 2:16. *Therefore no one must be continually judging you by food and by drink or in part of a feast or new moon or Sabbaths: 17. which are* **a shadow of the things that are coming, but the body making the shadow is of the Messiah.**

18. Let no one, who has a false humility himself and wants religious worship of angels, rob you of the prize which he has seen in a vision, puffed up without reason by what he saw, groundlessly inflated by his fleshly mind, 19. and if he does not hold fast the Head, from Whom the whole body, which is supported and joined together through the joints and bands, grows only with Divine growth.

Paul is writing this to former heathens who had no knowledge of their Jewish Roots, so he is advising them to keep their minds focused on Messiah, not to get drawn into disputes over Seasons of LORD* or dietary regulations. The congregants did not have Jewish leaders to teach them nor did they have books for reference. Scrolls the synagogues used were very expensive, more than a year's wages, so the house churches of the first century did not have the scrolls. Now we have pastors who have been trained in seminary or Bible College, but rarely trained on the Church's Jewish Roots. It is disgraceful that after two millennia we still have pastors and churches ignorant of Jewish Roots. Paul's advice is still valid for most Christians, who are not to be judged by food and drink, a feast, a new moon, or Sabbath. However, you will be judged on those things because Y'shua is still Jewish and the foundation and the gates of Heavenly Jerusalem are Jewish: the twelve Jewish apostles and the twelve tribes of Israel (Revelation 21:12).

Crowds Praising Y'shua and **another crowd** condemning Y'shua.

1. The Triumphal Entry – Luke 19:28. *Then after He said these things He was going before them, going up to Jerusalem. 29. And it happened as He neared Bethphage and Bethany by the mount called Olives, He sent two of the disciples 30. saying, "You must go into the village opposite, when you enter it you will find a colt tied, upon which nobody has ever sat. Then after you loose it you must lead it here. 31. And if someone asks you, 'Why are you loosing it?' You will say thus, that 'The Lord has need of it.'" 32. And when they went, those who were sent found just as He said to them. 33. And while they were loosing the colt its owners said to them, "Why are you loosing the colt?" 34. And they said, "The Lord has need of it." 35. Then they led it to Y'shua and after they put their prayer shawls on the colt they put Y'shua on it. 36. And while He was going they were spreading their prayer shawls on the road.*
Luke 19:37. *And while He was now nearing the slope of the Mount of Olives the **multitude of disciples**, rejoicing, were all beginning to praise God in a loud voice concerning all the miracles which they had seen, 38. saying,*

"'Blessed is the One Who comes,
the King in the name of the Lord:' (Psalm 118:26)
peace in heaven
and glory in the highest."

39. Then some of the Pharisees from the crowd said to Him, "Teacher, You must immediately rebuke Your disciples." 40. And answering them He said, "I say to you, if they are silent the stones will cry out."

The Triumphal Entry took place on the mile-long road from the Mount of Olives to Jerusalem. Thousands of people lined the road, all welcoming Y'shua.

Afterward in the courtyard of the governor's compound:

2. Luke 23:20. *And again Pilate called out to them, wanting to free Y'shua. 21 But they were shouting saying,* **"You must crucify, you must crucify Him right now!"** *22. And the third time he said to them, "For what evil did He do? I do not find guilt deserving of death in Him: therefore after I scourge Him I shall release Him." 23.* **But they were pressing upon him in loud voices asking for Him to be crucified, and their voices prevailed. 24.** *Then Pilate decided to do their request: 25. and he freed the one who was thrown in jail because of insurrection and murder, for whom they were asking, and he gave Y'shua over to their wishes.*

This meeting was in the courtyard of the Praetorium, a confined space in the city that probably held about two to three hundred people. The Jewish people who gathered there were all Hellenists whose world would have been shattered by the coming of Messiah, so they were shouting for His crucifixion.

It is important to understand the size and the nature of these crowds. Both crowds were Jewish people, but there was a huge difference in the size of the two crowds and in the belief system of each crowd. The Hellenists were not what we would call Observant Jews, but were nominal Jews, while the crowd of the Triumphal Entry were eagerly looking forward to the coming of Messiah, King.

Cycles of Scripture: The Books of Judges, Samuel, and Kings are good examples of scriptural events recycled. There were many cycles of going from being godly to back-sliding. After just a few generations, a new king would lead the people out of righteousness into idol worship. Then when the people cried out, a new king would lead them back to God.

Events prophesied have often happened more than once.

Jerusalem was first destroyed in 585 BC, rebuilt in 518 BC. It was again totally destroyed in 70 AD, then cleaned up and rebuilt in 135 AD under Emperor Hadrian who renamed it Aelia Capitolina. (See Book Order in the Glossary of the *One New Man Bible* for the full explanation of the threshing of Scripture.)

Seven Cycles of the Book of Judges referred to in the above article are listed here.

Disobedience:

Judges 3:1. *Now these are the nations which the LORD* left to test Israel by them, as many as had not known all the wars of Canaan, 2. only that generations of the children of Israel might know, to teach them war, at the least such as before they did not know anything about it. 3. Namely five leaders of the Philistines, all the Canaanites and the Sidonians and the Hivites lived in Mount Lebanon, from Mount Baal Hermon to the entrance of Hamath. 4. And they were to test Israel by them, to know whether they would listen to the commandments of the LORD*, which He commanded their fathers by the hand of Moses. 5. And the children of Israel lived among the Canaanite, the Hittite, the Amorite, the Perizzite, the Hivite, and the Jebusite: 6. and they took their daughters to be their wives, and gave their daughters to their sons and served their gods. 7. And the children of Israel brought anarchy in the eyes of the LORD* and forgot the LORD* their God and served their gods. 8. Therefore the anger of the LORD* was hot against Israel and He sold them into the hand of Cushan Rishathaim, king of Mesopotamia, and the children of* **Israel served Cushan Rishathaim eight years.**

1. Back to God!

Judges 3:9. *And when the children of Israel cried to the LORD*, the LORD* raised up a deliverer for the children of Israel, who delivered them,* **Othniel** *the son of Kenaz, Caleb's younger brother. 10. And the Spirit of the LORD* came upon him and he judged Israel and went out to war, and the LORD* delivered Cushan Rishathaim king of Mesopotamia into his hand, and his hand prevailed* *against Cushan Rishathaim. 11. Then **the land had rest forty years**. And Oth-niel the son of Kenaz died.*

Disobedience again!

Judges 3:12. *And again the children of Israel brought anarchy in the eyes of the LORD* and the LORD* strengthened Eglon the king of Moab against Israel because they had brought anarchy in the eyes of the LORD*. 13. And he gathered the children of Ammon and Amalek to himself and went and struck Israel and possessed the City of Date Palms, Jericho. 14. And the children of **Israel served Eglon the king of Moab for eighteen years**.*

2. Back to God!

Judges 3:15. *But when the children of Israel cried to the LORD*, the LORD raised a deliverer for them, **Ehud** the son of Gera, a Benjamite, a man with his right hand withered: and by him the children of Israel sent tribute to Eglon the king of Moab.*

Judges 3:30. *So Moab was subdued that day under the hand of Israel. And **the land had rest eighty years…***

Disobedience!

Judges 3:31. *And after him was Shamgar the son of Anat, who slew of the Philistines six hundred men with an ox-goad, and he also delivered Israel.*

Judges 4:1. *And when Ehud was dead the children of Israel again brought anarchy in the eyes of the LORD*. 2. And **the LORD* sold them into the hand of Jabin king of Canaan**, who reigned in Hazor, the captain of whose army was Sisera who lived in Haroshet Goyim. 3. And the children of Israel cried to the LORD*, for he had nine hundred chariots of iron and **for twenty years he mightily oppressed the children of Israel**.*

3. Back to God!

Judges 4:4. *And **Deborah**, a prophetess, the wife of Lapidot, judged Israel at that time. 5. And she lived under the date palm of Deborah between Ramah and Beit-*

El in Mount Ephraim, and the children of Israel came up to her for judgment. 6. And she sent and called Barak the son of Abinoam out of Kedesh Naphtali and said to him, Has not the LORD* God of Israel commanded, Go and draw toward Mount Tabor and take with you ten thousand men of the children of Naphtali and of the children of Zebulun? 7. And I shall draw to you Sisera, the captain of Jabin's army, with his chariots and his multitude to the river Kishon, and I shall deliver him into your hand.

Judges 5:31. *So let all Your enemies perish, LORD*! Those who love Him will be like the going forth of the sun in its might.*

Then **the land had rest forty years**.

Disobedience again!

Judges 6:1. *And the children of Israel brought anarchy in the eyes of the LORD*, and the LORD* delivered them into* **the hand of Midian for seven years**.

4. Back to God!

Judges 6:7. *And it was, when the children of Israel cried to the LORD* because of Midian, 8. that the LORD* sent a prophet to the children of Israel, who said to them, Thus says the LORD* God of Israel,* **I AM** *did bring you up from Egypt and brought you out of the house of bondage; 9. and I delivered you out of the hand of Egypt and out of the hand of all who oppressed you and drove them out from before you, and gave you their land. 10. And I say to you, I AM the LORD* your God. Do not revere the gods of the Amorite, in whose land you dwell, but you have not obeyed My voice. 11. And an angel of the LORD* came and sat under an oak which was in Afrah that belonged to Joash the Abiezrite, and his son* **Gideon** *threshed wheat by the wine press, to hide it from the Midianites. 12. And the angel of the LORD* appeared to him and said to him, the LORD* is with you, you mighty man of valor.*

Judges 8:28. *Thus Midian was subdued before the children of Israel, so that they lifted up their heads no more. And* **the country was quiet forty years in the days of Gideon**.

Disobedience again!

Judges 8:33. *And it was, as soon as Gideon was dead, that* **the children of Israel turned again and went astray after baalim** *and made Baal Berith their god.*

Judges 9:22. *When* **Abimelech had reigned three years over Israel**, *23. then God sent a bad spirit between Abimelech and the men of Shechem, and the men of Shechem dealt treacherously with Abimelech, 24. so the cruelty to the seventy sons of Jerubaal might come, and their blood would be laid on Abimelech their brother who slew them, and on the men of Shechem, who strengthened his hand to kill his brothers.*

5. Back to God!

Judges 10:1. *And after Abimelech,* **Tola** *the son of Puah, the son of Dodo, a man of Issachar rose to defend Israel, and he lived in Shamir in Mount Ephraim. 2. And he judged Israel* **twenty-three years** *and died and was buried in Shamir. 3. And after him rose* **Jair**, *a Gileadite, and he judged Israel* **twenty-two years.**

Disobedience again!

Judges 10:6. *Then the children of Israel again* **brought anarchy** *in the eyes of the LORD* and served baalim and Ashtarot, the gods of Syria, the gods of Sidon, the gods of Moab, the gods of the children of Ammon, and the gods of the Philistines and forsook the LORD*, and did not serve Him. 7. And the anger of the LORD was hot against Israel and He sold them into the hands of the Philistines and into the hands of the children of Ammon. 8. And that year of Jair's death, they crushed and oppressed the children of Israel, continuing for* **eighteen years**, *all the children of Israel that were on the other side of the Jordan in the land of the Amorite, which is in Gilead.*

6. Back to God!

Judges 10:15. *And the children of Israel said to the LORD*,* **We have sinned.** *Do to us whatever seems good to You, only deliver us, we pray you, this day. 16. And they put away the strange gods from among them and served the LORD*, and His very being was grieved by the misery of Israel.*

Judges 10:17. *Then the children of Ammon were gathered together and camped in Gilead. And the children of Israel assembled themselves together and camped in Mizpah. 18. And the people, the princes of Gilead, said to one another, What man is he who will begin to fight against the children of Ammon? He will be head over all the inhabitants of Gilead.*

Judges 11:1. *Now **Jephthah** the Gileadite was a mighty man of valor and he was the son of a harlot and Gilead begot Jephthah.*

Judges 12:7. *And **Jephthah judged Israel six years**. Then Jephthah the Gileadite died, and was buried in one of the cities of Gilead.*

Judges 12:8. *And after him **Ibzan** of Bethlehem judged Israel. 9. And he had thirty sons, and thirty daughters, whom he sent abroad, and took in thirty daughters from abroad for his sons. And he judged Israel **seven years**. 10. Then Ibzan died, and was buried at Bethlehem.*

Judges 12:11. *And after him **Elon**, a Zebulunite, judged Israel and **he judged Israel ten years**. 12. And Elon the Zebulunite died and was buried in Aijalon in the country of Zebulun.*

Judges 12:13. *And after him **Abdon** the son of Hillel, a Pirathonite, judged Israel. 14. And he had forty sons and thirty nephews who rode on seventy donkey colts and **he judged Israel eight years**. 15. And Abdon the son of Hillel the Pirathonite died and was buried in Pirathon in the land of Ephraim, in the mountain of the Amalakites.*

Disobedience Again!

Judges 13:1. *And the children of Israel **brought anarchy** in the eyes of the LORD* and the LORD* delivered them into **the hand of the Philistines forty years**.*

7. Back to God!

Judges 13:2. *And there was a certain man of Zarah of the family of the Danites, whose name was Manoah, and his wife was barren and had not borne. 3. And an angel of the LORD* appeared to the woman and said to her, Behold now, you are barren and have not borne, but you will conceive and bear a son (**Samson**).*

Judges 16:31. *Then his brothers and the entire house of his father came down and took him, and brought him up and buried him between Zarah and Eshtaol in the burying place of Manoah his father.*

And **he judged Israel twenty years**.

The price of disobedience was one hundred fourteen years of oppression versus two hundred ninety-six years of blessing.

We in the United States are doing the same things, back-sliding for some time, promoting abortion, homosexual rights, and bringing in hundreds of thousands of heathens, even encouraging heathen practices in schools. We need leaders who will restore the Judeo-Christian values on which this nation was founded, but in this republic that will only come when revival takes hold and the people demand, by voting, electing leaders who will restore us to greatness.

David's Reward by those who came to him when David was escaping from Saul.

1 Samuel 30:6. *And **David** was greatly distressed, for the people spoke of stoning him, because the soul of all the people was grieved, every man for his sons and for his daughters, but **David** encouraged himself in the LORD* his God.*

David's faith allows him to be gracious in the presence of those ready to kill him. Who were those who wanted to stone **David**?

1 Samuel 22:1. ***David** therefore left from there and escaped to the cave of Adullam, and when his brothers and all his father's house heard it, they went down there to him. 2. And **everyone who was in distress, everyone who was in debt, and everyone who was discontented gathered themselves to him** and he became a captain over them and there were with him about four hundred men.*

Many of those with **David** were malcontents, not an easy lot to lead.

Deborah Prophesies Jael (Yael), Judges 4:9. *And she said, I shall surely go with you, but the journey that you take will not be for your glory, for **the LORD* will sell Sisera into the hand of a woman**. And Deborah got up and went with Barak to Kedesh. 10. And Barak called Zebulun and Naphtali to Kedesh and he went up with ten thousand men in his footsteps and Deborah went up with him.*

Kedesh is in Naphtali's territory.

Judges 4:17. *But Sisera fled away on his feet to the tent of Jael the wife of Heber the Kenite, for there was peace between Jabin the king of Hazor and the house of Heber the Kenite.*

Judges 4:18. *And Jael went out to meet Sisera and said to him, Turn in, my lord, turn in to me.* ***Do not be in awe!*** *And when he had turned in to her in the tent, she covered him with a blanket.*

Judges 4:19. *And he said to her, Give me, I pray you, a little water to drink, for I am thirsty. And she opened a bottle of milk and gave him a drink, and covered him. 20. Again he said to her, Stand at the entrance of the tent and it will be when anyone comes and inquires of you and says, Is there anyone here? That you will say, No. 21. Then* ***Jael****, Heber's wife, took a tent peg and took a hammer in her hand and went softly to him and struck the peg into his temple and it pierced through into the ground, for he was fast asleep and weary. So he died.*

Judges 4:22. *And, behold, as Barak pursued Sisera,* ***Jael*** *came out to meet him and said to him, Come! I shall show you the man whom you are seeking. And when he came into her tent, behold, Sisera lay dead and the peg was in his temple.* Thus, Deborah's prophecy of verse 9 came to pass.

Do Not in Any Way be Awed! Do Not be Dismayed! The Hebrew negative command is very powerful, with no direct English equivalent. It is even stronger than saying "Do not dare to even think about..!" When you see the above quoted warnings in bold print, know that faith in God is what you need to replace the fear and dismay. Although usually translated "Fear not," the Hebrew means "to revere, to hold in awe." There is only One Whom we are to revere, to hold in awe, and we are not to be in terror of Him, but give the respect and honor to which He is due. Do not be awed by the size and strength of the enemy, but respect and revere the Awesome God we serve, Who will turn the situation around.

Do Not Murmur; Do Not Complain! Our Heavenly Father does not tolerate whining and complaining. He detests murmuring and complaining in general and especially when it is specifically against your boss, spouse, or sibling. In Exodus 15 and 16, the complaining is aimed at Moses, their boss.

Exodus 15:22. *So Moses brought Israel from the Reed Sea and they went out int the wilderness of Shur and they went three days in the wilderness and found n water. 23. And when they came to Marah, they could not drink of the waters o Marah, for they were bitter: therefore the name of it was called Marah. 24. An the people* **murmured** *against Moses saying, "What will we drink?" 25. And h cried to the LORD*, and the LORD* showed him a tree and he cast it into th waters, and the waters were made sweet. He made a statute and an ordinanc there for them and there he proved to them 26. and said, "If you will diligentl hearken to the voice of the LORD* your God and will do that which is right i His sight and will give ear to His commandments and keep all His statutes, I shal put none of these diseases upon you that I have brought upon the Egyptians, for AM the LORD* Who heals you."*

Exodus 15:27. *And they came to Elim, where there were twelve wells of wate and seventy palm trees, and they camped there by the waters.* **16.**1. *And they too their journey from Elim, and the entire congregation of the children of Israel cam to the wilderness of Sin, which is between Elim and Sinai, on the fifteenth day o the second month after their departing from the land of Egypt.*

After Victory, Complaining
Exodus 16:2. *And the whole congregation of the children of Israel* **murmured** *against Moses and Aaron in the wilderness. 3. And the children of Israel said to them, "Would that we had died by the hand of the LORD* in the land of Egypt when we sat by the pots of meat, when we ate bread to the full. For you have brought us out into this wilderness, to kill this whole assembly with hunger."*

Numbers 14:26. *And the LORD* spoke to Moses and to Aaron saying, 27. "How long will I bear with this bad congregation that* **murmurs against Me**? *I have heard the* **murmurings** *of the children of Israel, which they* **murmur** *against Me. 28. Say to them, 'As truly as I AM lives, says the LORD*, as you have spoken in My ears, so will I do for you: 29.* **your carcasses will fall in this wilderness and all that were numbered of you**, *according to your whole number, from twenty years old and upward, that have* **murmured against Me**. *30.* **Doubtless you will not come into the land, which I swore to make you dwell in, except Caleb the son of Jephunneh and Joshua the son of Nun.**

God will not abide murmurers. Instead of murmuring and complaining, it is most important to keep the faith, to know that God lets us go through hard times to strengthen our faith, and for each one of us to prove to himself that he can do what seems so hard. In this life we are not called to lie in a hammock on some comfortable beach, but to actually accomplish something with the life of each believer to be a testimony of God's strength as we work, bring up children, and face all manner of obstacles on the way. Have peace in all situations, bearing in mind Paul and Silas in the jail in Philippi, beaten and bloody, sitting in the stocks, singing Psalms, and not complaining. Then at midnight, God brought an earthquake, setting them free from the stocks, bringing the jailer to repentance, and ultimately to their release. (Read Trials in Glossary.)

Ebedmelech the Cushite was a high ranking official under King Zedekiah, but why is he called a servant in some translations?

Jeremiah 38:7. *Now when **Ebedmelech** the Cushite, **an officer** who was in the king's house, heard that they had put Jeremiah in the cistern, the king then sitting in the gate of Benjamin, 8. Ebedmelech went out of the king's house and spoke to the king saying, 9. My lord the king, these men have done evil in all that they have done to Jeremiah the prophet, whom they have cast into the cistern. And he is likely to die for hunger in the place where he is, for there is no more bread in the city. 10. Then the king commanded **Ebedmelech the Cushite** saying, Take thirty men from here with you and take Jeremiah the prophet up out of the cistern before he dies. 11. So **Ebedmelech** took the men with him and went into the house of the king under the treasury and took from there old worn cloths and old rotten rags and let them down by ropes into the pit to Jeremiah.*

Jeremiah 38:12. *And **Ebedmelech the Cushite** said to Jeremiah, Now put the old worn cloths and rotten rags under your armpits under the ropes. And Jeremiah did so. 13. So they drew up Jeremiah with ropes and took him up out of the pit, but Jeremiah remained in the court of the prison.*

The Hebrew word translated officer in verse 7 is *oved*, which in early Books was translated servant or slave, meaning bond servant. The meaning of oved changed with the times. By the time of the kings of Israel when it referred to a servant of the king, it meant someone of rank, like a cabinet officer in today's US government. That is why Ebedmelech had such quick access and respect from King Zedekiah. It is also important to note that this Ethiopian (Cushite) shows us there was no prejudice against black people.

Effective Prayer is seen in Genesis 24:10. *And the servant took ten camels of the came. of his master and departed, for all the goods of his master were in his hand, an he rose and went to Mesopotamia, to the city of Nahor. 11. And he made h camels kneel down outside the city by a well of water at the time of the evening the time that women go out to draw water. 12. And he said, "LORD* God of m master Abraham,* **Make something happen right in front of me today**, *an act gracefully with my master. 13. Behold, I am standing by the well of water an. the daughters of the men of the city come out to draw water. 14. And let it be tha the girl to whom I shall say, Let down your pitcher, please, so I can drink and sh will say, 'Drink, and I shall also give your camels drink.' Let the same be she tha You have appointed for Your servant Isaac and thereby will I know that You hav shown kindness to my master."*

To act gracefully is to look on Abraham with favor and loving kindness. Vers 12 is a quote from Rabbi Ben-Yehuda. Here comes God's swift reply:

Genesis 24:15. *And it happened* **before he had finished speaking that ther was Rebeccah** *(Rivkah) coming out, who was born to Bethuel son of Milkah, th wife of Nahor Abraham's brother, with her pitcher on her shoulder. 16. And th girl was very pleasant to look upon, a virgin, neither had any man known her And she went down to the well and filled her pitcher and came up. 17. And th servant ran to meet her and said, "Let me, I beg you, drink a little water fron your pitcher." 18. And she said, "Drink, my lord." And she hastened and let down her pitcher upon her hand and gave him a drink. 19. And when she had finishec giving him a drink she said, "I shall draw water for your camels also, until the; have done drinking." 20. And she hastened and emptied her pitcher into th trough and ran again to the well to draw water, and drew for all his camels.*

Then he asks about her. When she tells about her family, she also says there is room for the camels. He tells her Abraham is his master, so she runs home tc tell Laban who runs to meet Abraham's servant. When he tells Laban abou his mission and his prayer, he reveals the nature of his prayer:

Genesis 24:42. *And I came this day to the well and said, 'LORD*, God of my master Abraham, if now You make my way which I go successful, 43. Behold, I stand by the well of water and it will happen, that when the maiden comes forth to draw water and I say to her, 'Give me, please, a little water from your pitcher to drink.' 44. And she says to me, 'Both you drink, and I shall also draw for your camels.' Let the same one be the woman whom the LORD* has appointed for my* *master's son.' 45. And **before I had finished speaking in my heart**, behold, Rebeccah came forth with her pitcher on her shoulder and she went down to the well, and drew water and I said to her, 'Let me drink, please.'*

This extraordinarily successful prayer was **silent**, just prayed **in his heart**. God knows your every thought, so Paul wrote *For though we walk in the flesh we are not serving as soldiers according to the flesh, 4. for the weapons of our warfare are not fleshly but powerful in God for the tearing down of strongholds, tearing down reasonings 5. even every high thing being lifted up against the knowledge of God, and **taking captive every thought in obedience to Messiah**, 6. and being ready to punish every disobedience, when your obedience would be achieved:* (2 Corinthians 10:3–6). *Listen, O earth! Behold, **I AM** will bring evil upon this people, **the fruit of their thoughts**:* (Jeremiah 6:19).

God knows your every thought, so use your mind constructively with continual prayer!

Effective Prayer II is also in Genesis.

Genesis 25:20. *And Isaac was forty years old when he took Rebeccah to wife, the daughter of Bethuel the Syrian of Padanaram, the sister of Laban the Syrian.*

As later verses attest, there was a large twenty-year gap between verse 20 and verse 21. Since conception was so close to the entreaty, the gap must have been between verses 20 and 21.

Genesis 21:21. *And Isaac entreated the LORD* for his wife, because she was barren, and **the LORD* was entreated by him and Rebeccah his wife conceived**. 22. And the children struggled together within her and she said, "If it is so, why am I like this?" And she went to inquire of the LORD*. 23. And the LORD* said to her, "Two nations are in your womb and two kinds of people will be separated from your body, and the one people will be stronger than the other people and the elder will serve the younger."*

Genesis 25:26. *And after that his brother came out and his hand took hold of Esau's heel, and his name was called Jacob (Yaakov) and **Isaac was sixty years old when she bore them**. 27. And the boys grew and Esau was a skillful hunter, a man of the field, but Jacob was a plain man, living in tents.*

That was **effective prayer**! This was prayed after twenty years of marriage with no record of Rebeccah having asked for prayer.

Elizabeth, the mother of John the Immerser, was the daughter of an Aaronite priest as testified in Luke 1:5. *In the days of King Herod of Judea there was a certain priest named Zechariah from the division Abijah, and his wife was of the daughters of Aaron and her name was Elizabeth.*

Since Elizabeth and Miriam, the mother of Y'shua, were kin, there is a strong possibility that Miriam was also an Aaronite. Luke 1:35. *Then the angel said to her, "The Holy Spirit will come upon you and power of the Most High will cover you: for this reason then the Holy One Who is birthed will be called the Son of God. 36. And behold **your kin Elizabeth** has also conceived a son in her old age and this is her sixth month from her being called barren: 37. because with God nothing is impossible." (Genesis 18:14; Jeremiah 32:17,27; Job 42:2) 38. And Miriam said, "Behold the servant of the Lord: may it be according to your word. Then the angel left from her.*

That really begs the question because the father determines the tribal inheritance of the children. Y'shua's DNA is from His Father, God, so Y'shua is a Heavenly Priest. To the world Joseph was assumed to be His father, so to the world Y'shua was the Son of David. But in reality, Y'shua's father was not Joseph, but God. (See God Incarnate in Glossary.) Since Elizabeth was an Aaronite, if Elizabeth's father and Miriam's father were brothers, then Miriam was also an Aaronite, the perfect mother for the Son of God.

Elohim is a word used frequently in Scripture, but with vastly different meanings. Elohim is most often used for God, but can be translated false gods, judges, and leaders. The first use is:

Genesis 1:1. *In the beginning **God** created the heavens and the earth.*

Elohim is plural, so when it refers to God, it is called the Majestic Plural as we often hear from a politician speaking of some project in the plural, saying "We have said this before..." when it was just that person saying it.

Genesis 6:1. *And it was, when man began to multiply on the face of the earth, and daughters were born to them, 2. that the sons of the **leaders** saw the daughters of men, that they were fair and they took them for wives of all whom they chose.*

3. And the LORD said, "My spirit will not struggle forever with **man**, since he is but flesh. And his days will be one hundred twenty years." 4. There were giants in the earth in those days and also after that, when the sons of the leaders came in to the daughters of men, and they bore children to them, the same became mighty, macho, men who, from old, were men of bad reputation.*

While some claim different translations for Elohim here, not **leaders**, with something other than men, it is shown by God's statement in verse 3 that He will not struggle forever with **man**, that the progeny involved are human beings. The giants are sometimes called Nephilim, which is a Hebrew word for Giant, not meaning fallen angels or referring to some different species. Even today we talk about someone who has been very influential in a particular field as a **giant** in the field, so this is the metaphor for the **leaders** who held the power in their communities, with their sons taking full advantage of their fathers' influence.

Exodus 7:1. God makes Moses a god to Pharaoh:

And the LORD said to Moses, "See, I have made you a **god** to Pharaoh, and Aaron your brother will be your prophet.*

Exodus 22:6–8 sees **Elohim** translated **Judges** three times:

*Exodus 22:6. If a man delivers to his neighbor money or stuff to keep and it is stolen out of the man's house, if the thief is found, let him pay double. 7. If the thief is not found, then the master of the house will be brought to the **judges**, to see whether he put his hand to his neighbor's goods. 8. For all manner of trespass, whether it is for ox, for donkey, for sheep, for clothing, for any manner of lost thing, which another challenges to be his, the cause of both parties will come before the **judges**, and whom the **judges** will condemn, he will pay double to his neighbor.*

In Exodus 32:1 Elohim is used for false gods:

And when the people saw that Moses delayed coming down from the mountain, the people gathered themselves together to Aaron and said to him, Get up! Make gods for us that will go before us, for this Moses, the man who brought us up out of the land of Egypt, we do not know what has happened to him.

There are examples all throughout Scripture of these different translations for Elohim.

End of Egypt's Famine after just two years! The famine ended when the children o Israel arrived.

Genesis 47:23. *Then Joseph said to the people, "Behold, I have purchased you and your land for Pharaoh this day, **so here is seed for you and you will sow the land**.*

We know the famine ended at this time because seeds were not given during the famine, when no crop would grow. The famine had served God's purpose which was to bring the children of Israel to Egypt.

Eternal Life is the reward we are all seeking. When we leave this earthly home, we are expecting to join our ancestors in Heaven, which is to be a truly glorious experience. Y'shua said in John 17:3 *And this is **eternal life**, that they would know You, the only true God, and Whom You sent, Y'shua Messiah.*

To qualify for **Eternal Life,** we must have a vital relationship with the Living God. (See article on Bride in this chapter to get a deeper understanding o your commitment.)

Those who do not have **Eternal Life** include those stoned according to Torah for immorality, idol worship, or some other infraction. This sounds brutal to us, but that is what happens to those who commit various sins, iniquities, and transgressions and never repent. Though sinners are no longer stoned, they do not enter **Eternal Life**. They do not necessarily shorten their lives on Earth, but do lose **Eternal Life**.

Another example is the two killed by Phineas in Numbers 25:5. *And Moses said to the judges of Israel, "Slay everyone his men that were joined to Baal-Peor!' 6. And, behold, one of the children of Israel came and brought to his brothers a Midianite woman in the sight of Moses, and in the sight of the entire congregation of the children of Israel, who were weeping at the entrance of the Tent of Meeting. 7. And when Phineas, the son of Elazar, the son of Aaron the priest, saw, he rose up from among the congregation and took a spear in his hand, 8. and he went after the man of Israel into a tent and thrust both of them through, the man of Israel and the woman through her belly. So the plague was stayed from the children of Israel. 9. And those that died in the plague were twenty-four thousand.*

Those deaths now happen again at the Judgment Seat, Revelation 20:11. *Then I saw a great white throne and the One Who sits upon it, from Whose presence the earth and the sky fled and a place was not found for them. 12. Then I saw the dead, the great and the small, standing before the throne. And scrolls were opened, and **another scroll was opened**, which is of **life**, (Exodus 32:32,33; Psalm 69:29; Daniel 12:1) and the dead were judged according to their deeds, (Isaiah 59:18; Jeremiah 17:10; Psalm 28:4,62:13; Proverbs 24:12; Romans 2:6; 1 Corinthians 3:8) by what had been written in the scrolls. (Daniel 7:9,10) 13. Then the sea gave up the dead that were in it and Death and Hades gave up the dead, those in them, and each was judged according to his works. 14. Then **Death and Hades were thrown violently into the lake of fire. This is the second death, the lake of fire. 15. And if someone was not found written in the Book of Life, he was cast into the lake of fire.** (Isaiah 30:33)*

So the death sentences ordered in the Torah will be carried out after the Judgment Seat. Be sure your name is written in the Book of Life, guaranteeing you **Eternal Life**.

Faith and Works: Jacob 2:14. *What benefit is it my brothers, if someone would say he has faith, but does not have works? Is that faith able to save him? 15. If a brother or sister would be poorly clothed and is falling short of daily food 16. and if any of you would say to them from your plenty, "You must now go in peace, be warm and be filled," but would not give them their bodily needs, what is the benefit? 17. So then faith, if you would not have works, is dead in itself.*

Jacob 2:18. *But someone says, "You have faith, and I have works. You must now show me your faith without works, and I shall show you my faith by means of my works." 19. You believe that God is One, you do well: the demons also believe and shudder. (Matthew 8:29; Mark 1:24,5:7; Luke 4:34,8:28) 20. But are you willing to find out, O Senseless Man, that faith without works is unprofitable? 21. Was not our father Abraham vindicated by works, when he offered Isaac his son on the altar? 22. You see that his faith was working together with his works and that faith was made complete by his works, 23. also the Scripture was fulfilled saying, "And Abraham believed in God and it was reckoned to him as acts of loving kindness" (Genesis 15:6) and he was called a friend of God. 24. You must now see that a person is made righteous by means of works, and not only by faith. 25. And*

likewise also Rahab the idolatress, was she not made righteous by works, when sh
gave hospitality to the messengers and then sent them out another way? 26. For c
the body is dead without a spirit, so also faith without works is dead.

Everything you do counts! If a Christian's behavior has not changed, he doe
not have relationship with the Living God! It is not possible to make a list c
good things to do and live by, but every thought, every word, and every ac
tion must line up with God's perfect will. So far only One person has flowe
in that Spirit, but all of us must strive for that goal. Only the Spirit of Go
can transform each one of us. It is one step at a time, one day at a time, con
stantly improving each individual believer.

Many New Testament Scriptures confirm the necessity of Works! Check Mat
thew 7:21,16:27; Luke 8:21; John 5:29; Acts 26:20; Romans 2:10,25–29;
Corinthians 3:8; Ephesians 2:10; 2 Timothy 4:14; Titus 1:16,2:14,3:8. The
as you read through the whole Bible, make note of even more passages tha
confirm the need for works.

False Knowledge is something Paul cautioned Timothy to guard against.

1 Timothy 6:20. *O Timothy,* ***you must now guard the deposit****, the correc
knowledge and pure doctrine of the gospel, turning away for yourself from th
profane chatter and contradictions of what is* ***falsely called knowledge****,* (Isaiah
29:13; Psalm 118:8) *21. in which some missed the mark while professing abou
the faith.*

Isaiah 29:13. *Therefore the Lord said, Forasmuch as this people draws near wit*
*their mouth and honors Me with their lips, but has removed their heart far from
Me, and their reverence toward Me is* ***taught by the commandments of men***
(Matthew 15:8,9; 1 Timothy 6:20) *14. therefore, behold, I shall proceed to d
a marvelous work among this people, a marvelous work and a wonder: for th
wisdom of their wise men will perish, and the understanding of their prudent wil
be hidden.*

Psalm 8. *It is better to trust in the LORD* than to* ***put confidence in man****.*

Paul warns Timothy to be wary of what people teach about Scripture, since
the Word of God is not to be corrupted. He mentions profane chatter and
contradictions of what is falsely called knowledge, bringing confusion to the

congregations of the day. A similar situation is with us today, with many off-base interpretations being spread online and in print. To study commentary as a supplement to Scripture is fine, but Scripture itself is the defining base, not the commentary. To read commentary more than Scripture tilts you off-base. Paul said to guard the deposit, which is Scripture, the pure doctrine of the Good News. When Paul wrote this, there was no New Testament, the Hebrew Scriptures were the whole Good News. Commentary is just a group of comments on Scripture. Scripture must be the solid base on which to judge commentary.

Firstborn, both Sons and Livestock are to be taken from the Levites. The Firstborn of all livestock are only to be supplied by the Levites.

Numbers 18:14. *Everything devoted in Israel will be yours. 15. Everything that opens the womb in all flesh, which they bring to the LORD*, whether it is of men or beasts, will be yours. Nevertheless the **Firstborn** of man you will surely redeem, and the firstling of unclean beasts you will redeem. 16. And those that are to be redeemed from a month old you will redeem, according to your estimation, for the money of five shekels, after the shekel of the Sanctuary, which is twenty gerahs.*

Five shekels was a full month's wage, a sum that would strain many budgets today.

Numbers 3:40. *And the LORD* said to Moses, "Number all the **Firstborn** of the males of the children of Israel from a month old and upward and take the number of their names. 41. And you will take the Levites for Me, I AM the LORD*, **instead of all the Firstborn among the children of Israel and the livestock of the Levites instead of all the firstlings among the livestock of the children of Israel.**"*

Many people today dedicate every child to the LORD, vowing to bring the child up to revere and worship the LORD. That is very appropriate since each one of us is a Priest (Exodus 19:6).

Revelation 1:5b. *To the One Who loves us and has loosed us from our sins by His blood, 6. and made us a kingdom, **priests** to His God and Father,* (Exodus 19:6; Isaiah 61:6) *to Him be the glory and the power forever and ever. Amen.*

Fishers and Hunters are from Jeremiah 16:16. *Behold, I shall send for many fisher. says the LORD*, and they will fish them, then later I shall send for many hunt ers, and they will hunt them from every mountain and from every hill and ou of the holes of the rocks.*

The **Fishers** catch live; the **Hunters** kill.

This is speaking of Jewish people all over the world. We are now in a tim of transition when many Jewish people are being enticed by the **fishers** t make Aliyah to Israel by the attractiveness of having a Jewish State with grea education and a good environment for business. The **hunters** are already o the prowl and are speeding up the Aliyah of more. France is a good exampl of the **hunters** who are targeting Jews in different cities, shooting and us ing bombs when they can. French police are catching the **hunters**, and th courts are prosecuting them, but they have not been able to prevent all th attacks. Other countries are actively persecuting Jews, wanting them to leave Jeremiah was not prophesying these days, but his prophecy definitely applie to this very time in which we live.

Forty-one Moves in Forty Years meant the average stay of the Israelite camp wa eleven months, much longer than most of us would have guessed. The move and encampments are detailed in Numbers 33. Travel time from one camp site to the next would have taken multiple days, so there is no way to estimat the time of each camp with precision.

Numbers 33:1. *These are the journeys of the children of Israel when they went ou of the land of Egypt with their armies under the hand of Moses and Aaron. 2. An. Moses wrote their goings out according to their journeys by the commandment c the LORD*, and these are their journeys according to their goings out.*

Numbers 33:3. *And they departed from Rameses in the first month on the fif teenth day of the first month. On the day after the Passover the children of Israe went out with a high hand in the sight of all the Egyptians. 4. For the Egyptian buried all the firstborn that the LORD* had smitten among them: the LORD* also executed judgments upon their gods. 5. And the children of Israel left Ramese and pitched in Sukkot. (1) 6. Then they left Sukkot and pitched in Itam, (2 which is in the edge of the wilderness. 7. And they left Itam and turned again t Pi Ha\underline{h}irot, (3) which is before Baal Zephon, and they pitched before Migdol. 8 And they left Pi Ha\underline{h}irot and crossed through the midst of the sea into the wilder* *ness and went three days' journey in the wilderness of Itam and pitched in Marah. (4) 9. And they left Marah and came to Elim (5) and in Elim there were twelve fountains of water and seventy palm trees, and they pitched there. 10. Then they left Elim and camped by the Reed Sea. (6) 11. And they left the Reed Sea and camped in the wilderness of Sin. (7) 12. And they took their journey from the wilderness of Sin and camped in Dafkah. (8) 13. And they left Dafkah and camped in Alush. (9) 14. And they left Alush and camped at Refidim, (10) where there was no water for the people to drink. 15. And they left Refidim and pitched in the wilderness of Sinai. (11) 16. Then they left the desert of Sinai and pitched at Kibrot Hattaavah. (12) 17. And they left Kibrot Hattaavah and camped at Hazerot, (13) 18. and they left Hazerot and pitched in Ritmah. (14) 19. And they left Ritmah and pitched at Rimmon Perez. (15) 20. And they left Rimmon Perez and pitched in Libnah. (16) 21. And they left Libnah and pitched at Rissah. (17) 22. And they traveled from Rissah and pitched in Keheletah. (18) 23. Then they went from Keheletah and pitched at Mount Shefer. (19) 24. And they left Mount Shefer and camped at Haradah. (20) 25. And they left Haradah and pitched in Makehelot. (21) 26. Then they left Makehelot and camped at Tahat. (22) 27. And they departed from Tahat and pitched at Terah. (23) 28. And they left Terah and pitched in Mitkah. (24) 29. And they went from Mitkah and pitched in Hashmonah. (25) 30. And they departed from Hashmonah and camped at Moserot. (26) 31. And they left Moserot and pitched in Benai Jaakan. (27) 32. And they traveled from Benai Jaakan and camped at Hor Hagidgad. (28) 33. And they went from Hor Hagidgad and pitched in Jotbah. (29) 34. And they left Jotbah and camped at Avronah. (30) 35. And they left Avronah and camped at Ezion-geber. (31) 36. And they left Ezion-geber and camped in the wilderness of Zin, which is Kadesh. (32) 37. And they left Kadesh and pitched at Mount Hor, (33) in the edge of the land of Edom.*

Numbers 33:38. *And Aaron the priest went up on Mount Hor at the commandment of the LORD* and died there, in the fortieth year after the children of Israel came out of the land of Egypt, on the first of the fifth month. 39. And Aaron was a hundred twenty-three years old when he died on Mount Hor.*

Numbers 33:40. *And king Arad the Canaanite, who dwelled in the south in the land of Canaan, heard of the coming of the children of Israel. 41. And they departed from Mount Hor and camped in Zalmonah. (34) 42. And they left Zalmonah and camped in Punon. (35) 43. And they left Punon and pitched in Obot. (36) 44. And they left Obot and camped in Ije Haavarim, (37) in the border of Moab. 45. And they left Ijim and camped in Dibon Gad. (38) 46.*

And they traveled from Dibon Gad and camped in Almon Diblathaim. (39) 47. And they left Almon Diblathaim and camped in the mountains of Avarim, before Nebo. (40) 48. And they left the mountains of Abarim and camped in the plain of Moab by the Jordan near Jericho. 49. And they camped by the Jordan from Beit Jeshimoth to Abel Shittim (41) in the plains of Moab.

After Pi Ha<u>h</u>irot, they camped at various wilderness sites, never near any inhabited areas. All those stopping places are named so the world would know in later generations that this was indeed wilderness. The people lived in very large tents, not unlike the tents of the Bedouin seen in Israel today, so moving entailed a great deal of work, especially after the Tabernacle had been made.

Future Borders of Israel are given in Numbers 34:1.

And the LORD* spoke to Moses saying, 2. "Command the children of Israel and say to them,

"'When you come into the land of Canaan, this is the land that will fall to you for an inheritance, the land of Canaan according to its borders. 3. Then your south side will be from the wilderness of Zin along by the border of Edom and your south border will be the outermost end of the Salt Sea eastward, 4. and your border will turn from the south to the ascent of Akrabbim and pass on to Zin and from there it will be from the south to Kadesh Barnea, and will go on to Hazaraddar and pass on to Azmonah. 5. And the border will turn about from Azmonah to the river of Egypt, and from there it will go to the sea. 6. And as the western border, you will even have the Great Sea for a border: this will be your west border. 7. And this will be your north border, from the Great Sea you will point out for yourselves Mount Hor, 8. from Mount Hor you will point out to the entrance of Hamat, and from there the border will be to Zedadah, 9. and the border will go on to Ziphronah, and from there it will be at Hazar-Enan: this will be your north border. 10. And you will point out your east border from Hazar-Enan to Shefamah, 11. and the border will go down from Shefamah to Riblah, on the east side of Ayin, and the border will descend and will reach to the side of the lake of Kinneret eastward 12. and the border will go down to the Jordan, and from there it will go to the Salt Sea: this will be your land according to its borders all around.'"

Bringing an estimated two to three million people through any area would be an extraordinary undertaking. It is beyond imagination to think of the physical size of the group. How many square miles of land would they take up when they traveled with their animals – people and animals spread out over vast expanses of wilderness? When the people were in the camp, the animals were all outside, being shepherded, led to water and whatever grazing was available. The camp had to be some sight, with hundreds of thousands of enormous tents arranged around the Tabernacle.

The following map was drawn by Dr. Yigal Levin of Bar-Ilan University, printed in the Jerusalem Post. We are grateful for his perseverance through all the unknowns involved. Hamat, also spelled Hamath from the Greek, is at the far north and is in Syria today, although named here as part of Israel. Will these be the actual borders before the reign of Messiah? This is an exciting time to live and to ponder such things.

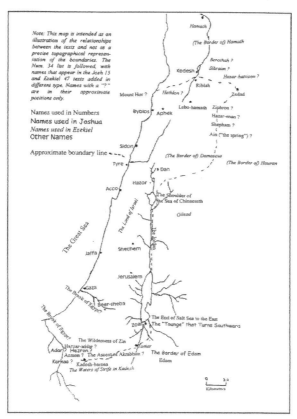

Gehazi, the Unclaimed Miracle Healing of Leprosy. After Elisha refused to take any reward for Naaman's healing, which was from leprosy, Gehazi's greed took over:

2 Kings 5:20. *But **Gehazi**, the young man of Elisha the man of God said, Behold, my master has spared Naaman this Syrian from taking at his hands that which he brought, but as the LORD* lives, I shall run after him and take something from him. 21. So **Gehazi** went down after Naaman. And when Naaman saw him running after him he got down from the carriage to meet him and said, Is all well?*

2 Kings 5:22. *And he said, All is well. My master has sent me saying, Behold, even now there are coming to me two young men of the sons of the prophets from Mount Ephraim. Please give them a talent of silver, and two changes of garments.*

2 Kings 5:23. *And Naaman said, Be content, take two talents. And he urged him and bound two talents of silver in two bags, with two changes of garments and laid them upon two of his young men, and they bore them before him. 24. And, when he came to the hill, he took them from their hand and deposited them in the house, then he let the men go and they departed.*

2 Kings 5:25. *Then he came and stood before his master. And Elisha said to him, Where were you, **Gehazi**? And he said, Your servant went neither here nor there.*

2 Kings 5:26. *And he said to him, Was not my heart with you, when the man turned from his carriage to meet you? Is it a time to take money and to take garments, olive trees, vineyards, sheep, oxen, men servants, and maid servants? 27. Therefore **the leprosy of Naaman will cling to you and to your seed forever. And he went out from his presence a leper as white as snow.***

The next time **Gehazi** is named is in 2 Kings 8:1. *Then Elisha spoke to the woman whose son he had restored to life saying, Arise! You and your household go and stay wherever you can, for the LORD* has called for a famine and it will also come upon the land for seven years. 2. And the woman got up and did according to the word of the man of God and she went with her household and stayed in the land of the Philistines for seven years. 3. And it was at the seven years' end that the woman returned from the land of the Philistines, and she went out to cry to the king for her house and for her land.*

2 Kings 8:4. *And the king talked with **Gehazi** the young man of the man of God saying, Now tell me, please, all the great things that Elisha has done. 5. And it was, as he was telling the king how he had restored a dead body to life, that, behold, the woman whose son he had restored to life cried to the king for her house*

*and for her land. And **Gehazi** said, My lord, O king, this is the woman and this is her son, whom Elisha restored to life.*

The king then ordered her property restored along with any crops, but how could **Gehazi** be there? A leper had to stay outside the city and could not associate with anyone else but other lepers. Could the answer lie in 2 Kings 7?

*2 Kings 7:3. And there were **four men with leprosy** at the entrance of the gate and they said to one another, Why are we sitting here until we die? 4. If we say, We will enter the city, then the famine is in the city and we will die there. And if we sit still here, we will also die. Now therefore come and let us fall to the army of the Syrians. If they save us alive, we will live and if they kill us, we will but die.*

2 Kings 7:5. And they rose up in the twilight to go to the camp of the Syrians, and when they had come to the outermost part of the camp of Syria, behold, no one was there. 6. For the Lord had made the army of the Syrians to hear a noise of chariots and a noise of horses, the noise of a great army, and they said to one another, Look, the king of Israel has hired against us the kings of the Hittites and the kings of the Egyptians to come against us. 7. Therefore they got up in the twilight and left their tents and their horses and their donkeys, even the camp as it was, and fled for their lives.

*2 Kings 7:8. And when these **lepers** came to the outermost part of the camp, they went into one tent and ate and drank and carried silver, gold, and garments from there, then went and hid it and came back and entered another tent and carried there also, and went and hid it. 9. Then they said to one another, **We are not doing well. This day is a day of good tidings and we are holding our peace. If we delay until the morning light, punishment will overtake us. Therefore now come, so we can go and tell the king's household.***

2 Kings 7:10. So they came and called to the gate keepers of the city and they told them saying, We came to the camp of the Syrians and, behold, there was not a man there, neither a sound of man, but horses tied and donkeys tied, and the tents as they were.

There can be no doubt, **Gehazi** was healed from his leprosy. The God of Mercy, Love, and Grace did heal him, but how? And why? Commentary suggests that **Gehazi** was one of the four lepers, and that the four were healed because they could have taken selectively from the gold and other valuables left by the fleeing Syrians and lived luxuriously, though still lepers, but chose instead to let everyone know that the siege was over. So God rewarded them by healing their leprous bodies. Thus **Gehazi** has **an Unclaimed Miracle Healing from Leprosy**.

God in Us is a major point that does not seem to register with many people. We read that in John 6:56. *The one who chews My flesh and drinks My blood* ***remain in Me and I in him***.

John 14:19. *Yet a little while and the world will no longer see Me, but you will see Me. Because I live you will also live. 20. In that Day you will know that **I am in My Father and you are in Me and I am in you**.*

John 15:4. ***you must now dwell in Me and I in you***. *Just as the branch is not able to bear fruit by itself unless it would remain in the vine, so **you could not bear fruit unless you would dwell continuously in Me**. 5. I am the vine, you are the branches. **The one who dwells in Me and I in him, this one bears much fruit**, because apart from Me you are not able to do anything. 6. Unless someone would dwell in Me, he is cast outside like the branch and it withers and they gather it and cast it into the fire and it is burned. 7. **If you would dwell in Me and My words would dwell in you, whatever you would wish you must immediately ask, and it will be done for you**.*

John 17:20. *I do not ask concerning them only, but also concerning those who believe in Me because of the disciples' message, 21. so that all would be one, just as You, Father, are in Me and I in You, that **they also would be in Us**, so that the world would believe that You sent Me.*

How can someone relate to that? Paul did just that. He died to self, so the God in Paul gave him peace when his body was in pain in the stocks of the Philippi jail. Stephen did also, so he had peace when he was being stoned. This dying to self was ordered to Abram in Genesis 12:1 when God said "Get yourself out of here." That referred to leaving Haran but also to Abram getting the **self** out of him.

Psalm 32:7. *You are **my hiding place**. You will preserve me from trouble. You will surround me with songs of deliverance. Selah. 8. I will instruct you and teach you in the Way which you will go. **I will guide you with My eye**.*

When God guides you with His eye, it is the God in you guiding you as you see through His eyes. As you become more like Him, you see more plainly what He sees.

Philippians 3:2. *Watch out for the dogs, watch out for the evil workings, watch out for the mutilation. 3. For we ourselves are the circumcision, those who serve by the Spirit of God and who boast in Messiah Y'shua and who do not trust in flesh, 4. although I have confidence even in my flesh. If any other thinks he has confidence in his flesh, I more: 5. circumcised at eight days old, from the nation of Israel, tribe of Benjamin, a Hebrew born of Hebrews, according to the sect of Pharisees, 6. with respect to zeal persecuting the congregation, regarding righteousness because I was blameless in legalism. 7. But whatever things were for me to gain, I have counted these things a loss because of the Messiah. 8. But no, rather then,* **I counted everything to be a loss because of the surpassing worth of the knowledge of Messiah Y'shua my Lord, for Whose sake I forfeited everything***, and I am counting myself, and those things, worthless, so that I shall gain Messiah's favor 9. to be found by Him, not having my righteousness from legalism, but through faith in Messiah, the righteousness of God based on faith, 10.* **to know Him and the power of His resurrection and the fellowship with His sufferings, when I have been rendered like Him in His death***, 11. if somehow I should attain to the resurrection from the dead.*

Colossians 1:24. *Now I rejoice in my sufferings on your behalf and I make up for His absence to take on the afflictions of the Messiah, in my flesh for the sake of His body, which is the congregation, 25. of which I have become a servant according to the divine office of God, the one that was given to me to bring the Word of God to completion in you, 26. the mystery that has been hidden away from the ages, and from the generations – but now it has been revealed to His saints, 27. to whom God desired to make known among the heathens the wealth of the glory of this mystery, which is* **Messiah in you***, the hope of glory: 28. which we are proclaiming, admonishing everyone and teaching everyone in all wisdom, so that we could present every person complete in Messiah: 29. and in which I toil, struggling, according to His working that which is being worked in me in power.*

Y'shua said *Therefore Y'shua was answering and was saying to them, "Most assuredly I say to you, the Son is not able to do anything by Himself except what* **He would see the Father doing***: for whatever that One would do, then the Son likewise does these things."* (Matthew 5:19)

In 1 Kings 18, Elijah looked through God's eyes to see the fire descending before he ordered the water to fill the troughs, and Elisha saw God's healing of Naaman before telling Naaman to dip seven times in the Jordan. That deep relationship with God comes only with total dedication to Him, in walking in repentance with every step.

God With Us is an amazing fact. No dead, false god can do anything, let alone go through difficult trials with those who worship the false god, but look what the Living God says:

2 Samuel 7:7. *In all the places where **I have walked with all the children of Israel** did I speak a word with any of the tribes of Israel, whom I commanded to feed My people Israel saying, Why have you not built Me a House of cedar? 8. Now therefore so shall you say to My servant David, Thus says the LORD* of Hosts, I took you from the sheepfold, from following the sheep to be ruler over My people, over Israel. 9. And I was with you wherever you went and have cut off all your enemies out of your sight and have made you a great name, like the name of the great men who are in the earth. 10. **Moreover I shall appoint a place for My people Israel and will plant them**, so they can dwell in a place of their own and not move any more. Neither will the children of wickedness afflict them any more, as before, 11. and as since the time that I commanded judges to be over My people Israel then I have caused you to rest from all your enemies. Also the LORD* tells you that the LORD* will make a house for you. 12. And when your days are fulfilled and you sleep with your fathers, I shall set up your seed after you, that will proceed out of your loins and I shall establish his kingdom. (Acts 2:30) 13. He will build a House for My name and I shall establish the throne of his kingdom forever. 14. I AM will be his Father and he will be My son. (2 Corinthians 6:18; Hebrews 1:5) If he sins, I will chasten him with the rod of men and with the stripes of the children of men. (Revelation 21:7) 15. But My loving kindness will not depart from him, as I took it from Saul, whom I put away before you. 16. And your house and your kingdom will be established forever before you. Your throne will be established forever.*

This passage states that God walked with Israel. He did not watch from afar. He did not ride in a chariot nor was He carried by cherubim, but God Himself walked with Israel. Our Heavenly Father then goes on in verses 12–16 to describe His plan for David, as He has a plan for you!

Jeremiah 29:11. *For **I AM** knows the thoughts, plans, and intentions that **I AM** thinking toward you, says the LORD*, thoughts of peace and not of evil, to give you a future and hope. 12. Then you will call upon Me and you will go and pray to Me and I shall heed you. 13. And you will seek Me and find Me, when you will search for Me with your heart.*

The bold **I AM** is the very powerful Anokhi. (See Anokhi in Glossary.)

God is with those who believe in Him with their whole heart, as a group and individually. That is so amazing that the Living God, the Heavenly Father, cares not only about the welfare of His congregation, but He cares about each one of us. He cares about you! He has a plan for you! His plan is to give you a future and hope.

Good and Bad is an expression used often in Scripture. What makes this especially intriguing is that **Good and Bad** are not opposites. Evil is the opposite of **Good** and Shalom is the opposite of **Bad**. What is **Bad** is not necessarily evil, but what is evil is necessarily **Bad**. If I miss-spell words and use poor grammar, that is bad, not evil. Scripture uses this expression quite often, with the first in Genesis.

Genesis 2:8. *And the LORD* God planted a garden eastward in Eden, and there He put the man whom He had formed. 9. And the LORD* God made to grow out of the ground every tree that is pleasant to the sight and good for food: also the tree of life in the midst of the garden, and the tree of knowledge of **good and bad**.*

1 Kings 3:7. *And now, LORD* my God, You have made Your servant king instead of David my father and I am but a little lad: I do not know how to go out or come in. 8. And Your servant is in the midst of Your people whom You have chosen, a great people, that cannot be numbered or counted for multitude. 9. Therefore give Your servant an understanding heart to judge Your people, so I can discern between **good and bad**, for who is able to judge this Your so great a people?*

There are at least a dozen other uses of **Good and Bad**, so understand that our Heavenly Father is concerned about **bad** behavior every bit as much as He is concerned about evil behavior.

Genesis 38:7. *And Er, Judah's firstborn, was **bad** in the eyes of the LORD* and the LORD* slew him.*

Bad behavior includes rudeness, carelessness, slacking on the job, not disciplining your children, wasting money, and much more, but you get the idea. Evil includes sins such as cheating, which is really stealing, and lying, which some do not consider sin. Y'shua said you will not lose **Eternal Life** by what you eat. But if you ignore Torah's food proscriptions, you are putting your life at risk because the forbidden foods will shorten your life. Doing **Bad Things** may well shorten your life and will certainly affect your Heavenly Reward.

Good Soil produces good fruit, but what about the parables of the sower?

Matthew 13:1. *In that day, after He left the house, Y'shua was sitting by the lake. 2. and immense crowds were gathered to Him, so that He got in a boat and sat down, and the entire crowd stood on the shore. 3. And He told them many things in parables saying, "Behold the sower of the seed came out to sow. 4. And while he was sowing some indeed fell by the way, and when the birds came they devoured them. 5. But some fell upon the rocky ground where it did not have much soil, and it sprang up right away because it had no depth of soil: 6. and when the sun rose it was burned, and because it did not have a root it was withered. 7. But some fell upon thorns, and the thorns came up and choked them. 8. But some fell upon **good ground**, and gave fruit, on the one hand a hundred times, on another sixty, and another thirty. 9. The one who has ears must listen continually."*

Matthew 13:18. *"Therefore you must now hear the parable of the sower. 19. For everyone who hears the message of the kingdom and does not understand, the evil one comes and snatches away what was sown in his heart, this one is what is sown by the way. 20. And the one sown upon the stony ground, this is the one who hears the message and immediately takes it with joy, 21. but it does not have a root in itself, but it is temporary, and when affliction or persecution comes because of the message, he is immediately caused to fall away. 22. And the one sown among the thorns, this is the one who hears the message, and the anxiety of the age and the deceitfulness of wealth (Matthew 6:24) choke the message and it becomes useless. 23. And the one sown upon the **good ground**, this is the one who hears the message and understands, who indeed bears fruit and makes on the one hand one hundred times, and on another sixty and another thirty."*

Matthew 7:16. *"**You will recognize people by their fruit.** Does anyone gather grapes from thorn bushes or figs from thistles? 17. In this way every good tree produces good fruit, but the rotten tree produces evil fruit. 18. A good tree is not able to produce evil fruit, nor a rotten tree to produce good fruit. 19. Every tree not producing good fruit is cut down and thrown into a fire. 20. Consequently you will indeed know them on account of their fruit."*

In verse 16 the Greek construction anticipates a negative response.

Since it takes **good soil** to produce good fruit, how can a person be made **good soil**? A person's fruit being recognized means what you do counts, relating to your bearing, dress, countenance, and reactions to various surprises; virtually everything you do and say. All those things shape your character, your visible fruit. So both **good and bad** things determine the quality of your fruit. Everything you think, say, and do counts. The important thing is to learn from your mistakes, to continually strive to become better. So far the earth has seen only one perfect person, Y'shua, so the rest of humanity is working on it. Like David we have to determine to get there as he said in Psalm 19:15 ***The words of my mouth and the meditation of my heart will be acceptable in Your sight, LORD*, my Rock and my Redeemer.*** When your thoughts and words line up with God, your actions will too. Your reactions to surprises when you do not have time to reflect, reveal your true fruit. Thus anger is a real test for all of us. Everything you do counts, so doing good things improves your fruit. Although you are not saved by good deeds, you do those things because you are saved, walking in the Spirit.

Going through tough times and overcoming obstacles builds character, giving you high quality fruit. What you have been through and are now going through are the things that build the quality of your soil. An example from the world is one I witnessed in the 1970s when we built a new home in the country. We had horses, so I built a temporary shed for shelter until I could afford to build a barn. I cleared a half acre of the sandy land in the sand hills of South Carolina for the corral by the shed. Each week for two years the sand was roto-tilled to bury the manure. After two years the barn was built and a new corral fenced by the barn. The old corral was planted, with that sand now rich soil, growing the biggest, sweetest cantaloupes I had ever seen. All the vegetables grown were astonishing in size and quality. So, if you are going through stuff now, be assured that while you persevere, you will in the end be **good soil**, producing wonderful fruit.

Helps in 1 Corinthians 12:28. *Now God indeed placed them in the congregation. First He placed apostles, second prophets, third teachers, then miracles, then gifts of healings,* **helps,** *administrations, kinds of tongues.*

The word **Helps** in this verse simply slips in unobtrusively, hiding in the verse. It is very easy to gloss over **Helps**, not understanding what Paul is saying. The word **Helps** is the literal translation of the Greek word Antilepsis, referring to **those responsible for the care of the poor and the sick.** Helps is not a general term for making one or more people in a congregation to just do whatever someone in leadership wants done. The **Helps** ministry is not to be misused, so take this definition seriously and apply **Helps** as Paul meant in 1 Corinthians 12.

Hezekiah's Destruction of an 8th Century BC Lachish Gate Shrine—from a September 28, 2016 Jerusalem Post article.

"The continuation of the building is constituted by the gate shrine, its walls treated with white plaster. Steps away, a staircase once ascended to a large room where there was a bench upon which offerings were placed.

"An opening was exposed in the corner of the room that led to the holy of holies," said Ganor. "To our great excitement, we found two four-horned altars and scores of ceramic finds consisting of lamps, bowls, and stands in this room. It is most interesting that the horns on the altar were intentionally truncated! "That is probably evidence of the religious reform attributed to King Hezekiah, whereby religious worship was centralized in Jerusalem, and the cultic high places that were built outside the capital were destroyed: 'He removed the high places, smashed the sacred stones, and cut down the Asherah poles... (II Kings 18:4).'" Moreover, besides cutting the horns on the altar, in an effort to further intensify the abolition of worship in the gate shrine, Ganor said a toilet was installed in the holy of holies as "the ultimate desecration of that place."

"A stone fashioned in the shape of a chair with a hole in its center was found in the corner of the room," he said. "Stones of this type have been identified in archaeological research as toilets. Evidence of abolishing cultic locations by installing a toilet in them is known in the Bible, as illustrated in the case of Jehu destroying the cult of Ba'al in Samaria: 'And they demolished the pillar of Ba'al, and demolished the house of Ba'al, and made it a latrine to this day

(II Kings 10:27).'" Ganor claimed this is the first time an archaeological find confirms this phenomenon.

"Laboratory tests we conducted in the spot where the stone toilet was placed suggest it was never used," he said. "Hence, we can conclude that the placement of the toilet had been symbolic, after which the holy of holies was sealed until the site was destroyed."

This article about the destruction of a shrine presages modern idolatry, which seldom brings stuff to present to gods, but emphasizes having stuff, to use and to show to others that we have the ability to gather all these things, fancy cars, big boys' toys, whatever society admires. This covetousness can even show up in churches.

How Old Was Isaac when Abraham took him to Mount Moriah to offer Isaac to God? How old was he when he married Rebeccah? Since we know the next event after he was offered on Mount Moriah was Sarah's death, then that gives us the timing.

> Genesis 23:1. *And Sarah was **a hundred twenty-seven years old**: these were the years of the life of Sarah.*

> Genesis 17:17. *Then Abraham fell upon his face and laughed, and said in his heart, "Will a child be born to him that is a hundred years old? And will **Sarah, who is ninety years old**, bear a child?"*

Sarah was **ninety** when Isaac was born, so Isaac was **thirty-seven** when Abraham took him to Mount Moriah.

How Old Were Jacob and Esau when Jacob left for Padan-Aram? They had to be about **seventy-six years old** at that time. We know Jacob's age when he arrived in Egypt. He was one hundred thirty years old when he met Pharaoh.

> Genesis 47:9. *And Jacob said to Pharaoh, "The days of the years of my pilgrimage are **a hundred thirty years**: few and bad have the days of the years of my life been, and have not attained to the days of the years of the life of my fathers in the days of their pilgrimage."*

Joseph was approximately **forty** because he was thirty when he began to reign and he had led through the seven years of plenty and two years of drought. He could not have been younger than **thirty-nine**, but could well have been a little older than forty. Using these figures would make Jacob ninety or a bit older when Joseph was born.

Genesis 30:22. *And God remembered Rachel and God hearkened to her, and opened her womb. 23. And she conceived and bore a son. Then she said, "God has taken away my reproach." 24. And she called his name Joseph (Yosef) and said, "The LORD* will add another son to me." 25. And it was, when* Rachel had borne Joseph that Jacob said to Laban, "Send me away, so I can go to my own place, and to my country. *26. Give me my wives and my children, for whom I have served you and let me go, for you know my service, what I have done for you.*

Joseph was born just prior to this request to leave Laban. It was another six years before Jacob was able to leave, to return to the land of Israel.

Genesis 31:40. *Thus I (Jacob) was; in the day the drought consumed me and the frost by night, and my sleep departed from my eyes. 41. I have thus been* **twenty years** *in your house. I served you fourteen years for your two daughters and six years for your livestock, and you have changed my wages ten times.*

Since Jacob had been with Laban for twenty years, he was about **ninety-six** when he left. The twins, Jacob and Esau, were **seventy-six** when Isaac blessed Jacob and sent him to Haran.

Huldah, a true prophetess of the LORD!

2 Kings 22:12. *And the king (Josiah) commanded Hilkiah the priest, Ahikam the son of Shafan, Achbor the son of Micaiah, Shafan the scribe, and Asaiah a servant of the king's, saying, 13. Go! Inquire of the LORD* for me and for the people and for all Judah, concerning the words of this scroll that has been found, for the wrath of the LORD* that is kindled against us is great because our fathers have not heeded the words of this scroll, to do according to all that is written concerning us.*

2 Kings 22:14. *So Hilkiah the priest, Ahikam, Achbor, Shafan, and Asaiah went to* **Huldah** *the prophetess, the wife of Shallum the son of Tikvah, the son of Harhas, keeper of the wardrobe. (Now she lived in Jerusalem, in the second quarter)*

and they spoke with her. 15. And she said to them, Thus says the LORD God of Israel, Tell the man who sent you to me, 16. Thus says the LORD*, Behold, I shall bring evil upon this place and upon its inhabitants, all the words of the scroll which the king of Judah has read 17. because they have forsaken Me and have burned incense to other gods, so they would provoke Me to anger with all the works of their hands. Therefore My anger will be kindled against this place, and will not be quenched. 18. But to the king of Judah who sent you to inquire of the LORD*, thus you will say to him, Thus says the LORD* God of Israel, As touching the words which you have heard, 19. Because your heart was tender and you have humbled yourself before the LORD*, when you heard what I spoke against this place and against its inhabitants, that they should become a desolation and a curse, and have torn your clothes and wept before Me, also **I AM** has heard you, says the LORD*. 20. Behold therefore, I AM will gather you to your fathers and you will be gathered to your grave in peace and your eyes will not see all the evil which I shall bring upon this place.*

And they brought back word to the king.

Josiah Leads Revival
2 Kings 23:1. *And the king sent, and they gathered all the elders of Judah and of Jerusalem to him. 2. And the king went up to the House of the LORD* and all the men of Judah and all the inhabitants of Jerusalem with him, the priests, the prophets, and all the people, both small and great. Then he read in their ears all the words of the scroll of the covenant which was found in the House of the LORD*. 3. And the king stood by a pillar and cut a covenant before the LORD*, to walk after the LORD* and to keep His commandments and His testimonies and His statutes with all their heart and their entire being, to perform the words of this covenant that were written in this scroll. And all the people accepted the covenant.*

King Josiah asked for a Word from the LORD, and he sure got it! Josiah believed the Word and acted on it, saving Jerusalem for that generation. **Huldah** was so highly honored by the leaders that the South Gate of the Temple was named for her. The South Gate opened from Solomon's Portico, the common entrance for the people.

Immorality is not to be tolerated in a congregation, taught to us by Paul in 1 Corinthians 5:9. *I wrote to you in the letter not to be associated with **immoral** people, 10. by no means are you able to avoid contact with the **immoralities** of this* *world or with covetous ones or swindlers or idolaters, for otherwise you would not have to come out of the world. 11. But now I write to you not to be associated if some brother would be called **immoral** or covetous or idolater or abusive or a drunkard or extortioner, and not to eat with such as this one: 12. for what allows me to judge those outside? Are you not judging those inside? 13. But God judges those outside. "You must immediately remove the **immoral** one from you."*

This could not be stated more clearly, yet there are congregations today with homosexual clergy, with couples living together out of wedlock, and others in various sins.

Instructions of the Jerusalem Council to the new congregations of former heathens

Acts 15:19. On this account I judge that we should not cause difficulty for those of the heathens who are turning to God, 20. but to instruct them to abstain from the pollutions of the idols and from immorality and from the meat of strangled animals and from the blood. (Leviticus 17:10) 21. For throughout every city from ancient generations Moses has those who preach him, since he is read in the synagogues on every Sabbath."

1. Pollutions from idols: this includes all idol worship, with covetousness especially noted as idol worship by Paul. (See Sins of Our Lives in Repentance.)
2. Immorality: this includes the moral teachings of Exodus chapters 21 and 22 and Leviticus chapters 18 through 20, with far more than just sexual sins. Read those chapters looking for the breadth of the commandments.
3. Meat from animals not killed by God's instructions, which direct the draining of blood from an animal.
4. Abstain from blood, from eating blood.

Some have defined these proscriptions in the narrowest terms, which is close to saying that anything goes, anything is okay. If that were true, Paul would not have written:

*Ephesians 5:1. Therefore you must continually be imitators of God as beloved children 2. and you must walk constantly in love, just as also the Messiah loved us and gave Himself over on our behalf, an offering and a sacrifice to God for a fragrant aroma. 3. But any **immorality or impurity or covetousness must not be named among you**, as is fitting for saints, 4. **nor foul speaking or foolish*** *talking or low jesting*, which things do not belong, but rather thanksgiving. 5. *For you know this very well, that anyone who practices immorality or uncleanness or covetousness, who is an idol worshipper, does not have any inheritance in the kingdom of the Messiah and God.*

In the Greek text, covetousness is specifically referred to as idol worship.

Paul, who carried the letter from the Jerusalem council to the congregations of former heathens, was specifically assigned to explain the council's decision concerning essential doctrines; therefore, the narrow readings of the proscriptions are definitely not correct.

Israel Sold! When Israel went after strange gods, God **Sold** them for the bargain price of Zero shekels.

Judges 10:6. *Then the children of Israel again brought anarchy in the eyes of the LORD* and served baalim and Ashtarot, the gods of Syria, the gods of Sidon, the gods of Moab, the gods of the children of Ammon, and the gods of the Philistines and forsook the LORD*, and did not serve Him. 7. And the anger of the LORD* was hot against Israel and He **Sold** them into the hands of the Philistines and into the hands of the children of Ammon. 8. And that year, of Jair's death, they crushed and oppressed the children of Israel, **continuing for eighteen years**, all the children of Israel that were on the other side of the Jordan in the land of the Amorite, which is in Gilead. 9. Moreover the children of Ammon crossed over the Jordan to fight also against Judah and against Benjamin and against the house of Ephraim, so that Israel was greatly distressed.*

Isaiah 50:1. *Or which of My creditors is it to whom I have **Sold** you? Behold, you have **Sold** yourselves because of your iniquities and your mother is put away because of your transgressions.*

Now the US has **Sold** itself and done so while paying other countries with absurd sums of our money, honoring false gods here and abroad. Only with deep national repentance will He redeem us.

Isaiah 52:3. *You have **Sold** yourselves for nought, and you shall be redeemed without money.*

Psalm 25:22. *Redeem Israel, O God, out of all his troubles.*

Redeem us, O LORD!

Psalm 130:8. *And He will redeem Israel from all its iniquities.*

Yes! We believe He will redeem us from all our iniquities and sins! (See National Sin in Glossary.)

Jethro, also called Hobab and Reuel, was Moses' father-in-law. It was Moses who invited Jethro to accompany Israel to the Promised Land (Numbers 10:29). *And Moses said to Hobab, the son of Reuel the Midianite, Moses' father-in-law, "We are journeying to the place of which the LORD* said, 'I shall give it to you.' Come with us for yourself and we will do you good, for the LORD* has spoken good concerning Israel."*

Numbers 10:30. *And he said to him, "I shall not go, but I shall leave for my own land and to my kindred."*

Numbers 10:31. *And he said, "**Do not leave us, I pray you!** For as you know we are to make camp in the wilderness and you have been as eyes for us. 32. And it will be, if you go with us – indeed it will be that what goodness the LORD* will do for us, He will do the same for you."*

Judges 1:16 tells us that Jethro did indeed go with the Israelites. *And the children of the Kenite, Moses' father-in-law, went up out of the City of Date Palms with the children of Judah into the wilderness of Judah, which is south of Arad, and they went and lived among the people.*

Judges 4:11 also confirms: *Now Heber the Kenite, from the children of Hobab the father-in-law of Moses, had separated himself from the Kenites and pitched his tent on the plain of Elon Bezaananim, which is by Kedesh (Kedshah).* (See Deborah Prophesies Jael in this chapter.)

Joseph Not Recognized by His Brothers. There are very good reasons that Joseph's brothers did not recognize him when they came to Egypt for food. Not only did they think he might be dead, but they knew that Joseph was a slave if he was alive. He would certainly not be the ruler of Egypt. Physically he was very different too, beyond whatever changes his appearance had during the twenty-two years since they had seen him. He left as a teenager and now was about forty years old. As a member of the royal household, Joseph had shaved all his head, eyebrows, and body hair. He shaved every day, so he was as bald as a billiard ball.

Genesis 42:7. *And Joseph saw his brothers and he recognized them, but made himself a stranger to them and spoke roughly to them. And he said to them, "Where did you come from?" And they said, "From the land of Canaan to buy food.* Genesis 42:28 tells us he was speaking to his brothers through an interpreter.

Back track a little.

Genesis 41:14. *Then Pharaoh sent and called Joseph and they brought him hastily out of the dungeon: and **he shaved** and changed his clothes and came in to Pharaoh.*

In an article in *Ancient Man and the First Civilizations; Egypt 2*: "Because of its hot climate, in Egypt shaving and hair removal was a regular part of daily grooming. The Egyptians had an unusual obsession with personal body hygiene. The great Greek historian/storyteller HERODOTUS, stated that the Egyptians bathed several times a day, and "set cleanness above seemliness."

"Clearly, being so clean all the time, was associated with fanatical behavior by outsiders. The ancient Romans thought that a lack of body hair, was some kind of terrible deformity. But not in Egypt, people there believed that body hair was shameful and unclean. Wild animals and barbarian people had hair, not the sophisticated, super-advanced Egyptian civilization."

That certainly explains how Joseph could recognize his brothers after twenty-two years and why they did not recognize Joseph.

Judah Goes First several times:

Numbers 10:11. *And it happened on the twentieth day of the second month in the second year that the cloud was taken up from off the Tabernacle of the Testimony. 12. And the children of Israel took their journeys from the wilderness of Sinai and the cloud rested in the wilderness of Paran. 13. And they took their first journey according to the commandment of the LORD* by the hand of Moses. 14. The standard of the camp of the children of **Judah went first** according to their armies, and Nahshon the son of Amminadab was over its army.*

Judges 1:1. *Now after the death of Joshua it happened that the children of Israel asked the LORD* saying. Who will go up for us against the Canaanites first, to fight against them?*

Judah Will Go First
Judges 1:2. *And the LORD* said,*
Judah will go up. Look, I have delivered the land into his hand.

Judges 1:3. *And Judah said to Simeon his brother,*
Come up with me to my portion, so we can fight against the Canaanites, then I likewise will go with you to your portion. So Simeon went with him. 4. And Judah went up and the LORD* delivered the Canaanites and the Perizites into their hand, and they slew ten thousand men of them in Bezek. 5. And they found Adoni Bezek in Bezek: and they fought against him, and they slew the Canaanites and the Perizites. 6. But Adoni Bezek fled and they pursued him, and caught him and cut off his thumbs and his big toes.

Judges 20:17. *And the men of Israel, besides Benjamin, were numbered four hundred thousand men that drew the sword: all these were men of war. 18. And the children of Israel rose and went up to the House of God and asked counsel of God and said, Who of us will go up first to the battle against the children of Benjamin?*

Judah Will Go First
And the LORD* said, Judah will go first.

Judges 20:19. *And the children of Israel rose up in the morning and camped against Gibeah. 20. And the men of Israel went out to battle against Benjamin and the men of Israel put themselves in array to fight against them at Gibeah. 21. And the children of Benjamin came forth out of Gibeah, and destroyed down to the ground of the Israelites that day twenty-two thousand men. 22. And the people, the men of Israel, encouraged themselves and set their battle again in array in the place where they put themselves in array the first day.*

Then another time **All Judah Goes First**:

The LORD's* Great Victory
2 Chronicles 20:1. *It happened after this also, that the children of Moab and the children of Ammon and with them others besides the Ammonites came against*

Jehoshaphat to battle. 2. Then some came who told Jehoshaphat saying, A great multitude is coming against you from beyond the sea on this side of the Dead Sea and, behold, they are in Hazazon-Tamar, which is En-Gedi. 3. And Jehoshaphat was awed and set himself to seek the LORD* and proclaimed a fast throughout all Judah. 4. And Judah gathered themselves together, to ask help from the LORD*, and they came to seek the LORD* out of all the cities of Judah. 5. And Jehoshaphat stood in the congregation of Judah and Jerusalem, in the House of the LORD*, before the new court 6. and said, LORD*, God of our fathers, are You not God in the Heavens? And You rule over all the kingdoms of the nations? And in Your hand is power and might, so that no one is able to withstand You? 7. Are You not our God, Who drove out the inhabitants of this land before Your people Israel and gave it forever to the seed of Abraham, who loves You? 8. And they lived there and have built You a Sanctuary there for Your name, saying, 9. If evil comes upon us, like the sword, judgment, or pestilence, or famine, we stand before this House and in Your presence, for Your name is in this House, and cry to You in our affliction, then You will hear and help. 10. And now, behold, the children of Ammon and Moab and Mount Seir, whom you would not let Israel invade when they came out of the land of Egypt, but they turned from them and did not destroy them. 11. See, I say, how they reward us, to come to cast us out of Your possession, which You have given us to inherit. 12. O our God, will You not judge them? For we have no power against this great company that comes against us; neither do we know what to do, but our eyes are upon You.

2 Chronicles 20:13. *And all Judah stood before the LORD*, with their little ones, their wives and their children.*

2 Chronicles 20:14. *Then the Spirit of the LORD* came upon Jahaziel the son of Jeiel, the son of Mattaniah, a Levite of the sons of Asaf, in the midst of the congregation. 15. And he said, Listen, all Judah, and you inhabitants of Jerusalem and you king Jehoshaphat, Thus says the LORD* to you,* **Do not be in awe! Do not be dismayed because of this great multitude!** *For the battle is not yours, but God's. 16. Tomorrow go down against them! Behold, they will come up by the hill of Ziz and you will find them at the end of the brook, before the wilderness of Jeruel. 17. You will not fight in this battle: set yourselves! Stand still and see the deliverance/salvation of the LORD* with you,* (Exodus 14:13) *O Judah and Jerusalem!* **Do not be in awe! Do not be dismayed!** *Tomorrow go out against them, for the LORD* will be with you.*

Worship

2 Chronicles 20:18. *And Jehoshaphat bowed his head with his face to the ground, and all Judah and the inhabitants of Jerusalem fell before the LORD*, worshipping the LORD*, 19. and the Levites, of the children of the Kohathites, and o. the children of the Korahites, stood up to praise the LORD* God of Israel with a* exceedingly loud voice.*

Believe

2 Chronicles 20:20. *And they rose early in the morning and went forth into the wilderness of Tekoa and as they went forth, Jehoshaphat stood and said, Listen to me, O Judah and you inhabitants of Jerusalem! Believe in the LORD* your God, and you will be confirmed, declared faithful! Believe His prophets, and you wil. succeed!*

Praise

2 Chronicles 20:21. *And when he had consulted with the people, he appointed singers to the LORD*, who would praise in the adornment of holiness as they wen. out before the army and to say, Give thanks to the LORD*, for His loving kindness endures forever. 22. And when they began to sing and to praise, the LORD* se. ambushes against the children of Ammon, Moab, and Mount Seir, who had come against Judah, and they were struck. 23. For the children of Ammon and Moab stood up against the inhabitants of Mount Seir, to utterly exterminate and destroy them: and when they had made an end of the inhabitants of Seir, everyone helped to destroy another.*

Succeed

2 Chronicles 20:24. *And when Judah came toward the watchtower in the wilderness, they looked at the multitude and, behold, there were dead bodies fallen to the earth and no one escaped. 25. And when Jehoshaphat and his people came to take away their spoil, they found among them in abundance both riches with the dead bodies and precious jewels, which they stripped off for themselves, more than they could carry away. And they were three days in gathering the spoil, it was so much. 26. And on the fourth day they assembled themselves in the valley of Berachah, for there they blessed the LORD*. Therefore the name of the same place was called, The Valley of Berachah, The Valley of Blessing, to this day. 27. Then they returned, every man of Judah and Jerusalem, and Jehoshaphat in the forefront of them, to go back to Jerusalem with joy, for the LORD* had made them to rejoice over their enemies. 28. And they came to Jerusalem with psalteries, harps, and trumpets to the House of the LORD*. 29. And the fear of God was on*

all the kingdoms of those countries, when they had heard that the LORD* fought against the enemies of Israel. 30. So the realm of Jehoshaphat was quiet, for his God gave him rest all around.

Judah led these times probably because of Jacob's prophecy in Genesis 49:

Genesis 49:8. *"Judah, you are he whom your brothers will praise: your hand will be on the neck of your enemies, your father's children will bow down before you. 9. Judah is a lion's whelp, from the prey, my son, you are gone up: he stooped down, he laid down like a lion and as an old lion. Who will rouse him up? 10. The* **Scepter will not depart from Judah, nor a Torah scholar from between his feet, until Shiloh comes**: *and the gathering of the peoples will be to Him. 11. Binding His foal to the vine and His donkey's colt to the choice vine, He washed His garments in wine and His clothes in the blood of grapes. 12. His eyes will be red with wine, and His teeth white with milk.*

The **Scepter** refers to the authority of the king. Shiloh represents Messiah, so Jacob is saying that Judah will rule until Messiah comes.

udging Others, Matthew 7:1. *"Do not **judge**, so that you would not be judged: 2. for in which judgment you **judge**, you will be **judged**, and in the measure in which you measure, it will be measured to you. (Romans 14:10–13) 3. Then why are you looking at the speck in your brother's eye, but you do not perceive the beam in your eye? 4. Or how will you say to your brother, 'You must let me cast the speck from your eye,' and there is this beam in your eye? 5. Hypocrite! First you must cast the beam from your eye, and then you will see clearly to cast out the speck from your brother's eye. 6. Do not give the sacred things to the dogs and do not cast your pearls before the swine, lest they will trample them with their feet, then when they turn they will tear you to pieces."*

Luke 6:37. *"And if you do not **judge**, then you would **not** be **judged**: and if you do not condemn, then you would **not** be condemned. You must set free, then you will be set free: 38. you must give, then it will be given to you: they will give a good measure, pressed down, shaken, poured into your bosom: for, in which measure you measure, it will be measured to you in return."*

Jacob 4:11. *You must not ever speak evil of one another, brothers. The one who speaks evil of a brother or **judges** his brother is speaking against Torah (Teaching) and is **judging** Torah (Teaching): if you **judge** Torah (Teaching), you are not a* *doer, but a **judge** of Torah (Teaching). 12. There is only One Torah-giver and **Judge** Who is able to save or to destroy: then who are you to **judge** your neighbor?*

Romans 2:1. *On this account you are without excuse, O Man, everyone who **judges**: for by what you are judging the other, you are condemning yourself. For you, the one who **judges**, are doing the same things. 2. But we know that the judgment of God is according to truth upon those who perpetrate things such as these. 3. And do you take this into account, O Man, the one who **judges** those who practice such things as these and does them that you will not escape from the judgment of God?*

Any time you speak critically of someone else, you are **judging** that person. When you do, you can be sure your turn will come when that criticism will be measured to you. Resist the impulse. (See Gossip/Slander in Glossary.)

Kingdom of God is described in Glossary, so read that. This article explores the meaning of Y'shua's order to preach the Kingdom.

Luke 9:1. *And after He summoned the twelve He gave them power and authority over all demons and to heal sicknesses 2. and He sent them to **preach the Kingdom of God** and to heal diseases. 60. **when you go you must proclaim the Kingdom of God far and wide.***

*The Torah (Teaching) and the Prophets were proclaimed until John: from then on the **Kingdom of God** is being preached and everyone enters it forcibly.* (Luke 16:16)

Clearly, preaching the **Kingdom** is a command of Y'shua's, but what is **preaching the Kingdom**? It involves healing and also includes deliverance. The **Kingdom** includes the Heavenly realm, but it also means that all the power of God is to be demonstrated and experienced right here, right now on earth, exactly as Y'shua did in His evangelism. Each believer who has been born again is to be trained immediately in deliverance from all bondage, to walk continually in the fullness of God, delivered from all sickness, congenital problems, spiritual bondage, and all else. That is the **Kingdom**, but while we hear reports from around the world of such things happening, the preaching of the **Kingdom** has not reached its potential. Many congregations are not even aware such things are possible, let alone being a goal we are all supposed to have. We have to believe the **Kingdom** before we can enter.

Then we can understand Matthew 11:12. *From the days of John the Immerser until now the* **Kingdom of the Heavens** *is taken by violence, and shares in the heavenly* **Kingdom** *are sought for with the most ardent zeal and the most intense exertion and violent men are seizing it, each one claiming eagerly for himself.*

We have to be like Jacob: *And Jacob was left alone, and a Man wrestled with him there until the breaking of the day. 26. And when the Man saw that He did not prevail against him, He touched the socket of his hip, and the socket of Jacob's thigh was out of joint as he wrestled with Him. 27. And He said, "Let Me go, for the day is breaking." And Jacob said, "I shall not let You go until You bless me."* (Genesis 32:25)

In verse 25, the Man is Y'shua. The Hebrew word, Ish, could also be translated Husband: He is our Bridegroom. Jeremiah 3:14 says He married Israel. Your Husband commands all to **Preach the Kingdom**.

Long Service was held as Ezra read the Torah and teachers taught on it so all would understand.

Nehemiah 8:1. *And all the people gathered themselves together as one man in the street that was in front of the Water Gate and they spoke to Ezra the scribe to bring the book of the Torah (Teaching) of Moses, which the LORD* had commanded to Israel. 2. And* **Ezra the priest brought the Torah** *(Teaching) before the congregation, both men and women, and all who could hear with understanding on the first day of the seventh month. 3. And* **he read** *there before the open place that was before the Water Gate* **from the daylight until midday**, *before the men and the women and those who could understand, and the ears of all the people were attentive to the book of the Torah (Teaching). 4. And Ezra the scribe stood on a platform of wood, which they had made for the purpose and beside him stood Mattithiah, Shema, Anaiah, Urijah, Hilkiah, and Maaseiah on his right hand; and on his left hand, Pedaiah, Mishael, Malchiah, Hashum, Hashbaddana, Zechariah, and Meshullam. 5. And Ezra opened the scroll in the sight of all the people; (for he was above all the people) and when he opened it, all the people stood up 6. and Ezra blessed the LORD*, the great God. And all the people answered, Amen. Amen! while lifting up their hands, and they bowed their heads and worshipped the LORD* with their faces to the ground. 7. Also Yeshua, Bani, Sherebiah, Jamin, Akkub, Shabbethai, Hodijah, Maaseiah, Kelita, Azariah, Jozabad, Hanan, Pelaiah, and the Levites caused the people to understand the Torah (Teaching), and the people stood in their place. 8. So they read in the* *scroll the Torah (Teaching) of God distinctly and gave the sense and caused them to understand the reading.*

This took place on the first Day of Memorial, now called Rosh Hashanah with the people standing for hours listening and absorbing all the words, the teachings of the LORD. The time of the year was September, so from sunup to midday would have been at least six hours of standing and listening. The people who were teaching are named in verse 7. All the people understood the words that were declared to them—verse 12.

Nehemiah 8:9. *And Nehemiah, who was the Tirshatha, Ezra the priest the scribe, and the Levites who taught the people said to all the people, This day is holy to the LORD* your God!* **Do not mourn or weep!** *For all the people wept when they heard the words of the Torah (Teaching). 10. Then he said to them, Go your way, eat delicacies and drink the sweet and send portions to those for whom nothing is prepared, for this day is holy unto our Lord!* **Do not be grieved, for the joy of the LORD* is your strength!** *11. So the Levites stilled all the people saying, Hold your peace, for the day is holy.* **Do not be grieved!** *12. And all the people went their way to eat and to drink and to send portions and to make great mirth, because they had understood the words that were declared to them.*

Tirshatha is the Persian title for the Provincial governor, Nehemiah. The delicacies of verse 10 are rich, fatty, sweet treats, like cheesecake or baklava, very delicious and very fattening. Some translations say "fat," eat the fat, but eating animal fat is forbidden by Torah. The Latin text is Pinguia, fatty meat. This fat, in the Hebrew text, is Mashmanyim, from olive oil, so it could have been something like baklava, which today is a common Middle Eastern dessert. This celebration is after the fast, Yom Kippur, so it is during Sukkot. The events of Nehemiah chapter 8 take place on more than one day, actually two weeks apart. Notice the portions are sent to those who were unable to attend the services in Jerusalem.

Love Matthew 22:34. *But when the Pharisees heard that He silenced the Sadducees they gathered together against Him, 35. and one of them, a teacher of Torah (Teaching), testing Him asked, 36. "Teacher, which is the greatest commandment in the Torah (Teaching)?" 37. And He said to him, "You will love the Lord your God with your whole heart and with your whole being* (Deuteronomy 6:5) *and with your whole mind: 38. this is the greatest and first commandment. 39. And the second is like it, 'You will love your neighbor as yourself.'* (Leviticus 19:18)

40. *The whole Torah (Teaching) and the Prophets are hanging on these two commandments."*

Leviticus 19:18. *You will not avenge or bear any grudge against the children of your people, but you will love your neighbor as yourself. I AM the LORD*!*

Galatians 5:14. *For the whole Torah (Teaching) has found its full expression in one saying, in this "You will love your neighbor as yourself."*

1 Corinthians 12:31b. *And yet I am showing you a better way. 13.1. If I speak in the tongues of men and of angels, but I do not have love, I have become sounds of brass or a clashing cymbal. 2. Now if I have a gift of prophecy and I would have known all mysteries and all knowledge and if I have all faith so as to move mountains, but I do not have **love**, I am nothing. 3. And I could give away all my belongings bit by bit to help the poor and if I should give over my body so that I could boast in it, but I do not have **love**, (Micah 6:8) I benefit nothing.*

These Scriptures barely scratch the surface of Scriptures referring to **Love**. Check this footnote to Leviticus 19:18: This command to **love** your neighbor as yourself is foundational for godly living. (See Matthew 5:43,19:19,22:39; Mark 12:31; Luke 10:27; Romans 13:9; Galatians 5:14; Jacob 2:8.)

What is the current condition of the Body of Christ in America? We have ordained minsters committing adultery, divorcing wives, wives of clergy divorcing husbands, clergy abusing children, clergy abusing the system by storing up money, sins of homosexuality and lesbianism, and virtually every sin is in the congregation to some extent. This ought not to be. The congregations of God have to show the world that believers are different because our fruit must be attractive to the world.

Every believer needs to seek the LORD for all one's needs, not all one's pleasures. Each one needs to follow Matthew 6:33. *But you must continually seek first the Kingdom of God and His righteousness, then all these things will be provided for you.*

Paul wrote in Ephesians 5:25. *Husbands, you must continually **love** your wives, just as the Messiah also **loved** the congregation and gave Himself over on her behalf, 26. so that He would sanctify His wife, the congregation, the bride, making her pure by washing with the word of Torah (Teaching), 27. in order that He* *would present for Himself the glorious congregation, not having spot or wrinkle or any of such things, but so that His bride would be holy and without blemish. 28. In this way husbands are obligated to love their own wives as their own bodies.* **The one who loves his own wife loves himself. 29. For no one ever hated his own flesh but nourishes and cherishes it, just as also the Messiah nourishes and cherishes the congregation, 30. because we are members of His body,** *31. "For this reason a man will leave his father and his mother and be faithfully devoted to his wife, and the two will be in one flesh."*

Many people have never known true **love**, never known a loving parent. Those people need to be delivered from the isolation, rejection, and loneliness of the lack of parental **love**.

What is this **love** that so many are lacking? *Webster's Dictionary* defines **love** as "a deep and tender affection for or attachment or devotion to a person or persons: a feeling of brotherhood and good will toward other people." The first definition is the foundation, the family relationship that everyone needs—parents, grandparents, siblings, and cousins. Without the foundation, it is very difficult for a person to **love** his neighbor or even to **love** himself. There are ministries relating to Father's Heart for those who do not have the foundation.

Loving your enemy is called for by Y'shua in Matthew 5:43. *"You heard that it was said, 'You will love your neighbor' and you will hate your enemy. 44. But I am saying to you, you must* **love** *your enemies and you must pray for those who persecute you,* (Proverbs 24:17,18) *45. so that you would become children of your Father, the One in the heavens, because He makes His sun rise on evil and good and rains on the righteous and unrighteous. 46. For if you would* **love** *those who* **love** *you, what reward do you have? Do not even the tax collectors do this? 47. And if you would respect only your brothers, what are you doing that is remarkable? Do not even the heathens do this? 48. Therefore you must be perfect as your heavenly Father is perfect."*

In this teaching, Y'shua uses enemies for His exhortation of righteous behavior, of the meaning of "**Love** your neighbor as yourself."

This is hands on ministry of **love** for someone in great need. It is not bringing hundreds of thousands of refugees to the United States. That is not **love**, but, at best, it is sympathy. It is not thinking through all the results, from infrastructure to security to jobs and a myriad of other factors. Believers are to **love** sinners, by showing **love**, bringing the sinner to repentance.

Believers are to **love** their neighbors as themselves, to truly help on an individual basis, giving care, comfort, and whatever is called for according to the need and within the ability of the giver.

Hate as *when the LORD* saw that Leah was **loved less**, he opened her womb, but Rachel was barren. 32. And Leah conceived and bore a son, and she called his name Reuben for she said, "Surely the LORD* has looked upon my affliction. Now therefore my husband will love me." 33. And she conceived again and bore a son and said, "Because the LORD* has heard that I am **hated**, he has therefore given me this son also and she called his name Simeon (Shimon)." 34. And she conceived again and bore a son and said, "Now this time my husband will be joined to me, because I have borne him three sons: therefore was his name called Levi." 35. And she conceived again and bore a son and she said, "Now I shall praise the LORD*." Therefore she called his name Judah (Y'hudah) and she left off bearing.* (Genesis 29:31–35)

In verse 31 the idiom is translated to read Loved Less. Verse 33 uses the word Hated, but the correct meaning is Loved Less. This same use is in Malachi 1:2. *I have loved you, says the LORD*. Yet you say, In what way have You loved us? Was not Esau Jacob's brother? says the LORD*, yet I loved Jacob 3. and I hated Esau and laid his mountains and his heritage waste for the jackals of the wilderness.*

God loves everyone, so He does not hate anyone, but those who adamantly reject Him are loved less.

Jacob's love for Leah grew over the years, so you can see the increasing love in the later chapters of Genesis.

Mark the Saint is a command in Ezekiel 9:4–8.

Mark the Saint
And the LORD said to him, Go through the midst of the city, through the midst of Jerusalem, and **set a mark** upon the foreheads **of the people who sigh and who cry over all the abominations that are done in its midst**.*

5. And to the others He said in my hearing,

Strike the Sinner
Go after him through the city, and <u>**strike**</u>*!* ***Do not let your eye spare! Do not have pity!*** *6. You (plural) will slay completely old and young, virgins, little children, and women!* ***Do not come near anyone upon whom is the mark!***

Begin at My Sanctuary
<u>***Begin at My Sanctuary.***</u> *Then they began with the elders who were in front of the House. 7. And He said to them, Defile the House and fill the courts!* ***Begin at My Sanctuary with the slain.*** *Go forth! And they went forth and slew in the city. 8. And it was, while they were slaying them, and I was left, that I fell upon my face and cried and said, Ah Adonai, LORD*! Will You destroy all the residue of Israel in Your pouring out of Your fury upon Jerusalem?*

The first three verses of this chapter set the stage for this operation, making this picture more vivid:

Ezekiel 9:1. *Then He cried in my ears with a loud voice saying, Cause those who have charge over the city to draw near, even every man with his destroying weapon in his hand. 2. And, behold,* ***six men came from the road of the higher gate which lies toward the north and each man a slaughter weapon in his hand and one man among them was clothed with linen, with a writer's inkhorn by his side.*** *And they went in and stood beside the bronze altar. 3. And the glory of the God of Israel went up from the cherub, upon which it was, to the threshold of the House. And He called to the man clothed in linen, who had the writer's inkhorn by his side.*

The man clothed in linen with the inkhorn by his side is the one who **Marks the Saint**. All six are armed and ready to **Strike the Sinners**. The verb **Strike** means "to hit with a fatal blow." This is death, not just an injury, but the final "lights out" with nothing to follow. The verb is in the Imperative mood, a direct command from God!

The next command is to begin at the Sanctuary! The first to go into oblivion will be the priests, those in ministry, noting that their judgment will be held to a higher standard.

Numbers 18:1. *And the LORD* said to Aaron, "You and your sons and your father's house with you will bear any iniquity in the Sanctuary, and you and your sons with you will bear any iniquity of your priesthood. 2. And bring your brothers also of the tribe of Levi, the tribe of your father, with you so they can be joined with you and minister with you, but you and your sons with you will minister before the Tent of Testimony. 3. And they will keep your charge and the charge of the entire Tent, only they will not come near the vessels of the Sanctuary and the altar, so neither they nor you would also die. 4. And they will be joined to you and keep the charge of the Tent of Testimony for all the service of the Tent and a stranger will not come near you. 5. And you will keep the charge of the Holy Place and the charge of the altar, so there will no longer be wrath upon the children of Israel. 6. And I AM, behold, I have taken your brothers the Levites from among the children of Israel. They are given to you as a gift for the LORD*, to do the service of the Tent of Meeting. 7. Therefore you and your sons with you will keep your priest's office for everything of the altar and within the veil, and you will serve. I have given your priest's office to you as a service of gift, and the stranger that comes near will be put to death."*

Back to Ezekiel chapter 9:

Ezekiel 9:9. *Then He said to me, The iniquity of the House of Israel and Judah is exceeding great and the land is full of blood and the city full of perversity for they say, The LORD* has forsaken the earth and the LORD* does not see. 10. And as for Me also, My eye will not spare, neither will I have pity, but I will pay back their way upon their head. 11. And see, the man clothed in linen, who had the ink well by his side reported the matter saying, I have done as You have commanded me.*

The Elders, those in the ministry, were to be struck first because they had brought idolatry into the Temple. Those who bring idolatry into the churches today are those who teach against Torah, who promote covetousness, acceptance of abortion, homosexuality, and other unholy teachings.

This should bring to repentance all those who are teaching against the Word of God, compromising with the world, justifying abortion, welcoming homosexuals without teaching the Biblical standard, and worshiping other gods, denying Torah, the Hebrew Scriptures.

Begin at the Sanctuary! Those in ministry will be judged and punished first. The priests, ministers and pastors are responsible that no iniquity (intentional sin) takes place in or about the holy place. There is a burden to know and to do what is right, to hold to the very highest standards—a higher standard than secular organizations.

Noah's Clean Animals that came into the box, with Scripture saying, "of every clean beast you will take by seven..." Were just seven animals of each clean specie taken?

Genesis 7:1. *And the LORD* said to Noah, "Come into the box, you and your entire house! For I have seen you righteous before Me in this generation. 2. Of every clean beast you will take to yourself* **by sevens, (pairs of) the male and his mate**: *and of beasts that are not clean by two, the male and his mate. 3. Also of* **fowls of the air by sevens, the male and the female**; *to keep seed alive upon the face of all the earth.*

Noah actually took **seven pairs** of each clean specie, **seven males and seven females, two by two**. The fowls are those that are edible, like chickens, turkeys, pheasants, and other game birds. Eagles, vultures, and other carrion eaters are not edible.

Genesis 7:7. *And Noah, his sons, his wife, and his sons' wives with him, went into the box because of the waters of the flood. 8. Of* **clean beasts** *and of beasts that are not clean, of fowls, and of everything that creeps upon the earth, 9.* **they came in two by two to Noah in the box, the male and the female**, *as God had commanded Noah.*

So now we know there were fourteen of each clean beast. All the clean animals, both mammals and fowls, graze and do not eat meat.

One Who Shares instead of **One Who Gives** is the spiritual gift in Romans 12:3. *For I say, through the grace that has been given to me, to everyone who is among you, not to think too highly of yourselves beyond which it is necessary to think, but to think to put a moderate estimate of yourself, in the same manner as God divided to each a measure of faith. 4. For just as we have many members in one body, but all the parts do not have the same function, 5. in this way, we, the many, are one body in Messiah, but each one part of one another. 6. And having different gifts according to the grace given to us, whether* **1** *Prophecy according to the proportion* *of his faith, 7. or 2 Ministry in his service, or the one who 3 Teaches in the teaching, 8. or the one who 4 Encourages in encouragement: the 5 **One Who Shares**, in sincerity without grudging, the 6 Protector or guardian giving aid in diligent eagerness, the one who is 7 Merciful in cheerfulness.*

The verb translated "one who shares" is "metadidomai" while to give is "didomai." The meaning of "metadidomai" is to share, not to give.

There have been teachings taken from other translations, concerning the one who gives because some translations have the **One Who Shares** as the **One Who Gives**, so the teaching goes that the giver has a lot of money and is generous, wanting to cover various costs. That misses the whole point of the **one who shares**, who may have very little, but whatever it is can be shared with someone in need.

Decades ago a friend told us that when her husband began his contracting business, they had very little money. One morning all she had for their three children and herself for breakfast was one cup of grits. Then her neighbor came and asked for something she could feed her five children, so our friend cooked her cup of grits and fed the eight children and two adults, with all ten fully satisfied. That is the **One Who Shares**, with God increasing that one cup.

Ephesians 4:28. *The one who steals must no longer steal, but rather let him toil as he works good things with his own hands so that he would have something to* ***Share*** *with the* ***One Who Has Need***.

Pairs in Hebrew are indicated by the suffix **ayim**. In Genesis 1:1 we have the Heavens, Sh'm**ayim**, indicating the visible heavens and the heavenly bodies that cannot be seen with the naked eye. In verse 2 we have the waters, M**ayim**, indicating the waters on the earth and those above the earth. In Genesis 32, Mahan**aim** is two camps. In another article, Jeremiah introduces two Jerusalems.

Parable of the Good Samaritan is an illustration that Y'shua made up, but it was based on true situations at a site of many robberies and personal attacks by robbers. This site is four and a half miles east of Jerusalem on the road to Jericho, where in Bible times it was very dangerous. The Romans built a fort there to protect travelers. Today there is a good-sized city of 37,000, named

Ma'ale Adumim. The Martyrius Monastery, founded in the seventh century, is there, as well as a museum.

Luke 10:25. Then behold some master of Torah (Teaching) stood up testing Him saying, "Teacher, what will I have to have done to inherit eternal life?" 26. And He said to him, "What has been written in the Torah (Teaching)? How do you read it?" 27. And he said, "'You will love the Lord your God out of your whole heart and with your whole being and with your whole strength and with your whole mind, and 'love your neighbor as yourself.'" (Deuteronomy 6:5, Leviticus 19:18) *28. And He said to him, "You answered correctly: you must do this and you will live eternally." 29. But because he wanted to justify himself he said to Y'shua,* **"Who in fact is my neighbor?"** *30. When He replied Y'shua said, "A certain man went down from Jerusalem to Jericho and fell among robbers, and then they stripped him, and after inflicting wounds went away, leaving him half dead. 31. And by chance there was a priest who came down by that way and when he saw him he crossed over to the other side: 32. and likewise also a man who was a Levite, as he came by the place, and when he saw him he crossed over. 33. And a certain traveling* **Samaritan** *came by him and when he saw him he was moved* **with compassion***, 34. and then he came over to him and bound up his wounds, pouring olive oil and wine, and after he put him on his own animal he led him to an inn and took care of him. 35. Then on the next day when he had to leave he gave two denarii to the innkeeper and said, 'You must take care of him, and whatever in addition you would spend, I shall repay to you on my return.' 36. Who of these three does it seem to you had become a neighbor of the one who fell among the robbers?" 37. And he said, "The one who had mercy on him." And Y'shua said to him, "You must go and you must habitually do likewise."*

For the priest and the Levite to deliberately avoid contact with the injured man was sinful, then to have a heathen show love to his neighbor heaped insult upon them. Y'shua picked a great location for His parable.

Parables are stories Y'shua made up to illustrate certain teachings. The Parable of the Good Samaritan makes good use of a very dangerous location where the Romans built an outpost to protect travelers. The listeners of Y'shua's message knew about this as a very dangerous place, where many robberies, beatings and even murders had taken place.

Patience Jacob 5:7. *Therefore you must now have* **patience***, brothers, until the coming of the Lord. See, the farmer expects the valuable fruit from the earth, when he has* *patience* over it until it has taken early rain and late rain. 8. You too must now *be patient*, you must strengthen your hearts, because the coming of the Lord has drawn near: 9. do not murmur, brothers, against one another so that you would not be judged: behold the Judge has been standing before the doors. 10. You must now take as an example, brothers, the suffering and the *patience* of the prophets, those who spoke in the name of the Lord. 11. Behold we consider blessed those who hold out: you have heard of the *patience* of Job and you have seen the Lord's reward, the end of Job's trial, because the Lord is sympathetic and compassionate.

When you hold onto prophetic words or a vision for ministry, feeling that the time is right, that you can do the work and are ready to go, you can be certain the timing is the LORD's, not ours, not yours.

There is a woman I know who was married to an evangelist. He died when she was in her mid-thirties, and she had many prophecies about her future mate, often thinking he would be coming along in a few weeks. She waited **patiently** for twenty-seven years before the LORD set up her wedding. You must **be patient**, no matter how long it takes. (See Isaiah 28:16 in Glossary.)

Persecution is a promise. John 15:18. *"If the world hates you, you know that it hated Me before it hated you. 19. If you were of the world, the world would love its own: but because you are not of the world, but I chose you from the world, the world hates you because of this. 20. You must continually remember the message, which I spoke to you, 'A servant is not greater than his master.' If they **persecuted** Me, then they will **persecute** you (Mark 10:30): if they kept My word, then they will keep yours.*

2 Timothy 3:12. *And all those who want to live in a Godly manner in Messiah Y'shua will be **persecuted**. (John 15:20)*

1 Peter 2:18. *You house slaves must be subject to your masters in every respect, not only to the good and gentle, but also to the unjust. 19. For this is grace, if, through consciousness of God, **someone bears patiently some grief of unjust sufferings**. 20. For what kind of credit is there if you are sinning and you will endure being beaten? **But if when you are doing good, and then you will endure suffering, this brings God's favor.***

It is no surprise that people love the prosperity message but often ignore **persecution**. Recent times have shown **persecution** right here in the United

States. Bakers have been given outrageous fines for not making cakes for same sex weddings. A Clerk of Court in Kentucky was jailed for refusing to sign a marriage license for a same sex couple. There are numerous other examples of **persecution** of Christians, some for simply quoting Scripture when the government of this country goes against the Judeo-Christian principles on which this country was founded.

In Muslim countries, many thousands of Christians have been and still are being tortured and killed just for being Christian. ISIS has killed hundreds of children who would not deny Y'shua.

Persecution has not reached its end in the United States. Are you ready to face a Decision for the Lord? To face a fine or imprisonment or worse?

Persistent Prayer is taught by Y'shua as well as a quick answer to prayer. We need to have faith, but we are not to be quitters. If at first you do not succeed, try, try again—and again.

Luke 11:5. *Then He said to them, "Who of you will have a friend and will go to him at midnight and would say to him, 'Friend, you must now lend me three loaves of bread, 6. since my friend came to me from a journey and I do not have anything to set before him:' 7. and answering from inside, he said, 'You must not cause me trouble: the door has already been shut and my children are with me in the bed: I am not able to get up to give it to you.' 8. I say to you, even if he will not get up to give to him because he is a friend, but because of his shamelessness when he gets up, he will give him what he needs. 9. And I say to you,* **You must continually ask and it will be given to you, you must continually seek and you will find, you must continually knock and it will be opened to you** *10. for everyone who asks takes and the one who seeks finds and for the one who knocks it will be opened. 11. And which of you if a son will ask his father for a fish will he then give him a snake instead of a fish? 12. Or also, if he will ask for an egg, will he give a scorpion to him? 13. If therefore you, who are evil yourselves, know how to give good gifts to your children,* **how much more the Father from heaven will give the Holy Spirit to those who ask Him.**"

It is wonderful when prayer is answered immediately as with Abraham's servant in his prayer in Genesis 24:12–14 and the prayer is answered in verse 15, but there are times the answer is not that swift. That is why Y'shua says to be persistent.

Even Y'shua prayed again in Mark 8:23. *Then taking the hand of the blind man, He led him outside the village and having spit in his eyes, after He placed His hands on him, He was asking him, "Do you see anything?" 24. And when he looked up he was saying, "I see men that are as trees I see walking." 25. Then He again laid hands upon his eyes, and he stared straight ahead and he was restored and he was looking at everything clearly.*

Do not feel your prayer is inadequate it you need to repeat it!

Prayer of Faith is also called for:

Mark 11:20. *And in the morning when they passed by they saw the fig tree withered from the roots. 21. And Peter, remembering, said to Him, "Rabbi, look! The fig tree which You had cursed has become withered." 22. And Y'shua said to them,* **"You must have faith in God. 23. Truly I say to you that whoever would say to this mountain, 'You must immediately be removed and you must immediately be cast into the sea,' and would not doubt in his heart but would believe that what he is saying is happening, it will be to him.** *24. Because of this I say to you, you must continually pray for everything, then for whatever you are asking,* **believe that you have taken it, and it will be there for you.** *25. And when you are standing praying, forgive whatever you have against anyone, in order that your Father Who is in the heavens would forgive you your trespasses.*

You must have **Faith** for any prayer to be effective, but why are some prayers effective immediately, but others take time and persistence? The answer must be that God's timing is what we often fail to sense or even consider. His plan is what counts, not our wants.

Isaiah 28:16. *Therefore thus says Adonai, the LORD*,*
Behold, I lay for a foundation in Zion a stone, a tried stone, a precious cornerstone, a sure foundation. He who believes will not make haste.

In the 12th century, Rabbi Ibn Ezra wrote, "In faith the faithful one will stand firm no matter how long it takes." (See Isaiah 28:16 in Glossary.)

It is essential to use both **Persistent Prayer** and the **Prayer of Faith**, whether or not you have a handle on God's timing.

Pruned as in John 15:1. *"I AM the true vine and My Father is the farmer. 2. He removes every branch in Me if it does not bear fruit, and He prunes every branch that bears fruit so that it would bear more fruit. 3. You are already pruned because of the Word which I have spoken to you: 4. you must now dwell in Me and I in you. Just as the branch is not able to bear fruit by itself unless it would remain in the vine, so you could not bear fruit unless you would dwell continuously in Me.*

When Y'shua said that, He was addressing His apostles and disciples, men and women who had been with Him more than three years, which is why He could say they had already been pruned. They had walked the length and breadth of Israel, listening to His teaching and conversing with Him every day. That is an enormous amount of time with instruction, admonishing, and demonstration all day, every day—exposure to the Holy One of Israel. This was not teaching by someone who was a college graduate or had some other earthly training. This teaching and the illustrations were by God Himself. That is something none of us can claim. For that reason each of us must be prepared for pruning. (See Trials in Glossary of the Bible, and Good Soil in this chapter.)

Rechabites, Jeremiah 35:18. *And Jeremiah said to the house of the Rechabites, Thus says the LORD* of Hosts, the God of Israel, Because you have obeyed the commandment of Jonadab your father and kept all his commandments and done according to all that he has commanded you 19. therefore,* **thus says the LORD* of Hosts, the God of Israel, Jonadab the son of Rechab will not lack a man to stand before Me forever**.

Jeremiah 35:1. *The word that came to Jeremiah from the LORD* in the days of Jehoiakim the son of Josiah king of Judah saying, 2. Go to the house of the* **Rechabites** *and speak to them and bring them into the House of the LORD*, into one of the chambers and give them wine to drink.*

The **Rechabites'** answer to the order to drink the wine was we will drink no wine because Jonadab said, *You will drink no wine, you, or your sons forever. 7. Neither will you build a house or sow seed or plant a vineyard or have any for yourself, but you will live in tents all your days, so you can live many days in the land where you are strangers. 8. Thus we have obeyed the voice of Jonadab the son of Rechab our father;* (Jeremiah 35:6–8)

Who were these greatly blessed **Rechabites** who were so obedient? They were descendants of Jethro, Moses' father-in-law, who brought his family to the Promised Land with the Israelites.

Resist the Devil! When anyone speaks of harmful things happening in his life, saying something like, "The devil (or Satan or enemy) has really been attacking me." Then that person has been authorizing the attacks, empowering the evil forces over which **we have authority**.

Matthew 28:16. *And the eleven disciples went into Galilee to the mountain which Y'shua appointed to them, 17. and when they saw Him they paid homage to Him but they doubted. 18. Then when Y'shua came He spoke to them, saying,* **"All authority has been given to Me in heaven and upon the Earth. 19. Therefore when you go, you must now make disciples of all the heathens, 20. teaching them to keep all the things that I have been commanding you:** (Amos 9:12) **and behold I AM with you all the days until the end of the age."**

Ignoring the authority all of us have, these are some things people say:
Every time I turn around, the enemy is attacking me.
Satan is attacking my business big time.
I must be doing something right because the devil is attacking at every turn.
Whenever we go to a powerful meeting, the enemy tries to stop us.

DO NOT GIVE GLORY TO SATAN! Every time someone brags or whines about things Satan—the devil, the enemy—is doing, that person is giving glory to Satan and not to God. **All authority was long ago given to Y'shua.** This is real spiritual warfare, but with one word of caution: this is for personal warfare, not going against principalities and powers. Daniel 10:13. *But the prince of the kingdom of Persia withstood me for twenty-one days, but lo, Michael, one of the chief princes, came to help me (Gabriel) and I remained there with the kings of Persia.* The warfare against principalities and powers is only for collective war with experienced leaders in charge. The following pertains to every believer.

Exodus 23:13. *And in all things that I have said to you be circumspect and you will not make mention of the name of other gods, nor let it be heard out of your mouth.* When anyone gives glory to the enemy, he is strengthening the attack and disobeying God!

161

Think about this! We are not to even mention, literally remember, the name of other gods! That means Satan, the devil, the enemy, Ishtar, or whatever. The repetition in verse 13 is for emphasis. (See Exodus 34:14; Joshua 23:7; Hosea 2:19; Zechariah 13:2.)

Matthew 28:18. *Then when Y'shua came He spoke to them, saying,* ***"All authority has been given to Me in heaven and upon the Earth.*** *19. **Therefore when** you go, you must now make disciples of all the heathens, 20. teaching them to keep all the things that I have been commanding you:* (Amos 9:12) *and behold I AM with you all the days until the end of the age."*

Therefore, each of us needs to use that authority to protect what we have, sending the attacker to the dry places of the earth. Matthew 12:43. ***When the unclean spirit would come out from a person, it comes through dry places seeking rest but does not find it.*** Today each believer has that authority, so use it! But whatever you do, do not give glory to Satan, the devil, the enemy—by whatever name you call him!

Jacob 4:7. *Therefore if you would be subject to God, you should **resist the devil** **and he will flee for his life from you,** 8. **draw near to God and He will** **draw near to you.** Cleanse your hands, you sinners, and purify your hearts, you double-minded!*

All glory goes to the LORD*!

Isaiah 42:8. ***I AM the LORD*. That is My name, and My glory I shall not*** ***give to another, nor My praise to graven images.***

Isaiah 45:20. *Assemble yourselves and come! Draw near together, you who escaped from the nations! Those who set up the wood of their graven image have no knowledge and they pray to a god who cannot save. 21. Tell, and bring them near. Yes let them take counsel together. Who has declared this from ancient time?! Who has told it from that time?! Has not the I AM, the LORD*?! And there is no other God besides Me, a Just God and a Deliverer. There is none besides Me.* (Mark 12:32) *22. **Look to Me and be delivered**, all the ends of the earth, for I AM God and there is no other. 23. I have sworn by Myself, the word has gone out from My mouth in acts of loving kindness and will not return, that to Me every knee will bow, every tongue will swear.* (Romans 14:11; Philippians 2:11) *24. Surely one will say, In the LORD* I have acts of loving kindness and strength. Men will* *come to Him and all who are incensed against Him will be ashamed. 25.* **In the LORD* will all the seed of Israel be made righteous and will glory.**

Each word you speak is important!

Matthew 12:36. *And I say to you that every idle word which men will speak will be paid back with regard to his account on Judgment Day: 37. for you will be justified, declared righteous, because of your words, and you will be condemned because of your words.* Each "you" in verse 37 is singular, just for you, yourself.

Psalm 19:15. **The words of my mouth and the meditation of my heart will be acceptable in Your sight, LORD*, my Rock and my Redeemer.**

Retreat is the word we use when going to a meeting to refresh, to spend time with God. Moses gave us this practice as an example even for today!

Exodus 33:4. *And when the people heard these bad tidings, they grieved and nobody put on his ornaments. 5. For the LORD* had said to Moses, "Say to the children of Israel, 'You are a stiff-necked people. I shall come up among you in a moment and consume you: therefore now take off your ornaments from yourselves, so I shall know what to do to you.'" 6. And the children of Israel stripped themselves of their ornaments by Mount Horeb. 7.* **Then Moses took the tent and pitched it outside the camp, afar off from the camp and called it the tent of meeting. And it was that everyone who sought the LORD* went out to the tent of meeting, which was outside the camp.**

Moses went to this tent of meeting when he really needed special time with the LORD, something to which each of us can relate. Joshua, though, took the really enviable part by staying there. The rest of the story is beautiful!

Exodus 33:8. *And it was, when Moses went out to the tent that all the people rose up and stood, each man at his tent entrance, and watched Moses until he went into the tent. 9. And it happened,* **as Moses entered the tent, the cloudy pillar descended and stood at the entrance of the tent and He talked with Moses. 10. And all the people saw the cloudy pillar stand at the tent entrance, and all the people rose up and worshipped, each man at his tent entrance. 11.** *And* **the LORD* spoke to Moses face to face, as a man speaks to his friend.** *And Moses returned again to the camp,* **but his servant Joshua, the son of Nun, a young man, did not leave the tent.**

Each of us needs a tent of meeting to spend time with the LORD! See the result!

Joshua, the young man, was probably forty-one; Moses eighty-one.

Exodus 33:14. *And He said, "My Presence will go with you and I shall give you rest."*

River of Egypt is not the Nile, but is a Wadi, which is a dry streambed most of the year. The Hebrew word is Nahalah, becoming a torrent in a hard rain. The River of Egypt is mentioned several times, including in Numbers 34 where it is part of the western border of Israel.

Ruah in Hebrew and Pneuma in Greek both mean Spirit, both mean Wind, and both mean Breath. Realizing this makes some verses even more interesting.

John 3:6. *What has been born of the flesh is flesh, and what has been born of the **Spirit** is spirit. 7. Do not be astonished that I said to you, 'It is necessary for you to be born from above.' 8. The **wind** blows where it wishes and you hear its sound, but you do not know where it comes from or where it is going: thus it is with everyone who has been born of the **Spirit**."*

Alternate: 3:6. What has been born of the flesh is flesh, and what has been born of the **Spirit** is spirit. 7. Do not be astonished that I said to you, 'It is necessary for you to be born from above.' 8. The **Spirit** blows where it wishes and you hear its sound, but you do not know where it comes from or where it is going: thus it is with everyone who has been born of the **Spirit**."

Acts 2:1. *And when the day of Shavuot had come they were all in one place to-gether. 2. And a sound came suddenly out of heaven as bringing a violent **wind** and it filled the whole House where they were sitting 3. and dividing tongues like fire were seen by them and the flames sat upon each one of them, 4. and all were filled by the Holy **Spirit** and began to speak in other languages just as the **Spirit** was giving them to speak out boldly.*

Alternate: **2:**1. And when the day of Shavuot had come they were all in one place together. 2. And a sound came suddenly out of heaven as bringing a violent **Spirit** and it filled the whole House where they were sitting 3. and dividing tongues like fire were seen by them and the *flames* sat upon each one of them, *4.* and all were filled by the Holy **Spirit** and began to speak in other languages just as the **Spirit** was giving them to speak out boldly.

Romans 8:8. *and those who are in the flesh are not able to please God. 9. But you are not in the flesh but in the Spirit, if indeed the **Spirit of God** dwells in you. But if someone does not have the **Spirit of Messiah**, this one is not His. 10. And if Messiah is in you, on the one hand your body is dead because of sin, but on the other hand the spirit is alive because of righteousness.*

Alternate: 8. and those who are in *the* flesh are not able to please God. *9.* But you are not in *the* flesh but in *the* Spirit, if indeed *the* **Breath of God** dwells in you. But if someone does not have *the* **Breath of Messiah**, this one is not His. *10.* And if Messiah *is* in you, on the one hand *your* body *is* dead because of sin, but on the other hand *the* spirit *is* alive because of righteousness.

Know that the **Breath of God** dwells in you.

Exodus 31:1. *And the LORD* spoke to Moses, saying, 2. "See, I have called by name Bezalel the son of Uri, the son of Hur of the tribe of Judah. 3. And I have filled him with the **Spirit of God** in wisdom, in understanding, in knowledge, and in all manner of workmanship: 4. to devise skillful works, to work gold, silver, and bronze, 5. and in cutting of stones, to set them, and in carving of timber, to work in all manner of workmanship.*

Alternate: 31:1. And the LORD* spoke to Moses, saying, *2.* "See, I have called by name Bezalel the son of Uri, the son of Hur of the tribe of Judah. *3.* And I have filled him with the **Breath of God** in wisdom, in understanding, in knowledge, and in all manner of workmanship: *4.* to devise skillful works, to work gold, silver, and bronze, *5.* and in cutting of stones, to set them, and in carving of timber, to work in all manner of workmanship.

Ezekiel 11:24. *Afterward the spirit took me up and brought me in a vision by the **Spirit of God** into Chaldea, to those of the captivity. So the vision that I had seen went up from me. 25. Then I told to those of the captivity all the things that the LORD* had shown me.*

Alternate: 11:24. Afterward the spirit took me up and brought me in a vision by the **Breath of God** into Chaldea, to those of the captivity. So the vision that I had seen went up from me. 25. Then I told to those of the captivity all the things that the LORD* had shown me.

Daniel 5:13. *Then Daniel was brought in before the king. The king spoke and said to Daniel, Are you that Daniel who is of the children of the captivity of Judah, whom the king my father brought out of Judah? 14. I have even heard of you, that the* **Spirit of God** *is in you, and light and understanding and excellent wisdom is found in you.*

Alternate: 5:13. Then Daniel was brought in before the king. The king spoke and said to Daniel, Are you that Daniel who is of the children of the captivity of Judah, whom the king my father brought out of Judah? 14. I have even heard of you, that the **Breath of God** is in you, and light and understanding and excellent wisdom is found in you.

1 Samuel 16:12b. *And the LORD* said, Arise! Anoint him for this is he. 13. Then Samuel took the horn of oil and anointed him in the midst of his brothers, and the* **Spirit of the LORD*** *came upon David from that day forward. So Samuel rose and went to Ramah.*

Alternate: 16:12b. And the LORD* said, Arise! Anoint him for this is he. 13. Then Samuel took the horn of oil and anointed him in the midst of his brothers, and the **Breath of the LORD*** came upon David from that day forward. So Samuel rose and went to Ramah.

It is very thought provoking when you consider that the very **Breath of the Living Breathing God, the LORD*,** dwells in you!

Self is a problem that must be overcome for each one of us. We die to self in order to accomplish our assignments from the LORD, so we can be more like Him. This separation, this dying to self, is seen in Genesis 12:1 when Abram was ordered to Canaan.

Genesis 12:1. *Now the LORD* had said to Abram,* **"Get yourself out of here!** *From your country and from your kindred and from your father's house to a land that I shall show you.*

The command for him to get going is simultaneously a call for Abram to put his personal desires out of the Way—out of the Way of the LORD! Getting rid of SELF is often painful, sometimes awkward, sometimes accompanied by falling and back-sliding, but a necessity for those who want God's perfect will in their lives.

Separated, Distinguished. God's People are to be perceptively, visibly different from all other people.

Exodus 33:12. *And Moses said to the LORD*, "See, You say to me, Bring up this people and You have not let me know whom You will send with me. Yet You have said, I know you by name and you have also found favor in My sight. 13. Now therefore, I plead with You, if I have found favor in Your sight, show me Your Way now, so I shall know You and I will find favor in Your sight and will see to it that this nation is Your people." 14. And He said, "My Presence will go with you and I shall give you rest." 15. And he said to Him, "If Your presence does not go with me, **do not take us up from here!** 16. How will it be known here that I and Your people have found favor in Your sight? Is it not because You go with us? So we will be separated, I and Your people, from all the people that are upon the face of the earth?"*

The difference is God's Presence, which is to be perceived by all who see the children of Israel. The Presence is with us as John recorded Y'shua: John 17:20. *"I do not ask concerning them only, but also concerning those who believe in Me because of the disciples' message, 21. so that all would be one, just as You, Father, are in Me and I in You, that they also would be in Us, so that the world would believe that You sent Me. 22. And I have given them the glory which You have given to Me, so that they would be one just as We are One: 23. **I in them and You in Me, so that they would have been brought into unity, so that the world would know that You sent Me and You loved them just as You loved Me.** 24. Father, the One Who gave to Me, I want that where I am those would be with Me, so that they would see My glory, which You have given to Me because You loved Me before the foundation of the world. 25. Righteous Father, even though the world did not know You, but I did know You, and these knew that You sent Me: 26. and I made Your name known to them and I shall make known, so that the love with which You loved Me would be in them and I would be in them."*

The Bride of Messiah is to be recognized as having the Presence of God, just as it was with Moses. Although it is the whole Body, the Body is made up of individuals, so each one has an obligation to maintain the Presence, by Faith,

Obedience. As Paul wrote in Philippians 2:14. *You must continually do every thing without grumbling or argument, 15. so that you would become blameless and pure, children of God who cannot be censured in the midst of a crooked and perverted generation, among whom **you are to shine like stars in the world 16. presenting as lights a message of life**, for my boasting in the Day of Messiah, that I did not run in vain and I did not labor in vain.*

The Presence of God should shine like a light in darkness as in Isaiah 60:1 ***Arise, and give Light! For your Light has come, and the Glory of the LORD* has shone like the sun upon you.*** *2. For, behold, the darkness will cover the earth and gross darkness the people, but the LORD* will rise like the sun upon you, and **His glory will be seen upon you.** 3. And nations (heathens) will come to your Light, and kings to the brightness of your rising like the sun* (Revelation 21:24)

Our ministry should mature like Y'shua's when He immersed and the dove came and lighted upon Him. After that He moved in Power and was easily recognized.

John 1:29. *The next day he saw Y'shua coming toward him and he said, "Behold the Lamb of God, the One Who takes away the sin of the world. 30. This is concerning Whom I said, 'A man is coming after me Who was before me, because He is more prominent than I.' 31. And I had not known Him, but, so that He would be revealed to Israel through this, I came immersing in water." 32. And John testified, saying that "I had seen the Spirit descending from heaven as a dove and it was staying on Him. 33. And I would not have known Him, but the One Who sent me to immerse in water, that One said to me 'Upon whomever you would see the Spirit descending and remaining upon Him, She is the One Who immerses in the Holy Spirit.' 34. And I saw and I had borne witness that this One is the Son of God."*

The Holy Spirit should come upon and remain on and in each of us.

Tampered Scriptures: Some of our New Testament verses were tampered with by copiers, with the changes still intact. One of these is John 19:14. *And it was preparation day for Passover; it was about the sixth hour. And he said to the Jewish Hellenists, "Behold your king."*

168

What Christians do not know is there is no Preparation Day for Passover. The Preparation Day in the Gospel accounts is for the weekly Sabbath, but those correcting the Greek text have not known that, and the addition of the word Passover has stayed in the text. (See Preparation Day in Myths and the full article in Glossary.)

Two Jerusalems, in Jeremiah 1:15. *For, lo, I shall call all the families of the kingdoms of the north, says the LORD*, and they will come and each one will set his throne at the entrance of the gates of Jerusalem and against its walls all around, and against all the cities of Judah.* What you cannot see here is the Hebrew spelling of Jerusalem, which is Jerusal**aim**, not spelled that way in English. What the different ending means is "Two Jerusalems," which Jeremiah uses throughout his prophecy. Therefore, in this and subsequent prophecies of the destruction of Jerusalem, Jeremiah is already talking about the rebuilding of Jerusalem!

But that is not all! There is a second meaning when you go deeper, that of a second Jerusalem from above:

Then one of the seven angels, of those who have the seven vials full of the seven last plagues, came and spoke with me saying, "You must come, I shall show you the bride, the wife of the Lamb." 10. Then he took me away in the spirit to a great and high mountain, and he showed me **the holy city, Jerusalem,** *(Ezekiel 40:2) descending out of the sky from God, 11. having the glory of God, her radiance like a precious stone as a crystal jasper stone. (Isaiah 60:1,2,19) 12. Having a great and high wall, which has twelve gates and upon the gates twelve angels and names that have been written upon the gates, which are the names of the twelve tribes of the Children of Israel: (Exodus 28:21) 13. on the east three gates and on the north three gates and on the south three gates and on the west three gates. (Ezekiel 48:30–35) 14. And the wall of the city had twelve foundations and upon them are twelve names of the twelve apostles of the Lamb. (Revelation 21:9)*

Jerusalem was first destroyed in 585 BC, rebuilt in 518 BC. It was again totally destroyed in 70 AD, then cleaned up and rebuilt in 135 AD under Emperor Hadrian who renamed it Aelia Capitolina. (See Book Order in Glossary for the full explanation of the threshing of Scripture.)

Vows are not to be taken lightly. The definition of a **vow** is "a solemn promise or a **vow**, especially one made to God dedicating one's self to an act, service, or way of life." Whether it is called a **vow, oath, pledge, faith promise,** or whatever, be careful.

Numbers 30:3. *If a man makes a vow to the LORD*, or swears an **oath** to bind himself with a bond, he will not break his word, he will do according to all that proceeds from his mouth.*

Deuteronomy 23:22. *When you **vow**, you will not be slow to pay it, for the LORD* your God will surely require it of you and it would be sin for you. 23. But if you refrain from **vowing**, it will not be a sin for you. 24. That which has gone out of your lips you will keep and perform, a freewill offering, according as you have **vowed** to the LORD* your God, which you have promised with your mouth.*

Ecclesiastes 5:3. *When you vow a vow to God, **Do not defer to pay it!** For He has no pleasure in fools. Pay that which you have **vowed**! 4. It is better that you do not vow, than you vow and do not pay. 5. **Do not allow your mouth to cause your flesh to sin! Do not say before the angel that it was an error!** Why should God be angry at your voice and destroy the work of your hands? 6. For in the multitude of dreams and many words there are also divers vanities, but revere God!*

Matthew 5:33. *Again you heard that it was said to the ancients, 'You will not swear falsely, and you will keep your **oaths** to the Lord.' 34. But I say to you not to **swear** at all: neither by heaven, because it is the throne of God, 35. nor by the Earth, because it is His footstool, nor by Jerusalem, because it is a city of the great King, 36. nor by your head may you **swear**, because you are not able to make one hair white or black. 37. But your word must consistently be, Definitely yes! or Definitely no! and what goes beyond these is from the evil one.*

Jacob 5:12. *But above all things, my brothers, do not **swear** either by heaven or by earth or any other oath: but with you it must be a "Definitely yes!" or a "Definitely no!" so that you would not fall under judgment.*

Be prudent! If you are asked to sign a **pledge** or any document, especially involving money, be certain beyond a shadow of a doubt that you will be able to do whatever is called for. If it is something you think you will be able to do, but are less than certain, you should add a qualification or not sign it at all.

Warfare in the Spirit is real. The first warfare for the congregation was in the Tabernacle in the wilderness:

Leviticus 4:21. *And the LORD* spoke to Moses saying, 22. Take also a census of the sons of Gershon, throughout the houses of their fathers, by their families, 23. you will number them from thirty years old and upward until fifty years old, all that enter to perform the* **Warfare***, to do the work in the Tent of Meeting.*

Leviticus 4:29. *As for the sons of Merari, you will number them after their families by the house of their fathers. 30. You will number them from thirty years old and upward even to fifty years old, everyone who enters the* **Warfare** *to do the work of the Tent of Meeting. 31. And this is the charge of their burden, according to all their service in the Tent of Meeting; the boards of the Tabernacle, its poles, its pillars and sockets, 32. the pillars of the court all around, their sockets, their pegs and their cords, with all their instruments and with all their service: and by name you will reckon the instruments of the charge of their burden.*

Leviticus 4:34. *And Moses and Aaron and the chiefs of the congregation numbered the sons of the Kohathites after their families, and after the house of their fathers, 35. from thirty years old and upward even to fifty years old, everyone that enters the* **Warfare** *for the service in the Tent of Meeting: 36. and those that were numbered of them by their families were two thousand seven hundred fifty. 37. These were those who were numbered of the families of the Kohathites, all that could do service in the Tent of Meeting, whom Moses and Aaron numbered according to the commandment of the LORD* by the hand of Moses.*

Each House of Levi served the LORD* with **warfare**: Gershon, Merari, and Kohath. The **warfare** continues throughout the Church today. **Warfare** is most noticeable in the second, third and fourth century Church as Jewish Roots were removed and heathen deities introduced, such as Ishtar to replace Passover. **Warfare** is visible in today's Church as we see denominations and various churches accepting abortion, homosexual perversion, and other ways of contravening commandments.

Read Paul's instructions to a congregation that ignored the Word of God: 1 Corinthians 5.1. *Actually it is heard there is* **sexual immorality** *among you, and* **such immorality** *which is not among the heathens, for someone to have his father's wife. 2. And you are proud and should you not rather be sad, that this work which I did could have been taken from among you? 3. For I indeed have already* *judged the one who did this as if I were present, although I am absent in the body but present in the spirit: 4. when you gather in the name of our Lord Y'shua and with my spirit with the power of our Lord Y'shua, 5.* **to give such a one as this over to Satan** *for destruction of the flesh, so that his spirit could be saved in the Day of the Lord. 6. Your boasting is not good. Do you not know that a little leaven leavens the whole lump of dough? 7.* **You must immediately cleanse the old leaven,** *so that you would be a new lump, just as you are unleavened: for also our Passover Messiah was sacrificed. 8. Thus we should celebrate not in old leaven and not in wickedness and evil but in unleavened purity and truth.*

2 Corinthians 7:8. *Because even if I did grieve you in my letter, I do not regret it: indeed if I were regretting, for I see that the letter, if even for a moment i grieved you, 9.* **now I rejoice,** *not because you were grieved but* **because you were grieved into repentance:** *for you were grieved according to God, so that you would no longer suffer loss through us. 10. For grief before God, not to be regretted, works repentance into salvation: but grief of the world brings about death 11. For behold this same thing, to have been grieved according to God brought about so great an eagerness in you, and rather an impatience to clear yourselves, and indignation, then fear, and longing, and zeal, and punishment. You stood together with yourselves in everything and have shown that you are blameless in the matter. 12. So if I then wrote to you, not on account of wrong doing and not on account of being wronged, but so your eagerness on our behalf would be revealed by you before God. 13. Because of this we have been encouraged.*

Y'shua said: Luke 8:19. *And His mother and brothers came to Him and they were not able to meet with Him because of the crowd. 20. And it was reported to Him, "Your mother and Your brothers have been standing outside wanting to see You." 21. And He said to them,* **"My mother and My brothers are these who hear and do the Word of God."**

We are to **do** the Word of God, not weaken it. (See Violent Believer in this chapter.)

Where Were the Apostles When the Holy Spirit Came Upon Them? Many assume they were in an upper room, but that could not have held one hundred twenty people, nor could thousands of people have been close enough to witness the miracle. The streets were too narrow and houses too small for that. The one place where thousands could have gathered in Jerusalem was Solomon's Colonnade, on the steps leading to the South entrance of the Temple.

Acts 2:1. *And when the day of Shavuot (Weeks) had come they were all in one place together. 2. And a sound came suddenly out of heaven as bringing a violent wind and it filled the whole **House** where they were sitting 3. and dividing tongues like fire were seen by them and the flames sat upon each one of them, 4. and all were filled by the Holy Spirit and began to speak in other languages just as the Spirit was giving them to speak out boldly. 5. And there were Jewish people staying in Jerusalem, devout people from all the nations under heaven. 6. And when this sound was made a multitude gathered and was amazed, because while they were speaking, they all were hearing in their own languages. 7. And they were astounded and amazed saying, "Look, are not all those who are speaking from Galilee? 8. Then how do we each hear in our own language with which we were born? 9. Parthians and Medes and Elamites and those who dwell in Mesopotamia, Judea, and even Cappadocia, Pontus, and Asia, 10. Phrygia, and also Pamphylia, Egypt and the parts of Libya around Cyrene, and the visiting Romans, 11. Cretes and Arabs, both Jewish people and proselytes. We hear them speaking the greatness of God in our languages." 12. And all were amazed and perplexed, saying to one another, "What does this mean?" 13. But others, mocking, were saying, "They are drunk because they have been filled with sweet new wine."*

The **House** is the Temple, which is frequently referred to in the Hebrew Scriptures as the **House**. Luke also refers to the Sanctuary as the **House** in his Gospel:

Luke 11:49. *Because of this the wisdom of God also said, 'I am sending prophets and apostles among them, and they will kill some of them, and they will persecute others,' 50. so that the blood of all the prophets, that which has been shed from the foundation of the world, would be required from this generation, 51. from the blood of Abel until the blood of Zechariah, who was killed between the altar and the **House**:*

Solomon's Colonnade was open for groups to meet, to teach, and to preach, so it would have been a natural place for one hundred twenty disciples to gather, waiting for the Holy Spirit. Under those steps archeologists have found hundreds of immersion pools where several thousand could immerse in less than a half hour.

Acts 2:37. *And when they heard this they were pierced in their hearts. They said to Peter and the rest of the apostles, "What could we do, men, brothers?" 38. And Peter said to them, "**You must immediately repent, and each of you must*** *immediately be immersed in the name of Y'shua Messiah, for forgiveness of your sins and you will take the gift of the Holy Spirit. 39. For the promise is for you and for your children and for all those in faraway places, whomever the Lord our God will call to Himself." 40. And he charged them in many other word and was urging them saying, "You must right now be rescued from this crooked generation." 41. Then indeed, those who accepted his message were immersed and there were added on that day **about three thousand lives**. 42. And they wer continuing steadfastly in the teaching by the apostles and in fellowship, in th breaking of bread and in prayers.*

The Center for Judaic Christian Studies estimated that because there were so many immersion pools, that those three thousand could have immersed in twenty minutes.

Violent Believer sounds inappropriate, but it is real! Look at:

Matthew 11:11. *Truly I say to you: there has not been born of women greater than John the Immerser: but the least in the Kingdom of the Heavens is greater than he. 12. From the days of John the Immerser until now **the Kingdom of the Heavens** is taken by **violence**, and shares in the **Heavenly Kingdom** are sough for with the **most ardent zeal** and the **most intense exertion** and **violent men are seizing it**, each one claiming eagerly for himself. 13. For all the Prophets and the Torah (Teaching) prophesied until John: 14. and if you want to accept it, he is Elijah, the one who was going to come. (Malachi 3:23) 15. The one who ha ears must continually listen.*

Luke 16:16. *The Torah (Teaching) and the Prophets were proclaimed until John from then on the Kingdom of God is being preached and **everyone enters in forcibly**.*

We are to be like Jacob who wrestled with our Bridegroom in Genesis 32:25.

And Jacob was left alone, and a Man wrestled with him there until the breaking of the day. 26. And when the Man saw that He did not prevail against him, He touched the socket of his hip, and the socket of Jacob's thigh was out of joint as he wrestled with Him. 27. And He said, "Let Me go, for the day is breaking." And Jacob said, "I shall not let You go until You bless me." 28. And the Man said to him, "What is your name?" And he said, "Jacob." 29. And He said, "Your name will no longer be called Jacob, but Israel, for as a prince you have power with God and with men, and you have prevailed." 30. And Jacob asked and said, "Tell me, I pray You, Your name." And He said, "Why do you ask after My name?" And He blessed him there. 31. And Jacob called the name of the place Peniel, for "I have seen God face to face and my life is preserved." 32. And as he passed over Peniel the sun rose upon him, and he was limping on account of his hip.

Our duty is to be determined to live a godly life, to obey the Spirit of all the commandments, rather than the letter of man-made rules. Our battle is not with flesh and blood, but as Paul wrote to the Ephesians:

Ephesians 6:10. *From now on, you must right away become strong in the Lord and in the power of His strength. 11. You must continually be clothed with the full armor of God to enable you to stand against the strategies of the devil: 12. because the* **wrestling for us is not with blood and flesh, but with the rulers, with the powers, with the world rulers of this darkness, with the spiritual forces of wickedness in the heavenlies.** *13. Because of this you must immediately take up the* **full armor of God**, *so that you would be able to resist in the evil day and when you have completely achieved all things, to stand. 14. Therefore you should stand, after you have girded around your waist the belt of truth and have put on the breastplate of righteousness 15. and have put sandals on your feet in preparation for the gospel of peace, 16. in all things having taken up the long shield of faith, with which you have been enabled to extinguish all the burning arrows of the evil one: 17. and you must immediately take up the helmet of salvation and the sword of the Spirit, which is the Word of God. 18. Through every prayer and entreaty, by praying always in the Spirit, and being alert in Him, by means of every perseverance and entreaty concerning all the saints 19. and on my behalf, that a word would be given to me as often as I open my mouth to speak, to make known the mystery of the Good News with boldness, 20. concerning which I am an ambassador in chains, so that in this I would have boldness as there is need for me to speak.*

So the **violence** is **Spiritual Violence**—Not to fight with your neighbor, but to do spiritual warfare with our common enemy.

JEWISH ROOTS

Eve Created Equal to Adam: Men have used passages in Scripture to exalt themselves over women, but males and females were created to be equal and to complement one another. We are not created to be identical, but each gender has qualities or specific characteristics needed for our different roles.

Genesis 2:18. *And the LORD* God said, "It is not good that the man, Adam, should be alone. I shall make a helper for him, corresponding to him."*

The word translated Corresponding is Kenegdo, meaning "equal to and adequate for." Any assignment given to Adam, Eve was equal to the task and adequate for her role in completing that task. There is no place for male chauvinism here. Male and female were created to be equal.

Ephesians 5:21. **(Wives and Husbands)** *Being subject to one another in reverence of Messiah, 22. wives to their own husbands as to the Lord, 23. because a husband is head of his wife as also the Messiah is head of the congregation, He is savior of the body: 24. but as the congregation is subject to the Messiah, so also should wives be subject to their husbands in everything. 25. Husbands, you must continually love your wives, just as the Messiah also loved the congregation and **gave Himself over on her behalf**, 26. so that He would sanctify His wife (the congregation) the bride, making her pure by washing with the word of Torah (Teaching), 27. in order that He would present for Himself the glorious congregation, not having spot or wrinkle or any of such things, but so that His bride would be holy and without blemish. 28. In this way husbands are obligated to love their own wives as their own bodies. The one who loves his own wife loves himself. 29. For no one ever hated his own flesh but nourishes and cherishes it, just as also the Messiah nourishes and cherishes the congregation, 30. because we are members of His body. 31. "For this reason a man will leave his father and his mother and be **faithfully devoted to his wife**, and the two will be in one flesh."* (Genesis 2:24)

32. This mystery is great: now I say this in Messiah then in respect to the congregation. 33. But then you one by one, each must continually love his own wife just as himself, and that the wife should respect her husband.

Some translations say a wife must respect her husband, but that is not what Paul wrote. Paul wrote **should** respect, with a subjunctive verb in a *hina* clause, a very common usage.

There are two neat, hidden truths in the next verses:

Genesis 2:22 Footnote: God created the universe, made man, but He built Eve. The root for build has the same letters as the root for discern, so Hebrew scholars say that is why women are more sensitive spiritually than men.

Genesis 3:20 Footnote: Eve's name in Hebrew is Havah, said to come from Hayya, said to mean A Living Thing, but Hayya really means Beast. Literally, Havah means farm or village, so this name refers to Adam and Eve's domain.

Gleaning is ordered in Leviticus 23, the only verse in that chapter not about the Seasons of the LORD. Gleaning was very important, so the poor could have access to good, fresh produce. The LORD shows great compassion for the poor with gleaning and the third tithe, which is laid up especially for them and for the priests who are given the task of distributing to the poor. (See Tithe in Glossary.)

Leviticus 23:22. *"And when you reap the harvest of your land, you will not wholly reap the corners of your field when you reap, neither will you gather any gleaning of your harvest. You will leave them for the poor and for the stranger. I AM the LORD* your God!"*

Gleaning was a life saver to Naomi and Ruth when they came from Moab to Israel because Naomi had relatives around Bethlehem. Both were widows, having to glean for whatever they could eat. Their timing was good because it was the time of the barley harvest.

Ruth 1:22. *So Naomi returned and Ruth the Moabitess, her daughter-in-law, with her, who returned from the country of Moab and they came to Bethlehem in the beginning of barley harvest.*

Ruth 2:2. And Ruth the Moabitess said to Naomi, Let me now go to the field an **glean grain** *after him in whose sight I shall find grace. And she said to her, Go my daughter.*

Ruth chose the right field to glean because that field was owned by Boaz:

Ruth 2:8. Then Boaz said to Ruth, Listen, my daughter. **Do not go to glean i another field!** *Do not go from here, but stay here close by my maidens.*

Read about the blossoming relationship between Ruth and Boaz in chapte three of the Book of Ruth. What a beautiful story this is, with Ruth and Boa later becoming progenitors of Y'shua!

The compassion of our Heavenly Father is shown in Matthew 25:34. *The the King will say to those on His right hand, 'Come, the blessed of My Father you must now inherit what has been prepared for you in the kingdom from th foundation of the world. 35. For I was hungry and you gave Me to eat, I wa thirsty and you gave Me to drink, I was a stranger and you took Me in, 36. an I was poorly clothed and you clothed Me, I was sick and you visited Me, I wa in prison and you came to Me.' 37. Then the righteous will answer Him saying 'Lord, when did we see You hungry and we fed You, or thirsty and we gave Yo something to drink? 38. And when did we see You a stranger and we took Yo in, or poorly clothed and we clothed You? 39. And when did we see You sick or i prison and we came to You?' 40. Then the King will say to them,* **'Truly I say t you, in so much as you did anything for one of these, the least of My broth ers, you did it for Me.'**

Hebraic Thinking. This article is from the book, *Thinking Hebraically* by Alyosha Ryobinov, a very important mindset for westerners, reprinted here with hi permission.

"The word דעומ *(moed)* is used in Leviticus 23:2 referring to appointed time of God. There is a weekly appointed time with God called תבש *(Shabbat* and yearly appointed times that include Passover, Unleavened Bread, Sheaf o First Fruits, Feast of Weeks, and what Scripture calls the memorial blowing of trumpets, and then the Day of Atonement and finally, the Feast of Booths There are seven of these appointed times, not including *Shabbat*. Shabbat i the weekly דעומ *(moed)*.

Note that in Genesis God said, "Let there be lights in the firmament of the heavens to divide the day from the night; and let them be for signs and seasons, and for days and years" (Genesis 1:14). What was being set in order there are God's appointments and not four seasons of the year. As was said earlier, the word for sign is תוא *(ot)* which also means miracle. Miracles or signs often occurred in the past on God's appointed times. And there's no reason to believe they can't happen now or in the future during those same appointed times.

These םידעומ *(moedim)* are really cycles of God which He Himself arranged on the fourth day of His creation. The fourth day is when the cycles in general were set in place when God created the sun, moon and stars. We know that the planets rotate. Everything in the universe cycles. It would be impossible to measure time in the first three days of creation since there was no sun and moon. We can begin to measure time only from the fourth day of creation.

Since the םידעומ *(moedim)* are the cycles of God, this means that God Himself operates in these cycles. Two thousand years ago believers got away from these cycles due to the influence of Constantine and the church fathers. But God never abandoned the cycles. He still operates in them, and if we begin to understand the cycles as His appointed times to be with us we begin to see that our lives also cycle according to the םידעומ *(moedim)*, whether we understand their significance or not."

Think on these things.

Hebraic Thinking 2. This is a commentary by Rabbi Ben-Yehuda that shows another fine example of Hebraic thinking.

Proverb 24:21. *My son, revere the LORD* and the king.* ***Do not meddle with those who are given to change!***

"To a question about the word king, R. Ben-Yehuda replied: There is no question in my mind that the "king" is NOT connected to "the Lord"—as in the Hebrew text the word 'my son' is placed between 'Lord' and 'king.' So, one might ask, why keep the king in the same breath with 'revere the Lord'—and we know that it is to be read in one breath by the traditional musical notes, known as "trop." Two possibilities: (1) This sets the priorities for the pious man: your first obligation is to the Lord, and only if that obligation is discharged, obey the king. (2) The whole book is known as "The Wisdom of Solomon"—a book of instruction left by the wise king to his son and future king of Israel. The Hebrew text was originally without vowels, and therefore "VAMELEKH" (and king) could also be read "UM'LOKH"—which would render the meaning "and reign!" In this reading we can find instruction from the father to his son, "Revere the Lord and you shall continue to reign." (Which, of course, he failed to do—and didn't keep his kingdom…)

"Because the LORD* is named first, the king cannot make any law that goes against the word of the LORD*; the people have to obey the word of the LORD*. Those given to change are in rebellion and are not to be followed."

What a blessing to have this insight to a verse that many of us gloss over, a verse that is meaningful for believers in the United States today when our government has regulations with the force of law that oppose our Biblical commandments. The Hebrew Scriptures are filled with verses from which so much can be gleaned.

Is Torah for Today? There can be no valid argument denying Torah for it is the basic foundation of both Christianity and Judaism. Here are just a few of the Scriptures attesting to the Torah.

Matthew 5:17. *"Do not think that I came to do away with, or to bring an incorrect interpretation to, the **Torah** or the Prophets: I did not come to do away with but to bring (spiritual) abundance, for the **Torah** (Teaching) to be obeyed as it should be and God's promises to receive fulfillment. 18. For truly I say to you, until the sky and the Earth would pass away, **not** one yod or one vav could **ever** pass away from the **Torah** (Teaching), until everything would come to pass. (Luke 16:17; Romans 3:29–31; Hebrews 10:28) 19. Therefore, whoever would break one of the least of these commandments, and would teach people this way, will be called least in the Kingdom of the Heavens: but whoever would do the commandments and would teach them, will be called great in the Kingdom of the Heavens. 20. For I say to you that unless your righteousness would be present in abundance more than that of the scribes and Pharisees, you could not enter the Kingdom of the Heavens."*

Luke 8:19. *And His mother and brothers came to Him and they were not able to meet with Him because of the crowd. 20. And it was reported to Him, "Your mother and Your brothers have been standing outside wanting to see You." 21.*

And He said to them, **"My mother and My brothers are these who hear and do the Word of God."**

John 5:37. *And the One Who sent Me, the Father, that One had testified concerning Me. But you have neither heard His voice at any time nor seen His appearance, 38. and you do not have* **His message** *remaining in you, because you do not believe in this One Whom He has sent. 39. You must examine the Scriptures, because you think you have eternal life in these: and these are those Scriptures that testify about Me: 40. and you do not want to come to Me so that you would have eternal life.*

John 14:15. *If you love Me, you will keep* **My commandments***:*

John 15:10. *If you would keep* **My commandments***, you will dwell in My love,* **just as I have kept the commandments of My Father** *and I dwell in His love.*

Romans 3:29. *Or is He God only of Jewish people? And not also of heathens? Indeed also of heathens, 30. since God is One, He will make righteous the one circumcised by his faith, and the one uncircumcised through his faith. 31. Therefore do we cancel* **Torah** *(Teaching) through faith? God forbid! But we cause* **Torah** *(Teaching) to stand.*

Hebrews 10:28. *Anyone who has set aside the* **Torah** *(Teaching) of Moses dies without pity on testimony by two or three witnesses:*

That cannot be stated any more clearly. **Torah** is for today and forever!

Lot Was Not All That Righteous. Scripture does not tell us much about Lot's behavior, but we can catch a glimpse from his choice of the best land when Abraham gives Lot first crack. Lot did not defer to his uncle or offer to divide the best and share the Jordan Valley, but he gladly chose the Jordan Valley when given the chance.

Genesis 13:5. *And Lot also, who went with Abram, had flocks, herds, and tents. 6. And the land was not able to bear them, so they could dwell together, for their possessions were great, so that they could not dwell together. 7. And there was strife between the herdsmen of Abram's cattle and the herdsmen of Lot's cattle. And the Canaanites and the Perizzites then dwelled in the land.*

181

Genesis 13:8. *And Abram said to Lot, "**There must be no strife**, I pray you, between me and you, and between my herdsmen and your herdsmen, for we are brothers. 9. Is not the whole land before you? Separate yourself from me, I pray you, if you will take the left hand, then I shall go to the right, or if you go to the right hand, then I shall go to the left."*

Genesis 13:10. *And Lot lifted up his eyes, and looked at the whole plain of the Jordan, that it was well watered everywhere before the LORD* destroyed Sodom and Gomorrah, even like the garden of the LORD*, like the land of Egypt, as you come to Zoar. 11. Then Lot chose for himself all the plain of the Jordan and Lot journeyed east, and they separated themselves the one from the other.*

Genesis 13:12. *Abram lived in the land of Canaan and Lot lived in the cities of the plain and pitched his tent toward Sodom. 13. But the people of Sodom were exceedingly bad and sinners before the LORD*.*

One key word in verse 5, **ALSO**, shows that Lot went with Abram because he was kin, that Lot was not one of Abram's disciples. Lot was the most righteous in Sodom, but was not what he ought to have been.

Mankind was created in Genesis, in the image of God, both male and female. The process is explained in the second chapter.

Genesis 1:26. *Then God said, "**We will make mankind in our image, after our likeness and have dominion over the fish of the sea, over the fowl of the air, over the cattle, over all the earth, and over every creeping thing that creeps upon the earth."** 27. So God created mankind in His own image; He created him in the image of God. **He created them male and female.** 28. And God blessed them and God said to them, "**Be fruitful! Multiply! Fill the earth! Subdue it and have dominion over the fish of the sea and over the fowl of the air and over every living thing that moves upon the earth!"***

Being made in the image of God has two meanings. First, the physical resemblance. Two, the very nature of God that mankind can have the same love, the feelings and emotions of God. Since He created both male and female here, the second chapter reveals just how He did that.

Genesis 2:18. *And the LORD* God said, "It is not good that the man, Adam, should be alone. I shall make a helper for him, corresponding to him." 19. And* *out of the ground the LORD* formed every beast of the field and every fowl of the air, and brought them to Adam to see what he would call them, and whatever Adam called every living creature, that was its name. 20. And Adam gave names to all cattle, to the fowl of the air, and to every beast of the field, but for Adam there was not found a helper for him.*

Genesis 2:21. *And the LORD* God caused a deep sleep to fall upon Adam, and he slept. And He took one of his ribs and closed up the flesh in its place. 22. And He built the rib, which the LORD* God had taken from man, into a woman and brought her to the man. 23. And Adam said, "This is now bone of my bones and flesh of my flesh. She will be called Wife (Ishah), because she was taken out of Husband (Ish). 24. Therefore a man will leave his father and his mother and will cling to his wife, and they will be one flesh."*

Those verses complete the narrative of Genesis regarding the creation of mankind.

Moses Lets Pharaoh Know Who God is when Pharaoh's army is drowned in the Reed Sea.

Look at Pharaoh's attitude when Moses and Aaron first went to Pharaoh:

Exodus 5:1. *And afterward Moses and Aaron went in and told Pharaoh, "Thus says the LORD* God of Israel, 'Send My people away! So they can hold a feast to Me in the wilderness.'" 2. And Pharaoh said, "**Who is the LORD*** that I should obey His voice to send Israel out? **I do not know the LORD***, neither will I send Israel away."*

Then there is the Exodus with the song of Moses:

Exodus 15:3. *The LORD* is a Man of War! The LORD* is His name. 4. He has cast Pharaoh's chariots and his army into the sea, his chosen captains also are drowned in the Reed Sea. 5. The depths have covered them, they sank to the bottom like a stone. 6. Your right hand, LORD*, has become glorious in power. Your right hand, LORD*, has dashed the enemy in pieces. 7. And in the greatness of Your excellency You have overthrown those who rose up against You. You sent forth Your wrath, which consumed them as stubble. 8. And with the blast of Your nostrils the waters were gathered together, the floods stood upright as a heap, the depths were solidified in the heart of the sea. 9. The enemy said, 'I shall pursue,*

I shall overtake, I shall divide the plunder. My lust will be satisfied upon them
I shall draw my sword; my hand will destroy them.' 10. You did blow with you
wind, the sea covered them: they sank like lead in the mighty waters. 11. Wh
is like You, LORD*, among the gods?! Who is like You, glorious in holiness, fear
ful in praises, doing wonders?! 12. You stretched out Your right hand, the eart
swallowed them. 13. You in Your loving kindness have led out the people that Yo
have redeemed. You have guided them in Your strength to Your Holy Habitation

Commentary says Moses called from the eastern side to pharaoh on the western side of the sea. **"You asked Who the LORD* was. Now you know."**

Never, Never, Never Fear God. *God is love, and the one who dwells in love dwells in*
God and God lives in him. 17. By this, love has been made complete among us
so that we would have fearless confidence in the Day of Judgment, because jus
*as that One is, we ourselves are like Him in this world. 18. There is **no fear i***
*love but **complete love casts fear outside**, because **fear has to do with punish***
***ment, and the one who fears has not been made complete in love**. (1 John*
4:16–18)

Verse 18 tells us that fear has to do with punishment, that anyone who fear
has not been made complete in love. While some translations have numerous passages saying "Fear God" and "Fear the Lord," the word Fear in those
verses came from the Latin text, which was the source of our early English
translations. Even Hebrew-English dictionaries and lexicons have added Fea
to the meaning of the Hebrew word Y'reh, so it is often translated Fear, but
the Hebrew meaning is Revere. This is a night and day difference because we
call the Lord our Heavenly Father, Whom we are to revere but we are not to
be afraid of Him.

Today many children and adults have never known a loving earthly father,
so they are not able to relate to our Loving Father in Heaven. Reading other
Bible passages that speak of fear of the Lord or fear of God reinforces the
problem for those who have not known a loving father. There are a number
of very strong ministries whose call is to teach Christians to relate to the
God of Love, our Father. Those ministries are performing a very valuable
service, enabling those who never knew a loving father to be able to relate to
their Heavenly Father. It is amazing to me how many people have grown up
without a loving father. Many of those who still have a problem relating to

our Loving God are being blessed by the ministries that have the mission to impart Father's Love.

Fear of the Lord is appropriate for idolaters and unbelievers as in 2 Chronicles 17:10. *And the **fear of the LORD* fell upon all the kingdoms of the lands that were all around Judah**, so that they did not make war against Jehoshaphat.*

Only one time does Scripture report a backslidden believer to fear the LORD:

2 Chronicles 19:4. *And Jehoshaphat lived in Jerusalem and he went out again through the people from Beer Sheba to Mount Ephraim, and **brought them back to the LORD* God of their fathers**. 5. And he set judges in the land throughout all the fortified cities of Judah, city by city, 6. and said to the judges, Take heed what you do, for you do not judge for man, but for the LORD*, Who is with you in the judgment. 7. Therefore now let the **fear of the LORD*** be upon you! Take heed and do it, for there is no iniquity with the LORD* our God, nor respect of persons, nor taking of bribes.*

These are backslidden Israelites, not total heathens.

A believer is never, never, never to fear God. A believer is to revere God, the most Loving Father ever.

One Hundred Forty-Four Thousand of Revelation 7:

Who are these? What do they represent?

The second question must be answered first because John wrote in a style that used symbols and metaphors. The number 144,000 represents Perfection of Divine Government and Perfect Reign. One hundred forty-four represents Perfection of Divine Government. One thousand represents Perfect Reign. This is a description of two things: Heavenly Reign and Messianic Reign. Thus, Revelation Chapter 7 is about those two governments, not about Jewish young men.

Revelation 7:1. *After these things I saw four angels standing upon the four corners of the earth, holding the four winds* (Jeremiah 49:36; Ezekiel 37:9; Zechariah 6:5; Daniel 7:2) *of the earth so that the wind could not blow upon the earth and not upon the sea nor even upon any tree. 2. And I saw another angel going up*

*from the east, having a seal of the Living God, and in a loud voice he cried out
to the four angels to whom it was given to destroy the earth and the sea 3. saying
"Do not harm the earth or the sea or the trees, until we could seal the servants of
our God upon their foreheads.* (Ezekiel 9:4; Revelation 9:4,14:1,22:4) *4. Then
I heard the number of those who had been sealed, a hundred forty-four thousand
that they had been sealed from every tribe of the children of Israel:*

Twelve Jewish tribes, 12,000 each: 12 is perfect government, 1,000 is perfect
reign, so this is not about the number of people, but all about the two Perfect
Reigns.

Revelation 7:9. *After these things I looked, and there was an enormous crowd
which no one was able to number, from all nations and tribes and peoples and
languages, standing before the throne and before the Lamb, who had been clothed
with white robes and they had date palms in their hands..*

Revelation 7:13. *And one of the elders answered, saying to me, "Who are these
clothed in white robes and where did they come from?*

So, who are these people?

Revelation 7:14. *And I said to him, "My lord, you know." Then he said to me,*
"These are those who came out of the Great Affliction (Daniel 12:1) *and they
washed their robes and they made them white in the blood of the Lamb."*

What is the Great Affliction?

1. Those who came through the Tribulation without spot or blemish.
2. Those who came through life's problems, temptations without spot or
   blemish. These are the conquerors of the seven congregations of Revelation chapters 2 and 3.
3. All believers who have kept the faith through all of life's challenges.

Why are they Jewish?

The answer here lies in Revelation 21:9. *Then one of the seven angels, of those
who have the seven vials full of the seven last plagues, came and spoke with me
saying, "You must come, I shall show you the bride, the wife of the Lamb." 10.
Then he took me away in the spirit to a great and high mountain, and he showed*

me the holy city, Jerusalem, (Ezekiel 40:2) descending out of the sky from God, 11. having the glory of God, her radiance like a precious stone as a crystal jasper stone. (Isaiah 60:1,2,19) 12. Having a great and high wall, which has twelve gates and upon the gates twelve angels and names that have been written upon the gates, which are the names of the twelve tribes of the Children of Israel: (Exodus 28:21) 13. on the east three gates and on the north three gates and on the south three gates and on the west three gates. (Ezekiel 48:30–35) 14. And the wall of the city had twelve foundations and upon them are twelve names of the twelve apostles of the Lamb.

Remember, all twelve Apostles of the foundation are Jewish.

The New Jerusalem is founded on the Jewish apostles of Messiah, and entry is only through the Jewish gates, the twelve tribes of Israel. That is the reason for Revelation 7:4. *Then I heard the number of those who had been sealed, a hundred forty-four thousand, that they had been sealed from every tribe of the children of Israel:*

Each Gate has one or more Jewish Gate-Keepers who have a duty to admit only those who are qualified.

The Church has a very real need to return to its Jewish Roots, including honoring the Seasons of the LORD*.

One New Man is named in Ephesians, speaking of the merger of the Jew and the non-Jew:

Ephesians 2:14. *For He is our peace, the One Who has made both things into one and Who has loosed the dividing wall of the fence, cause of the enmity to His flesh, 15. by His nullifying the tradition of the commandments by decrees, so that He could create the two, Jewish and non-Jewish, into **One New Man**, establishing peace 16. so He could reconcile both in one body to God through the cross, as God killed their enmity by means of Him, Y'shua. 17. And when He came He proclaimed the Good News of peace to you, to those far away, and peace to those near: 18. because through Him we both have the introduction to the Father by means of one Spirit. 19. Therefore then, you are no longer aliens and strangers, but you are fellow citizens of the saints and members of the household of God, 20. building upon the foundation of the apostles and prophets, Messiah Y'shua being His cornerstone, 21. in Whom the whole building being constructed is being fit to-*

gether into a holy sanctuary in the Lord, 22. and in Whom you are built togethe into a habitation of God by the Spirit.

The Bride of Messiah has been grafted into the Jewish olive tree, so the non Jews are the yet-to-be believers gathered in by End-Time evangelism. Ortho dox Jewish Rabbi Shlomo Riskin, a few years ago at a Day of Unity of Chris tians and Jews in Jerusalem, said that the two birds of Genesis 15:10 wer not divided, but released with one bird representing Christians, the othe representing Jews. They were released to take God's love to the world.

There is a vicious, malicious, incorrect doctrine still finding adherents toda saying the New Testament replaced the Torah and all the Hebrew Scriptures Those promoting that false doctrine apparently have not read Hebrews 10:28

Hebrews 10:28. ***Anyone who has set aside the Torah (Teaching) of Mose dies without pity on testimony by two or three witnesses: 29. how muc more worthy of punishment do you suppose the one will be who trod down th Son of God and who looked upon the blood of the covenant, by Whom he wa sanctified, as defiled, and has insulted the Spirit of Grace? 30. For we know th One Who said,***

"Vengeance is Mine, I shall repay." (Deuteronomy 32:35)
And again,

"The Lord will judge His people." (Deuteronomy 32:36; Psalm 135:14)
31. It is fearful to fall into the hand of the Living God.

That fateful event will take place for those who reject their Jewish Roots! Th **One New Man** is steadily being established right now.

Racial Prejudice is not demonstrated in Scripture, though some think it is from th criticism of Moses' wife Zipporah.

Numbers 12:1 *And Miriam and Aaron spoke against Moses because of the Ethio pian woman whom he had married, for **he had married an Ethiopian wom an**. 2. And they said, "Has the LORD* indeed spoken only with Moses? Has H not spoken also with us?" And the LORD* heard. 3. (Now the man Moses wa very humble, more than all the men on the face of the earth.)*

What is not apparent to those who do not understand Hebrew is that the reason for the criticism of Zipporah is her name. Zipporah means Bird, so it is said she twittered incessantly like some birds. The next two Scriptures show there was no racial prejudice in high places in ancient Israel.

Jeremiah 38:7. *Now when **Ebedmelech the Cushite, an officer** who was in the king's house, heard that they had put Jeremiah in the cistern, the king then sitting in the gate of Benjamin, 8. Ebedmelech went out of the king's house and spoke to the king saying, 9. My lord the king, these men have done evil in all that they have done to Jeremiah the prophet, whom they have cast into the cistern. And he is likely to die for hunger in the place where he is, for there is no more bread in the city.*

King Zedekiah immediately ordered Ebedmelech to take thirty men and raise Jeremiah out of the pit. This easy access to the king was because Ebedmelech was an officer in the government. Some translations say Ebedmelech was a servant of the king, but that word, Oved, for centuries had been used when referring to officers in the governments of kings.

Zephaniah 1:1. *The word of the LORD* which came to **Zephaniah the son of Cushi**, the son of Gedaliah, the son of Amariah, the son of Hezekiah, in the days of Josiah the son of Amon, king of Judah.*

Zephaniah was a member of the royal household, a great-grandson of Hezekiah. His father's mother or grandmother was an Ethiopian. Skin color was not an issue in ancient Israel and should not be an issue anywhere in this day and age.

Red Heifer is much sought after by all who are looking for the Third Temple. The ashes of the **Red Heifer** will be needed to cleanse the Temple Mount and the Third Temple before the Temple can be used.

Numbers 19:1. *And the LORD* spoke to Moses and to Aaron saying, 2. "This is the **ordinance** of the teaching which the LORD* has commanded saying, Speak to the children of Israel, so they will bring you a red heifer without spot, in which there is no blemish, upon which a yoke has never come, 3. and you will give it to Elazar the priest so he can bring it outside the camp, and one will slay it before his face 4. And Elazar the priest will take of its blood with his finger and sprinkle of its blood directly in front of the Tent of Meeting seven times, 5. and one will*

burn the heifer in his sight, its skin, its flesh, and its blood, he will burn with it.
dung. 6. And the priest will take cedar wood, hyssop, and scarlet and cast it into
the midst of the burning of the heifer. 7. Then the priest will wash his clothes and
he will immerse his flesh in water, and afterward he will come into the camp and
the priest will be unclean until the evening. 8. And the one who burns it will
wash his clothes in water and immerse his flesh in water, and will be unclean
*until the evening. 9. And **a man who is clean will gather up the ashes** of the*
heifer and lay them up outside the camp in a clean place, and it will be kept for
the congregation of the children of Israel for a water of sprinkling: it is an offering
*of purification. 10. And **the one who gathers the ashes of the heifer will wash***
***his clothes and be unclean until the evening**, and it will be for the children of*
Israel and for the stranger that lives among them, for a statute forever.

What is a heifer? A heifer is a young female bovine under three years old that
has not given birth to a calf. That age limit presents a problem because until
the Third Temple is being built, no one knows when the **Red Heifer** will be
called for, so how can a supply of the heifers be planned?

There is always excitement over the appearance of a **Red Heifer**, especially
when one is found in Israel, but here are some points that need consideration.
First, the heifer must be born in Israel because any shots, tattoos, and halters
that would be necessary for international travel would disqualify the heifer
from being used for the cleansing. Second, the heifer must be observed from
birth by qualified Levites to be sure the stringent requirements for the care
of the **Red Heifer** are faithfully observed. The third problem is there must
be other qualified heifers ready at the time when the **Red Heifer** is needed,
when the Third Temple is ready for dedication. That is because the heifer
will be kept at a site that is reasonably close to the Mount of Olives where
it will be offered. The heifer has to lead the way to the place where it will be
offered without any halter or other device to lead it. If the heifer stumbles or
if it turns in a wrong direction, it is disqualified and must be replaced. The
Levites need a breeding stock of red cows to be sure of having a ready supply
of **Red Heifers**.

There is no reason given for the effectiveness of the ashes, so this whole operation is just one of obedience to the commands of the LORD.

The priest who gathers the ashes that are to be used for cleansing is, himself,
made unclean for doing that, adding to the mystery of this process.

Reward for Ruth came quickly with her diligent care of her mother-in-law.

Ruth 2:11. *And Boaz answered and said to her, It has fully been told to me all that you have done for your mother-in-law since the death of your husband, and how you have left your father and your mother and the land of your birth and have come to a people which you have not known. 12. The LORD* will repay* **your work and a full Reward** *will be given you by the LORD* God of Israel, under* **Whose wings you have come to take refuge.**

The **Reward** was really overwhelming. First, having a field in which she was invited to glean, protected while there, then married to Boaz. But the crown was giving birth to a son who was an ancestor of Y'shua. All this was from her conversion to the Hebrew God and her godly lifestyle.

Under the LORD*'s wings is a statement of intimacy with Him, indicating conversion to worship of the LORD*. Her **conversion** was when she answered Naomi:

Ruth1:14. *And they lifted up their voices and wept again and Orpah kissed her mother-in-law, but Ruth clove to her. 15. And she said, Behold, your sister-in-law has gone back to her people and to her gods. You return after your sister-in-law. 16. And Ruth said,* **Do not plead with me to leave you** *or to return from following after you, for wherever you go, I shall go. And where you lodge, I shall lodge.* **Your people are my people, and your God is my God.**

(See note on Ruth 3:9 in the Bible.)

Seven Blessings in Joel are beautiful!

Seven Blessings
Joel 2:23. *You children of Zion, rejoice exuberantly! Rejoice in the LORD* your God! For He has given you the Teacher of Acts of Loving Kindness and* **(1)** *the* **Teacher** *will cause the rain to come down for you,* **the former rain and the latter rain** *as at the first. (Double Blessing) 24.* **(2)** *And the floors will be* **full of wheat** *and the vats will* **overflow with wine and oil.** *(Abundance) 25.* **(3)** *And* **I shall restore to you the years** *that the locust, the canker worm, the caterpillar, and the palmer worm have eaten, (Restoration) My great army which I sent among you. 26.* **(4)** *And* **you will eat in plenty and be satisfied,** *(Never a*

191

Lack) and praise the name of the LORD* your God, **(5) Who has dealt won***drously with you,* (Miracles) *and* **(6) My people will never be ashamed.** *(Re*
spect) 27. And you will know that **(7) I AM in the midst of Israel,** *(Divin*
Presence) and I AM the LORD* your God, and no one else is, and My people wi
never be ashamed.

Praise the LORD we are grafted in, so these blessings apply to all believers!

Sh'ma Israel!

Deuteronomy 6:4. *"Listen! Obey, O Israel! The LORD* is our God! The LORD*
is One! 5. And you will love the LORD* your God with all your heart, wit
your very being, and with all your might. (Matthew 22:37; Mark 12:33; Luk
10:27) *6. And these words, which I am commanding you this day, will be in you*
heart 7. and you will teach them diligently to your children, and you will talk o
them when you sit in your house, when you walk by the way, when you lie down
and when you rise up. 8. And you will bind them as a sign upon your hand, an
they will be as frontlets between your eyes. 9. And you will write them on th
doorposts of your house and on your gates.

The gates are the city gates, showing that all inhabitants are to revere th
LORD*.

Deuteronomy 11:13. *"And it will be, if you will listen diligently to my com*
mandments which I command you this day, to love the LORD* your God, an
to serve Him with all your heart and with your entire being, 14. that I shall giv
you the rain of your land in its due season, the first rain and the latter rain, so yo
can gather in your grain, your wine, and your oil. 15. And I will provide grass i
your fields for your cattle so you can eat and be full. 16. Take heed to yourselves
so your heart will not be deceived, and you turn aside and serve other gods an
worship them."

Deuteronomy 11:17. *"Then the LORD's* wrath would be kindled against yo*
and He would shut up the heavens so there would be no rain, and so the lan
would not yield its fruit, and you would perish quickly from off the good lan
which the LORD* is giving to you.

Deuteronomy 11:18. *"Therefore you will lay up these my words in your hear*
and in your inner being, and bind them for a sign upon your hand, so they ma

be as frontlets between your eyes. 19. And you will teach them to your children, speaking of them when you sit in your house, when you walk by the way, when you lie down, and when you rise up. 20. And you will write them upon the doorposts of your house and upon your gates, 21. so your days and the days of your children will be multiplied in the land which the LORD* swore to your fathers to give them, as the days of heaven upon the earth."

Numbers 15:37. *And the LORD* spoke to Moses saying, 38. "Speak to the children of Israel and bid them to make fringes for themselves in the wings of their garments throughout their generations and that they put upon the fringe of the border a thread of blue, 39. and it will be to you for a fringe, that you may look upon it and remember all the commandments of the LORD* and do them, and that you do not seek after your own heart and your own eyes, after which you used to go astray, 40. so you will remember and do all My commandments and be holy to your God. 41. I AM the LORD* your God, Who brought you out of the land of Egypt, to be your God: I AM the LORD* your God."*

The prayer shawl is brought by God after the murmuring and disobedience of the people following the spies' report when God wanted to kill them all. Moses' intercession saved them, but this 15th chapter of Numbers is all about reminding them of His commandments and promises, ending with the prayer shawl's reminder with the fringes. The wings of a prayer shawl are very significant, used to cover the bride at a wedding. (See Ruth 3:9. See Prayer Shawl in Glossary.)

Those verses on the Prayer Shawl conclude the Sh'ma, which is said by Jewish people every day. The Sh'ma is an excellent reminder for all believers, every day.

Symbolism can be superficial, which is not pleasing to God.

Hosea 6:4. *O Ephraim, what will I do to you? O Judah, what will I do to you? For your goodness is like a morning cloud and as the early dew it goes away. 5. Therefore I have hewn them by the prophets. I have slain them by the words of My mouth (Ephesians 6:17) and your judgments are like the light that goes forth. 6.* **For I desire loving kindness and not sacrifice, and the knowledge of God more than burnt offerings.**

Verse 6 is a lesson for all of us: our Heavenly Father wants to see our love for our neighbor much more than He wants our **religious symbolism**.

Mark 12:32. *And the scribe said to Him, "Quite right! Teacher, You said in truth that 'He is One and there is not another except Him:' 33. and **to love Him out of his whole heart and out of his whole mind and out of his whole strength and to love his neighbor as himself is greater than all burnt offerings and sacrifices.***"

Hebrews 10:5. *On account of which, when He came into the world He said,*
"You did not want sacrifices and offerings,
but You did make ready a body for Me:
6. and You did not take pleasure in a whole burnt offering
on behalf of sin.

Symbolism can easily become **Legalism**. (See Legalism in Glossary.)

Transgender Dressing is not permitted.

Deuteronomy 22:5. *The woman will not wear that which pertains to a man neither will a man put on a woman's garment, for all that do so are an abomination to the LORD* your God.*

This does not mean a woman cannot wear slacks, but that a woman cannot dress to look like a man, nor a man dress to look like a woman.

Two Priests judged Israel, Eli and Samuel.

Their sons were wicked:

1 Samuel 2:12. *Now the sons of Eli were wicked men. They did not know the LORD*. 13. And the priest's custom with the people was when any man offered sacrifice, the priest's servant came while the flesh was in boiling, with a flesh hook of three teeth in his hand 14. and he stuck it into the pan or kettle or caldron or pot. All that the flesh hook brought up the priest took for himself. So they did in Shiloh to all Israel who came there. 15. Also before they burned the fat, the priest's servant came and said to the man who sacrificed, Give flesh to roast for the priest, for he will not have sodden flesh from you, but raw. 16. And if any man said to him, Let them not fail to burn the fat presently then take as much as your being*

desires. Then he would answer him, No, but you will give it to me now. And if not, I shall take it by force. 17. Therefore the sin of the young men was very great before the LORD*, for the men abhorred the offering of the LORD*.

1 Samuel 8:1. *And it was, when Samuel was old, that he made his sons judges over Israel. 2. Now the name of his firstborn was Joel, and the name of his second, Abijah. They were judges in Beer Sheba. 3. But his sons did not walk in his Ways, but turned aside after unjust gain and took bribes and perverted justice.*

Eli's sons could have inherited the Judgeship but for Samuel. Then Samuel's sons could have inherited the Judgeship except the people asked for a king. Saying Eli's sons did not know the LORD* means that they did not have a personal relationship with Him. You have to think that the behavior of Samuel's sons helped to bring about the people's desire for a king.

The leadership of Israel belongs to Judah, not Priests, from Genesis 49:8. *"Judah, you are he whom your brothers will praise: your hand will be on the neck of your enemies, your father's children will bow down before you. 9. Judah is a lion's whelp, from the prey, my son, you are gone up: he stooped down, he laid down like a lion and as an old lion. Who will rouse him up? 10.* **The scepter will not depart from Judah,** *nor a Torah scholar from between his feet, until Shiloh comes: and the gathering of the peoples will be to Him."*

The Scepter not departing means that the future royal leadership of Israel will always belong to Judah. The Torah scholar being at his feet means Judah will always be loyal to the LORD*. **The word Shiloh is a composite of the words Sh' loh, a gift to him, a reference to the King Messiah, to whom all nations will bring gifts.**

Two Foundations. The Greek New Testament translates two very different words as Foundation. These are:

1. Themelios often refers to the foundation of a building, whether it is a home, a public building or a city wall. This is a foundation laid out by men—square, rectangular, round or any other shape. The sturdiness of the structure depends on the quality of this foundation. Themelios is used seven times in the New Testament in referring to the foundation of a structure. Themelios is used other times in speaking of the foundation of biblical principles.

2. <u>Katabole</u> always refers to the foundation of the world. It is used ten times in the New Testament in referring to the foundation of the world. Katabole speaks of the foundation of the Earth as something cast down forcefully, with God raising His arm then dropping it quickly, like FOOMP! And there is the foundation of our world! A typical verse is Matthew 25:34. *Then the King will say to those on His right hand, Come, the blessed of My Father, you must now inherit what has been prepared for you in the kingdom from the Foundation of the World.*

It is fascinating that every time a New Testament author refers to the Foundation of the World, he uses Katabole. Now look at Genesis 1:1 in a slightly different way: In *the* beginning God created the heavens, then He raised His arm and cast down the Foundation of the Earth!

Two More Foundations based on the Greek word **Themelios**:

1. <u>Themelios</u> often refers to the foundation of a building, whether it is a home, a public building or a city wall. This is a **foundation** laid out by men—square, rectangular, round or any other shape. The sturdiness of the structure depends on the quality of this foundation. Themelios is used seven times in the New Testament in referring to the foundation of a structure.
2. Themelios is used other times in speaking of the **Foundation of biblical principles**. These are the sure doctrines of God.

Ephesians 2:17. *And when He came He proclaimed the Good News of peace to you, to those far away, and peace to those near: 18. because through Him we both have the introduction to the Father by means of one Spirit. 19. Therefore then, you are no longer aliens and strangers, but you are fellow citizens of the saints and members of the household of God, 20. building upon the Foundation of the apostles and prophets,* ***Messiah Y'shua being His Cornerstone,*** *21. in Whom the whole building being constructed is being fit together into a* ***Holy Sanctuary in the Lord,*** *22. and in Whom you are built together into a habitation of God by the Spirit.*

1 Timothy 6:17. *You must continually command those who are rich in the present age not to be proud and not to hope in riches in uncertainty, but in God, the One Who supplies richly everything for our enjoyment, 18. and that they are to do good works, to be rich in good works, to be generous, sharing, 19. and in this way*

*to be storing up for themselves a good **Foundation** for the coming age, so that they would really take hold of life.*

Hebrews 11:8. *By trusting, Abraham, when he was called, obeyed to come out to a place which he was going to take for an inheritance, and he came out not knowing where he was going.* (Genesis 12:1–5) *9. By trusting, he sojourned in the land of the promise, dwelling as a stranger in tents with Isaac and Jacob, the fellow heirs of this promise:* (Genesis 23:4,26:3,35:12,27) *10. for he was waiting for the city that has* **Foundations, of which God was the designer and builder**.

These **Foundations** are even better than the best building Foundations engineered by people. Our Jewish God is the Designer and Builder of our **Biblical Foundations**. The whole **Foundation** of our belief system is Jewish, the reason this article is in Jewish Roots.

Urim and Tummim were worn by the High Priest to determine God's plan for different situations.

Exodus 28:30. *Urim (pronounced ooreem) refers to light and Tummim (pronounced toomeem) refers to 'made perfect' for these two objects with the Name of God on each, in order to bring His plan to light.*

1 Samuel 30:6. *And David was greatly distressed, for the people spoke of stoning him, because the soul of all the people was grieved, every man for his sons and for his daughters, but David encouraged himself in the LORD* his God. 7. And David said to Abiathar the priest, Ahimelech's son, Now please, bring the ephod here for me. And Abiathar brought there the ephod to David. 8. And David inquired of the LORD* saying, Will I pursue after this troop? Will I catch up with them?*

And He said, Pursue! For you will absolutely catch up with them! You will certainly rescue them!

Abiather tuned into the Holy Spirit, ordering David to pursue the Amalekites, saying he would surely prevail.

Va'ethanan, the name of the weekly Torah portion beginning Deuteronomy 3:23, has much deeper meaning than shows in the text. The Story begins in Numbers 20 when the people are murmuring because there is not enough water. Then Moses is told to speak to a rock.

Numbers 20:6. *Then Moses and Aaron went from the presence of the assembly to the entrance of the Tent of Meeting, and they fell upon their faces and the glory of the LORD* appeared to them. 7. And the LORD* spoke to Moses saying, 8. "Take the staff and gather the assembly together, you and Aaron your brother, and **speak to the rock** before their eyes and it will give forth its water and you will bring water out of the rock to them: so you will give the congregation and their beast drink."* (Deuteronomy 3:23)

Moses Disobeys
Numbers 20:9. *Then Moses took the staff from before the LORD*, as He commanded him. 10. And Moses and Aaron gathered the congregation together before the rock and he said to them, "Listen now, you rebels! Must we fetch you water out of this rock?" 11. And Moses lifted up his hand and with his staff he **struck the rock twice**, and the water came out abundantly, and the congregation and also their beasts drank.*

Numbers 20:12. *And the LORD* spoke to Moses and Aaron, "Because you did not believe Me, to sanctify Me in the eyes of the children of Israel, therefore you will not bring this congregation into the land which I have given them." 13. This is the water of Meribah, because the children of Israel strove with the LORD* and He was sanctified among them.*

Now, in Deuteronomy, Moses comes face to face with not being able to enter the Promised Land, so he pleads with God:

Va'ethanan
Deuteronomy 3:23. ***And I implored*** *the LORD* at that time saying, 24. "My Lord, LORD*, You have begun to show Your greatness and Your mighty hand to Your servant, for what god is in heaven or on earth that can do according to Your words and according to Your might? 25. I beg You, let me go over and see the good land that is beyond the Jordan, that goodly mountain and Lebanon." 26. But the LORD* ignored, passed by, my plea for your sake and would not hear me. And the LORD* said to me, 'Let it be enough for you! Speak no more to Me of this matter.'"*

In Va'ethanan Moses implores the LORD with a verb that is asking for grace, a pardon. Hanan means to be gracious, so he is actually asking for a pardon for striking the rock instead of speaking to it. Implore here is a very strong plea for God's grace, for a pardon for his disobedience in not speaking to the rock.

The depth in these verses is much deeper as Moses begs the LORD* to let him cross over the Jordan, using the verb Ayin-Vet-Resh, which means to cross or to pass over something. That verb is the source of the word Hebrew because the Hebrews are the people who crossed over the river to establish the Promised Land, Israel. The LORD* then uses the same verb and passes over Moses' request, so Moses is denied entry to the long-sought Promised Land.

What God Hates is listed in Proverbs 6.

> Proverbs 6:16. *The LORD* hates these six things, and seven are an abomination to Him: 17.* **1** *a proud look,* **2** *a lying tongue,* **3** *hands that shed innocent blood,* *18.* **4** *a heart that devises wicked imaginations,* **5** *feet that are swift in running to evil,* *19.* **6** *a false witness who speaks lies, and* **7** *the one who sows discord among brothers.*

1 Number one is Pride! That is because pride automatically belittles someone or whole groups of people. Pride says "I am better than you!" Jewish teaching has, for thousands of years, considered humility an essential foundation for a lifestyle of service to the LORD*.

2 Those who have a problem with Truth have a very real problem relating to the LORD. Be cautious of those people regarding all your relationships, business or social.

3 That murder ranks third surprises some because we put great stress on murder, ranking it higher than Pride and Lies. Notice this is Innocent blood because the LORD promotes capital punishment for those who deserve it.

4 Take every thought captive (2 Corinthians 10:5) because what is in your heart is known to God. That you think of doing or saying something evil is judged by God as if you had actually done it! Matthew 5:27. *"You heard that it was said, 'You will not commit adultery.' 28. But I am saying to you that everyone who looks at a woman with desire for her has already committed adultery with her in his heart.*

5 This is running to evil, which can be without thinking or planning the evil when someone says "Let's do .." and you go without a thought.

6 Bearing false witness was the primary cause of Joseph being sold into slavery. Genesis 37:2. *These are the descendants of Jacob. Joseph, seventeen years old, was tending the flock with his brothers and he was a lad with the sons of Bilhah and with the sons of Zilpah, his father's wives. Joseph brought to their father very evil reports about them.* These very evil reports were slander. Joseph was exaggerating bad reports about his brothers. This slander by Joseph opened the door for Potiphar's wife to slander Joseph. Exaggeration is often involved with gossip. It is hard for exaggeration not to be involved with gossip. (See Gossip Slander in Glossary.)

7 Sowing discord is very common—on the job, within any group, whether social or whatever, especially if one person or two are ambitious and think they know better than the leaders. This is all too common in church, the spirit involved in many church splits.

This list of things that God hates is certainly not the complete list. But it calls out the worst, so we can mull them to understand God's desire for relationship with each of us. It puts into perspective—especially showing us that **Pride** is often—the motivator for all manner of sins.

Willing Heart is required to give an offering to God.

Exodus 25:1. *And the LORD* spoke to Moses, saying, 2. "Speak to the children of Israel, that they will bring Me an offering: you will take My offering from every man who gives it **Willingly with his Heart**.*

Exodus 35:5. *Take from among you an offering to the LORD*. Whoever is of a **Willing Heart** (2 Corinthians 9:7) will bring it, an offering for the LORD*; gold, silver, bronze, 6. blue, purple, scarlet, fine linen, goats' hair, 7. rams' skins dyed red, badgers' skins, acacia, 8. oil for the light, spices for anointing oil, for the sweet incense, 9. onyx stones, and stones to be set for the ephod and for the breast plate. 10. And every wise-hearted among you will come and make all that the LORD* has commanded; 11. the Tabernacle, its Tent and its covering, its hooks, its boards, its bars, its pillars, its sockets, 12. the Ark, its poles, the cover, the veil of the covering, 13. the table and its poles, all its vessels, the showbread, 14. the menorah also for the light, its furniture, its lamps with the oil for the light, 15* *the incense altar, its poles, the anointing oil, the sweet incense, the hanging for the door at the entrance of the Tabernacle, 16. the altar of burnt offering with its bronze grate, its poles, all its vessels, the laver and its base, 17. the hangings of the court, its pillars and their sockets, the hanging for the entrance of the court, 18. the pegs of the Tabernacle, the pegs of the court and their cords, 19. the crocheted garments, to do service in the Holy Place, the holy garments for Aaron the priest, and the garments of his sons to minister in the priest's office."*

2 Corinthians 9:6. *And this, the one who sows sparingly will also reap sparingly, and the one who sows bountifully will also reap bountifully. 7. Each just as he chose in his heart, not reluctantly or from compulsion: for* **God loves a Cheerful Giver**.

Never begrudge an **offering** to the LORD, but rejoice that you have the appropriate offering for the occasion.

1 Chronicles 29:11. *Yours, O LORD*, is the greatness and the power and the glory, the victory and the majesty, for all that is in the heavens and in the earth is Yours. Yours is the kingdom, LORD*, and You are exalted as Head above all. 12. Both riches and honor are of You and You reign over all, and in Your hand is power and might and in Your hand is to make great and to give strength to all. 13. Now therefore, our God, we thank You and praise Your glorious name. 14. But who am I and what is my people that we should be able to offer so willingly in this way?* **For all things come of You and of Your own have we given You.**

REPENTANCE

Repentance in the Hebrew Scriptures uses several idioms for **Repent**.

Shuv, meaning return, is one of the most common Hebrew idioms for **Repentance**. Shuv is the masculine, second person singular imperative: a command to you, personally to **Repent**.

T'shuva is the common reference to the month of Elul as the time of repentance leading up to the Day of Memorial (Rosh Hashanah). The modern use of T'shuva is for the call to repent, but technically T'suva is the masculine, third person singular, future tense: **He (Y'shua) will Return!**

Anav is often translated humble, poor, or meek, all of which are idioms for **Repentant**. Matthew 5:3. *Blessed are the **Repentant**, because theirs is the Kingdom of the Heavens.* The Greek text reads **Poor in Spirit**.

Dal means Poor. Isaiah 11:4. *but He will judge the **Poor (Repentant)** with righteousness and decide with equity for the **Humble (Repentant)** of the earth and He will strike the earth with the rod of His mouth, and with the breath of His lips He will slay the wicked.*

When you are reading a Bible, check each one of these words to determine if **Repent** or **Repentance** is appropriate in that context.

Continuously Repent as in Matthew 4:17. *From then on Y'shua began to preach and to say, **You must continuously repent**: for the Kingdom of the Heavens has come near.* The tense used in the Greek tells us to walk in repentance every day, even though we know we have been sanctified and made righteous by the Blood of the Lamb. This is because we have not been perfected, but we are to strive to be better today than we were yesterday as we become more like Him. (See Ephesians 5:1–5.)

1 Timothy 1:15. *The statement is faithful and worthy of all approval, that Messiah Y'shua came into the world to save sinners, of whom I am foremost. 16. But I received mercy because of this, so that Messiah Y'shua would show all patience with me first, for an example for those who were going to believe in Him for eternal life. 17. Now to the Eternal King, Immortal, Invisible, the Only God, be honor and glory forever and ever. Amen.*

Hebrews 3:12. *You must beware, brothers, lest a heart evil with unbelief will be in some of you, causing you to fall away from the Living God, 13. but you must continually exhort yourselves throughout each day, until the Day is called, so that none of you would be hardened by sin's deceitfulness:*

John 8:31. *Therefore Y'shua was saying to the Jewish people who believed in Him, "If you would remain in My Word, you are truly My disciples 32. and you will know the truth, and the truth will make you **free.**" 33. They answered Him, "We are Abraham's seed and we have never been slaves: how do You say that 'You will become **free.**'" 34. Y'shua answered them, "I most definitely say to you that everyone who commits sin is a slave of sin. 35. And the slave does not stay in the house forever, the son does stay forever. 36. If therefore the Son would set you **free**, you will truly be **free**. 37. I know that you are Abraham's seed: but you are seeking to kill Me, because My message does not take hold in you. 38. I am saying what I have seen from the Father: but you are doing what you heard from your father."*

The word translated Free means to be set free **from** something, **from sin**.

Day of Atonement, Only for Sin in Error: Exodus 34:5. *And the LORD* descended in the cloud and stood with him there and proclaimed the name of the LORD*. 6. And the LORD* passed by before him and proclaimed, "The LORD*, the LORD* God, merciful and gracious, patient, and abundant in loving kindness and truth, 7. keeping loving kindness for thousands, forgiving **Iniquity**, **Transgression**, and **Sin**, and Who will by no means clear the guilty, visiting the **Iniquity** of the fathers upon the children and upon the children's children, to the third and to the fourth generations.*

The above verses give the Hebrew grading of Sin: **Iniquity** (avon) is intentional sin, the perpetrator knows it is sin, but does it anyway; **Transgression** (fesha) is sin committed to anger God; and **Sin** (hata'ah) is committed i ignorance, unintentionally. In the *One New Man Bible* the Hebrew wor for sin is always translated sin, with the word for iniquity always translate iniquity, and the word for transgression always translated transgression. (Se Sin in Glossary.)

Leviticus 4:1. *And the LORD* spoke to Moses saying, 2. Speak to the children o Israel, saying,*

*"If someone **sins through ignorance** against any of the commandments of th LORD*, things which ought not to be done and will do against any of them:*

*3. If the priest that is anointed **sins**, putting guilt for the **sin** on the people, the let him bring for his **sin**, which he has **sinned**, a young bull without blemish t the LORD* for a **sin** offering.*

Matthew 12:33. *You must make the tree good and its fruit good, or you mus make the tree rotten and its fruit rotten: for the tree will be known by its frui 34. Children of vipers, how are you, since you are evil, able to speak good thing For the mouth speaks from the abundance of the heart. 35. The good man cas out good from his good treasure box and the evil man casts out evil from his ev treasure box. 36. And I say to you that every idle word which men will speak wi be paid back with regard to his account on Judgment Day: 37. for you will b justified, declared righteous, because of your words, and you will be condemne because of your words.*

Colossians 3:5. *Therefore you must right now put to death the earthly part which are immorality, uncleanness, passion, evil desires, and covetousness, whic is idol worship, 6. because of which the wrath of God is coming upon the son of the disobedient. 7. Among whom you also once walked, when you were livin in these things: 8. but now then you must immediately put everything off from yourself, anger, passion, wickedness, depravity, malice, blasphemy, slander, evi obscene, abusive speech from your mouth: 9. you must not ever lie to one another since you stripped off the old man with his deeds 10. and by putting on your new self, which is being renewed in knowledge according to the image of the One Wh created the universe, 11. where there is not one Greek or Jewish, circumcision o uncircumcision, barbarian, Scythian, slave, free, but then Messiah is all things t all those.*

Ephesians 5:1. *Therefore you must continually be imitators of God as beloved children 2. and* **you must walk constantly in love, just as also the Messiah loved us and gave Himself over on our behalf, an offering and a sacrifice to God for a fragrant aroma.** *3. But any* <u>immorality</u> *or* <u>impurity</u> *or* <u>covetousness</u> *must not be named among you, as is fitting for saints, 4. nor* <u>foul speaking</u> *or* <u>foolish talking</u> *or* <u>low jesting</u>*, which things do not belong, but rather thanksgiving. 5. For you know this very well, that anyone who practices* <u>immorality</u> *or* <u>uncleanness</u> *or* <u>covetousness</u>*,* <u>who is an idol worshipper</u>*, does not have any inheritance in the kingdom of the Messiah and God.*

These passages point out some things we do every day, especially foolish talking, low jesting, and anger like when someone cuts you off in traffic. Coveting your friend's new car is sin. In both Colossians 3:5 and Ephesians 5:5, covetousness is specifically referred to as idol worship. All these and many other things are sin—things we do without thinking. These must be repented, which is why Y'shua said, "You must continuously repent." (Matthew 4:17) How many of us walk in repentance every day? This is why Christians need to honor Yom Kippur, which atones for unintentional sin. Iniquity and Transgression since they are intentional, known by the sinner immediately, require repentance immediately. Anyone living in sin knows it is sin, but makes excuses, and while those excuses may ease the conscience, they are not repentance. Repentance requires the sinner to immediately change behavior, so all the world can be made aware of the change.

Exodus 30:10. *And Aaron will make atonement upon the horns of it (altar) once in a year with the blood of the* **Sin Offering** *of atonements: once in the year will he make atonement upon it throughout your generations: it is most holy to the LORD*.*

Numbers 29:7. *And you will have on* **the tenth of this seventh month a holy convocation, and you will afflict your souls***: you will not do any work. 8. You will offer a burnt offering to the LORD* for a sweet savor, one young bull, one ram, seven lambs of the first year; they will be to you without blemish, 9. and their grain offering will be of fine flour mixed with oil, three tenths of an ephah to a bull, two tenths to one ram, 10. one tenth for each lamb of the seven lambs, 11. one he goat for a sin offering besides* **the sin offering of atonement***, the continual burnt offering, its grain offering, and their drink offerings.*

The above two verses are the only ones that name **Sin** in the passage with the word **"atonement,"** and in both cases they use the word for **unintentional sin**. That ties the Day of Atonement to **unintentional sin**, strengthened by Hebrews 9:6, which specifically refers to **sin committed in ignorance**.

Hebrews 9:1. *Now truly the first covenant had both regulations for service and the earthly Sanctuary. 2. Indeed a Tabernacle was prepared. The first room in it had the menorah and the table and the bread of the presence, which first room is called "Holy:" 3. but after the second veil in the tent, the one called "Holy of Holies," 4. there was a golden altar of incense and the Ark of the Covenant, which was covered entirely in gold, and had in it the gold jar with the manna and the rod of Aaron that budded and the tablets of the covenant, 5. and above it two cherubim of glory that overshadowed the mercy seat: I shall not now speak in detail about this.*

Hebrews 9:6. *And such as these indeed were the furnishings in the first Tabernacle, and so the priests always entered, fulfilling the services, 7.* ***but in the second room, the Holy of Holies, once a year, only the <u>High Priest, not without blood, which he offered on behalf of both himself and the people for the Sins committed in Ignorance</u>,*** *8. although the Holy Spirit made this clear, the way into the Holy of Holies had not yet been revealed while the first Tabernacle was still standing, 9. which was a symbol for the present time, according to which both gifts and sacrifices were brought which were not able to perfect the conscience of the worshipper, 10. they were only regulations of flesh on food and drink and different immersions, imposed until the time of the new order.*

Leviticus 8:13. *And Moses brought Aaron's sons, put tunics on them, belts on them, turbans on them, as the LORD* commanded Moses. 14. And he brought the bull for the* **Sin** *(Unintentional Sin)* ***offering****, and Aaron and his sons laid their hands on the head of the bull for the* **Sin offering***. 15. And he slew it and Moses took the blood and put it upon the horns of the altar round about with his finger and purified the altar, and poured the blood at the bottom of the altar and sanctified it to make atonement upon it. 16. And he took all the fat on the innards, the lobe above the liver, the two kidneys and their fat and Moses burned it on the altar. 17. But the bull and its hide, its flesh, and its dung, he burned with fire outside the camp, as the LORD* commanded Moses.*

If your congregation does not honor Yom Kippur, you now know that you are to honor that yourself with the whole month Elul, the 29 or 30 days before the Day of Memorial (Rosh Hashanah) to be spent in repentance, then during the Ten Days of Awe between the Day of Memorial and Yom Kippur, focusing even more on repentance, so all the sinful thoughts, words and deeds done without knowing would be erased from your record.

Sinning deliberately is not forgiven on Yom Kippur because that iniquity or transgression by its very nature is known. When a person commits iniquity or transgression, deliberately committing that deed, the perpetrator knows what was done, that it is an act against God and must be dealt with separately.

Keep the Whole Torah as Jacob exhorts:

Jacob 2:8. *If you really fulfill the royal Torah according to the Scriptures, "You will love your neighbor as yourself,"* (Leviticus 19:18) *you do well: 9. but if you show partiality, you are working sin, being exposed as a transgressor under the Torah (Teaching). 10. **For whoever would keep the whole Torah (Teaching) but would stumble in one thing, has become guilty of all.** 11. For the One Who said, "Do not commit adultery," also said, "Do not commit murder:" but if you do not commit adultery but do commit murder, you have become a transgressor of Torah (Teaching). 12. So you must continually speak, and so you must act as one going to be judged through the law of freedom. 13. For judgment without mercy is to be given for the one who does not do mercy: mercy, full of glad confidence, has no fear of judgment.*

It is not possible to pick and choose what we are to obey, although there are some commandments that are not appropriate for today, such as stoning for not observing Sabbath, or capital punishment for immorality. (See Ignored Commandments in Glossary.)

These verses in Leviticus are passed over or not read at all:

Leviticus 19:13. *You will not defraud or rob your neighbor. The wages of him that is hired will not stay with you all night until the morning. 14. You will not curse the deaf, or put a stumbling-block before the blind, but will revere your God. I AM the LORD*! 15. You will do no unrighteousness in judgment: you will not respect the person of the poor, or honor the person of the mighty: in righteousness you will judge your neighbor. 16. You will not go up and down as a talebearer among your people neither will you stand against the blood of your neighbor. I AM the LORD*!*

Gossip is expressly forbidden as is favoritism in judgment for either rich or poor. (See Gossip/Slander in Glossary.)

Ordination of the Priests was seven days of repentance, a process followed on the eighth day by an appearance of the **Glory of the LORD* Himself**.

Aaron and His Sons Anointed

Leviticus 8:1. *And the LORD* spoke to Moses saying, 2. "Take Aaron and his sons with him, the garments, the anointing oil, **a bull** for the **sin offering, two rams**, and a basket of **unleavened bread**, 3. and **gather the whole congregation** together at the entrance of the Tent of Meeting."*

Leviticus 8:4. *And Moses did as the LORD* commanded him and the assembly was gathered together at the entrance of the Tent of Meeting. 5. And Moses said to the congregation, "This is the thing that the LORD* commanded to be done."*

Leviticus 8:6. *And Moses brought Aaron and his sons and immersed them in water. 7. And he **put the tunic on him and put the belt around him and clothed him with the robe and put the ephod on him and put the belt of the ephod on him, and fastened it. 8. And he put the breastplate on him, then he put the Urim and the Tummim in the breastplate. 9. And he put the turban on his head and upon the turban, over his forehead he put the gold plate, the holy crown,** as the LORD* commanded Moses. 10. And Moses took the anointing oil and anointed the Tabernacle and all that was in it, and sanctified them. 11. And he sprinkled it upon the altar seven times and anointed the altar and all its vessels, both the laver and its foot, to sanctify them. 12. And he poured the anointing oil upon Aaron's head and anointed him, to sanctify him.***

Leviticus 8:13. *And Moses brought **Aaron's sons, put tunics on them, belts on them, turbans on them**, as the LORD* commanded Moses. 14. And he brought the **bull for the sin offering**, and **Aaron and his sons laid their hands on the head of the bull for the sin offering**. 15. And he slew it and Moses took the blood and put it upon the horns of the altar round about with his finger and purified the altar, and poured the blood at the bottom of the altar and sanctified it to make atonement upon it. 16. And he took all the fat on the innards, the lobe above the liver, the two kidneys and their fat and Moses burned it on the altar. 17. But the bull and its hide, its flesh, and its dung, he burned with fire outside the camp, as the LORD* commanded Moses.*

Leviticus 8:18. *And he brought the **ram for the burnt offering** and **Aaron and his sons laid their hands on the head of the ram**. 19. And he killed it and Moses sprinkled the blood all around on the altar. 20. And he cut the ram into pieces and Moses burned the head and the pieces and the fat. 21. And he washed the innards and the legs in water and **Moses burned the whole ram on the altar: a burnt offering for a sweet savor, an offering made by fire to the LORD***, as the LORD* commanded Moses. 22. And he brought the **second ram, the ram of consecration and Aaron and his sons laid their hands upon the head of the ram**. 23. And he slew it and Moses took its blood and put it upon the **tip of Aaron's right ear, upon the thumb of his right hand, and upon the big toe of his right foot**. 24. And he brought **Aaron's sons, and Moses put some of the blood on the tip of their right ear, upon the thumbs of their right hands, and upon the big toes of their right feet**, and Moses sprinkled the blood upon the altar round about. 25. And he took the fat, the rump, all the fat on the innards, the lobe above the liver, the two kidneys and their fat, and the right shoulder, 26. and from the basket of unleavened bread that was before the LORD*, he took **one unleavened cake, a cake of oiled bread, and one wafer, and put them on the fat and upon the right shoulder. 27. And he put all upon the palms of Aaron's hands and upon the palms of his sons' hands, and waved them, a wave offering before the LORD*. 28. And Moses took them from off their hands and burned them on the altar upon the burnt offering. They were consecrations for a sweet savor, an offering made by fire to the LORD***. 29. And Moses took the breast and waved it for a wave offering before the LORD*, for it was Moses' share of the ram of consecration, as the LORD* commanded Moses. 30. And **Moses took of the anointing oil and of the blood which was upon the altar, and sprinkled it on Aaron, upon his garments, upon his sons, and upon his sons' garments with him, and sanctified Aaron, his garments, his sons, and his sons' garments with him**.*

The blood on their ears represents **listening** to the LORD*. The blood on the thumb and the big toe represent **service to mankind**.

Seven Day Process of Sanctification
Leviticus 8:31. *And Moses said to Aaron and to his sons, "You must boil the meat at the entrance of the Tent of Meeting, and you must eat it there with the bread that is in the basket of consecrations, as I commanded," saying Aaron and his sons will eat it. 32. "And that which remains of the flesh and of the bread you will burn with fire. 33. And **you will not go out of the entrance of the Tent of Meeting in seven days, until the days of your Consecration (Ordination)***

are at an end: He will Consecrate (Ordain) you for seven days. 34. As He has done this day, so the LORD* has commanded to do, **to make atonement for you. 35. Therefore you will stay at the entrance of the Tabernacle of the Congregation day and night seven days and keep the charge of the LORD* so you won't die: for so I have been commanded." 36.** *So Aaron and his sons did all the things which the LORD* commanded by the hand of Moses.*

The LORD* to Appear
Leviticus 9:1. *And it happened on the* **eighth** *day that Moses called Aaron and his sons and the elders of Israel. 2. And he said to Aaron, "Take for yourself a* ***young calf for a sin offering and a ram without blemish for a burnt offering and offer them before the LORD*. 3.*** *And to the children of Israel you will speak saying, Take for yourselves a* **he goat for a sin offering and a calf and a lamb, both of the first year, without blemish, for a burnt offering, 4. also a bull and a ram for peace offerings, to sacrifice before the LORD* and a grain offering mixed with oil, for today the LORD* will appear to you."**

Leviticus 9:5. *And they took what Moses commanded before the Tent of Meeting (Tabernacle) and the whole congregation drew near and stood before the LORD*. 6. And Moses said, "This is the thing that the LORD* commanded that you should do and the* **Glory of the LORD* will appear to you."**

Leviticus 9:7. *And Moses said to Aaron, "Go to the altar and* **offer your sin offering and your burnt offering, and make atonement for yourself and for the people: and offer the offering of the people and make atonement for them, as the LORD* commanded." 8.** *Aaron therefore went to the altar and slew the calf of the sin offering, which was for himself. 9. And the sons of Aaron brought the blood to him and he dipped his finger in the blood, and put it on the horns of the altar, and poured out the blood at the bottom of the altar, 10. but the fat, the kidneys, and the lobe above the liver of the sin offering, he burned upon the altar, as the LORD* commanded Moses. 11. And the flesh and the hide he burned with fire outside the camp. 12. And he slew the burnt offering and Aaron's sons presented the blood to him, which he sprinkled all around on the altar. 13. And they presented the burnt offering to him, with the pieces of it and the head, and he burned them on the altar. 14. And he washed the innards and the legs and burned them on the burnt offering on the altar.*

The LORD's* Appearance
Leviticus 9:23. *And **Moses and Aaron came in the Tent of Meeting, then went out and blessed the people, and the Glory of the LORD* appeared to all the people. 24. And a fire came out from before the LORD* and consumed the burnt offering and the fat on the altar and all the people saw it, and they shouted and fell on their faces.***

This elaborate process, taking seven days, was well worth the time and the expense. Those animals and all that time were expensive, especially all the repentance by Aaron, his sons and all the people. Repentance is what wins forgiveness. Repentance cannot be emphasized enough for us today. Instead of the blood of the bulls, the rams and the other animals offered we have the one offering of Y'shua's blood, which is still being poured out for us today, but **without repentance there is not forgiveness**.

Many of us today would love to see the **Glory of the LORD*** come like it did in these verses and in the others that are named in **Fire and Glory** in the Glossary of the *One New Man Bible*—but who is willing to pay the price and waiting and **Repenting** at the Tabernacle until the eighth day for **His Glory** to come? All Israel had gathered at the Tabernacle. How can that be done today?

Seasons of the LORD*: The seasons, literally appointed times, described in the Glossary are the Scriptural seasons that Y'shua, and all the New Testament authors, celebrated. The Fall Season is based on **Repentance**. There is not one word in the New Testament suggesting the Church should stop honoring these holy days. The Church started drifting away from its Jewish Roots in the second century. Then in the fourth century at the Council of Nicea, the Church made those changes official, confirming Easter instead of Passover. Easter was the celebration of the fertility goddess Ishtar in Syria and Babylon. Christmas substituted for the Roman winter solstice celebration of the Roman god Saturn. These times of the Lord—Seasons—are listed in Leviticus 23, with the first being the Sabbath. (See Hebraic Thinking in Jewish Roots. See Seasons of the LORD* in Glossary.)

Sin in Our Lives is significant and each person needs to deal with sin. Matthew 4:17. *From then on Y'shua began to preach and to say, "You must continuously repent: for the Kingdom of the Heavens has come near."*

The tense used in the Greek tells us to walk in repentance every day, even though we know we have been sanctified and made righteous by the Blood of the Lamb. This is because we have not been perfected, but are to strive to be better today than we were yesterday as we become more like Him. Why did Y'shua say to continuously repent? Few of us acknowledge there is **Sin** in our lives. Think about the following verses written by Paul:

Romans 1:28. *And since they did not see fit to have true knowledge of God, God gave them over into an unrighteous mind, to do the shameful things, 29. since they were filled with every unrighteousness, wickedness, avarice, desire to injure, full of envy, murder, contention, deceit, evil habits, whisperers, 30. slanderers, God-haters, insolent, arrogant, braggart, contriving evil, refusing to obey parents, 31. without understanding, covenant breaking, without natural affection, without mercy: 32. who, although they know the ordinances of God thoroughly, because they are practicing such things as these that are worthy of death, not only are they doing them but they are also applauding others who do them.*

Ephesians 5:1. *Therefore you must continually be imitators of God as beloved children 2. and you must walk constantly in love, just as also the Messiah loved us and gave Himself over on our behalf, an offering and a sacrifice to God for a fragrant aroma. 3. But any immorality or impurity or covetousness must not be named among you, as is fitting for saints, 4. nor foul speaking or foolish talking or low jesting, which things do not belong, but rather thanksgiving. 5. For you know this very well, that anyone who practices immorality or uncleanness or covetousness, who is an idol worshipper, does not have any inheritance in the kingdom of the Messiah and God.*

Idol Worshipper refers specifically to covetousness.

Covetousness is twice referred to as idol worship and is a very, very major sin in today's Church, from the pew sitter who wants to match someone else's fashion, or car, or house, or TV, or whatever to the pastor who wants bragging rights to the best attendance at the next meeting of local pastors; all are guilty of the sin of covetousness.

How many of all those things do we do subconsciously as we go about our daily routines? We pretty well control the really heavy things, like immorality, or do we? If a man looks at a woman with lust, which is the same as committing the deed, he is guilty. Matthew 5:27. *You heard that it was said, 'You will not commit adultery.'* (Exodus 20:13) 28. *But I am saying to you that everyone who looks at a woman with desire for her has already committed adultery with her in his heart.* This was a common teaching in Y'shua's day, that looking at a woman with desire in your heart equaled adultery. Then look over a long list of things we think, say, and do because "immorality" includes a broad range of sins. Paul addressed this in 2 Corinthians 10:3. *For though we walk in the flesh we are not serving as soldiers according to the flesh, 4. for the weapons of our warfare are not fleshly but powerful in God for the tearing down of strong-holds, tearing down reasonings 5. even every high thing being lifted up against the knowledge of God, and taking captive every thought in obedience to Messiah, 6. and being ready to punish every disobedience, when your obedience would be achieved.*

Jeremiah 6:19. *Listen, O earth! Behold, **I AM** will bring evil upon this people, <u>the fruit of their thoughts</u>, because they have not heeded My words or My Torah (Teaching), but rejected it.* (See Psalm 19:15.)

It is not just thoughts that get us into trouble, but our tongues do too. Jacob 3:2. *For we all stumble in many things. If someone does not stumble in the act of speaking, this is a perfect man, able to bridle his whole body. 3. And if we put bridles in the mouths of horses for them to obey us, we also guide their whole body. 4. And look at the ships, which are so large and are driven by a strong wind, they are guided by a very small rudder, where the helmsman wishes, 5. in the same way the tongue is also a little member and boasts great things.* (Psalm 39:2)

Sin progresses from thought to word to deed, but these stages are equal. To think of murdering someone equals murder to our heavenly Father. To speak any evil equates to doing it.

Think about the things on this list:
Course jesting
Evil, immoral thoughts
Vengeful thoughts
Cursing, placing curses
Leading, causing someone to sin. Matthew 18:7
Anger
Cheating
Drugs
Speeding

Gossip
Slander
Rude manners, in traffic or in a crowd
Accepting mistakes in our favor, i.e. if given too much change

(Read Chapters 18, 19, and 20 in Leviticus for even more.)

This list, supplementing the lists in Romans 1 and Colossians 3, gives you some idea that you are less than perfect—which is because each of us is less than perfect. So far only One Perfect Person has walked the Earth. The rest of us need to follow the example of our Jewish Apostolic forefathers and use the month of Elul to repent, in preparation for the Day of Memorial and Yom Kippur.

PATRIARCHS, MOSES, JUDGES, AND KINGS

Patriarchs, Moses, Judges, and Kings are the normal people who populate our Bible. Not one of them was perfect, with each one showing very human traits. False gods are superhuman, but our God uses anointed humans with common failings.

Abraham is introduced to us in Genesis 11:31. *And Terah took Abram his son and Lot the son of Haran, his son's son, and Sarai his daughter-in-law, his son Abram's wife, and they left with them from Ur of the Chaldees to go to the land of Canaan, and they came to Haran and lived there.*

Genesis 11:32. *And the days of Terah were two hundred five years, and Terah died in Haran.*

Lekh-L'kha
Genesis 12:1. *Now the LORD* had said to Abram, "**Get yourself out of here!** From your country and from your kindred and from your father's house to a land that I shall show you. 2. And I shall make a great nation of you, and I shall bless you and make your name great and you will be a blessing. 3. And I shall bless those who bless you and curse the one who curses you: and in you will all families of the earth be blessed." (Numbers 24:9; Galatians 3:8) 4. So Abram departed, as the LORD* had spoken to him and Lot went with him, and Abram was seventy-five years old when he left Haran. 5. And Abram took Sarai his wife and Lot his brother's son and all their possessions that they had gathered, and the souls that they had made in Haran: and they left to go into the land of Canaan, and they came into the land of Canaan. (Hebrews 11:8) 6. And Abram passed through the land to the place of Shechem, to the oak of Moreh. And the Canaanites were then in the land.*

He was content to stay in Haran after being sent to Canaan, but stopped in Haran.

Genesis 12:10. *Then there was a famine in the land and Abram went down into Egypt to sojourn there, for the famine was grievous in the land. 11. And it happened when he came near to enter Egypt that he said to Sarai his wife, "Behold now, I know that you are a beautiful woman to look upon. 12. Therefore it will be, when the Egyptians will see you that they will say, 'This is his wife.' And they will kill me, but they will save you alive. 13. Say, I pray you, that you are my sister so it may be well with me for your sake and my soul will live because of you.*

Genesis 12:14. *And it was that when Abram had come into Egypt, the Egyptians beheld the woman that she was very beautiful. 15. The princes of Pharaoh also saw her, and commended her before Pharaoh and the woman was taken into Pharaoh's house. 16. And he treated Abram well for her sake and he had sheep, oxen, he-donkeys, men servants, maid servants, she-donkeys, and camels. 17. And the LORD* plagued Pharaoh and his house with great plagues because of Sarai Abram's wife. 18. And Pharaoh called Abram and said, "What is this that you have done to me? Why did you not tell me that she was your wife? 19. Why did you say, 'She is my sister?' so that I took her to be my wife. Now therefore behold your wife, take her and go your way." 20. And Pharaoh commanded his men concerning him. And they sent him away, and his wife, and all that he had.*

Abraham has a failing of faith at this time as he claims the sister arrangement and ignores the fact that Sarai is his wife.

Genesis 16:1. *Now Sarai, Abram's wife, bore him no children, but she had a handmaid, an Egyptian, whose name was Hagar. 2. And Sarai said to Abram "Look now, the LORD* has restrained me from bearing. Please, go in to my maid. It may be that I may obtain children by her." And Abram heeded the voice of Sarai.*

This is another lack of faith, which Abraham repeats in Genesis 20:2. **Isaac** also uses the sister ploy in Genesis 26:7.

Jacob erred by showing strong favoritism to Joseph:

Genesis 37:1. *And Jacob settled in the land of his father's sojourning, in the land of Canaan. 2. These are the descendants of Jacob. Joseph, seventeen years old, was* *tending the flock with his brothers and he was a lad with the sons of Bilhah and with the sons of Zilpah, his father's wives. Joseph brought to their father very evil reports about them. 3. Now **Israel loved Joseph more than all his children**, because he was the son of his old age and **he made him a long tunic**. 4. And when his brothers saw that their father loved him more than all his brothers, they hated him and could not speak peaceably to him.*

Jacob encouraged Joseph's slandering of his brothers, then compounded that by making the long tunic for him. The long tunic was a sign of rank, making Joseph, the second youngest, to outrank the ten older brothers.

Moses, who was part of so many miracles in Egypt and the wilderness, was guilty of disobedience late in the game.

Numbers 20:6. *Then Moses and Aaron went from the presence of the assembly to the entrance of the Tent of Meeting, and they fell upon their faces and the glory of the LORD* appeared to them. 7. And the LORD* spoke to Moses saying, 8. "Take the staff and gather the assembly together, you and Aaron your brother, and <u>speak to the rock</u> before their eyes and it will give forth its water and you will bring water out of the rock to them: so you will give the congregation and their beasts drink." 9. Then Moses took the staff from before the LORD*, as He commanded him. 10. And Moses and Aaron gathered the congregation together before the rock and he said to them, "Listen now, you rebels! Must we fetch you water out of this rock?" 11. And Moses lifted up his hand and with his staff he <u>struck the rock twice</u>, and the water came out abundantly, and the congregation and also their beasts drank. 12. And the LORD* spoke to Moses and Aaron, **"Because you did not believe Me, to sanctify Me in the eyes of the children of Israel, therefore you will not bring this congregation into the land which I have given them."** 13. This is the water of Meribah, because the children of Israel strove with the LORD*, and He was sanctified among them.*

Moses, who did so many things right, was punished for his disobedience here. That should make all of us aware that we have no reason to be presumptuous about our relationship with God. Keeping Moses from entering the Promised Land was extraordinary punishment for that one infraction when Moses was so frustrated with his people. (See Va'e<u>th</u>anan in Jewish Roots.)

Joshua was anointed to lead Israel into the Promised Land:

Deuteronomy 34:9. *And Joshua the son of Nun was full of the spirit of wisdom, for Moses had laid his hands upon him. And the children of Israel hearkened to him and did as the LORD* commanded Moses.*

Joshua's biggest mistakes seem to have been when he thought for himself instead of praying to find out God's plan. That sounds like us, does it not?

Joshua 7:1. *But the children of Israel dealt treacherously regarding the accursed thing, for Achan, the son of Carmi, the son of Zabdi, the son of Zerach of the tribe of Judah, took some of the accursed thing and the anger of the LORD* was kindled against the children of Israel. 2. And **Joshua sent men from Jericho to Ai, which is beside Beit-Aven, on the east side of Beit-El, and spoke to them saying, Go up and view the country. And the men went up and viewed Ai** 3. And they returned to Joshua and said to him, **Do not have the whole army go up!** But let about two or three thousand men go up and strike Ai, and do not make all the people labor there for they are few. 4. So about three thousand men of the people went up there and they fled before the men of Ai. 5. And the men of Ai struck about thirty-six men of them, for they chased them from in front of the gate to the quarries and struck them at the descent, then the hearts of the people melted and became like water.*

Joshua sent the men to spy out Ai, then thought *We can do this.* Joshua did not even think about praying, so God gave the day to Ai. Another action without prayer. (See "Seven Cycles in the Book of Judges" under Teachings.)

Samuel had problems because of his undisciplined sons, a common trait in many families.

1 Samuel 8:1. *And it was, when Samuel was old, that **he made his sons judges over Israel.** 2. Now the name of his firstborn was Joel, and the name of his second, Abijah. They were judges in Beer Sheba. 3. But his sons did not walk in his Ways, but turned aside after unjust gain and took bribes and perverted justice 4. Then **all the elders of Israel gathered themselves together and came to Samuel at Ramah 5. and said to him, Behold, you are old and your sons are not walking in your ways.** Now set a king for us to judge us like all the nations. 6. But the thing displeased Samuel when they said, Give us a king to judge us. And Samuel prayed to the LORD*. 7. And the LORD* said to Samuel, listen to the voice of the people in all that they say to you, for they have not rejected you, but they have rejected Me, that I should not reign over them.*

Step **1** was to promote his sons who were not walking with the Lord.

Step **2** was the elders asking for a king in place of Samuel.

Step **3** was God saying, "They have not rejected you, but they have rejected Me." So the sinning of Samuel's sons caused the people to reject the LORD! That brought in a king who made things worse by his disobedience with the Amalekites.

Saul, by his disobedience, led the people of Israel to come close to total destruction hundreds of years later.

1 Samuel 15:1. *Samuel also said to Saul, the LORD* sent me to anoint you king over His people, over Israel. Now therefore listen to the voice of the words of the LORD*. 2. Thus says the LORD* of Hosts, I remember what Amalek did to Israel, how he laid wait for him on the road, when he came up from Egypt. 3.* ***Now go and strike Amalek and utterly destroy all that they have, and do not spare them, but slay both man and woman, infant and suckling, ox and sheep, camel and donkey.*** *4. And Saul gathered the people together and counted them in Telaim, two hundred thousand foot soldiers, and ten thousand men of Judah. 5. And Saul came to a city of Amalek and laid wait in the valley. 6. And Saul said to the Kenites, Go! Leave! Go down from among the Amalekites! Lest I destroy you with them for you showed loving kindness to all the children of Israel, when they came up out of Egypt. So the Kenites departed from among the Amalekites. 7. And Saul struck the Amalekites from Havilah until you come to Shur, which is over against Egypt. 8. And he took* **Agag** *the king of the Amalekites alive, and utterly destroyed all the people with the edge of the sword. 9. But Saul and the people spared* ***Agag, the best of the sheep, of the oxen, of the fatlings, the lambs, and all that was good and would not utterly destroy them, but everything that was vile and refuse, that they destroyed utterly.***

The LORD* Regrets Making Saul King

1 Samuel 15:10. *Then the word of the LORD* came to Samuel saying, 11. I regret that I have set up Saul to be king, for* **he has turned back from following Me and has not performed My commandments.** *And it grieved Samuel and he cried to the LORD* all night. 12. And when Samuel rose early to meet Saul in the morning, Samuel was told saying, Saul came to Carmel and, behold, he set himself up a place and has gone about and passed on and gone down to Gilgal. 13. And Samuel came to Saul and Saul said to him, Blessed be you of the LORD*! I have performed the commandment of the LORD*. 14. And Samuel said,* **What then is this bleating of the sheep in my ears and the lowing of the oxen**

which I am hearing? 15. *And Saul said, They have brought them from the Ama*
lekites, for the people spared the best of the sheep and of the oxen, to sacrifice to th
LORD* your God and the rest we have utterly destroyed. 16. Then Samuel said t
Saul, Stay! I shall tell you what the LORD* has said to me this night.

And he said to him, Say on.

1 Samuel 15:17. *And Samuel said, When you were little in your own sight wer*
you not made the head of the tribes of Israel, and the LORD* anointed you kin
over Israel?! 18. And the LORD* sent you on a journey and said, Go and ut
terly destroy the sinners, the Amalekites, and fight against them until they ar
consumed. 19. Why then did you not obey the voice of the LORD*, but did hurr
upon the loot and did bad things in the eyes of the LORD*? 20. And Saul sai
to Samuel, Yes, I have obeyed the voice of the LORD*, and have gone the wa
which the LORD sent me and have brought **Agag** the king of Amalek and hav*
utterly destroyed the Amalekites. 21. But the people took sheep and oxen of th
loot, the chief of the things which should have been utterly destroyed, to sacrifice t
the LORD* your God in Gilgal. 22. And Samuel said, Has the LORD* as grea
delight in burnt offerings and sacrifices as in obeying the voice of the LORD*
Behold, to obey is better than sacrifice, to listen is better than the fat of rams. 23
For rebellion is like the sin of witchcraft, and stubbornness is like idolatry an
*image worship. **Because you have rejected the word of the LORD*, He ha***
***also rejected you from being king.** 24. And Saul said to Samuel, I have sinned*
for I have transgressed the commandment of the LORD* and your words, becaus
I was awed by the people and obeyed their voice. 25. Now therefore, I pray you
pardon my sin and turn again with me so I can worship the LORD*.

Saul's disobedience led to the near disaster told in the Book of Esther, with
Haman, the descendant of Agag, making the way to annihilate all of Israel.

Esther 3:1. *After these things king Ahasuerus promoted Haman the son o*
Hammedatha the Agagite and advanced him, and set his seat above all the prince
who were with him.

Due to Saul's disobedience at least one of Agag's sons escaped to have a descendant nearly bring such a horrible tragedy for Israel.

David brought problems to Israel by his disobedience, his desire for pleasure
coupled with his sons' lack of discipline.

2 Samuel 11:1. *And it happened at the return of the year, at the time when kings go forth to battle, that David sent Joab and his servants with him, and all Israel. And they destroyed the children of Ammon and besieged Rabah. But David still stayed in Jerusalem. 2. And it was at evening that David got up from his bed and walked on the roof of the king's house, and from the roof he saw a woman immersing herself. And the woman was very beautiful to look at. 3. And David sent and inquired after the woman. And someone said, Is this not Bathsheba, the daughter of Eliam, the wife of Uriah the Hittite? 4. And David sent messengers and took her and she came in to him, and he lay with her. She was purified from her uncleanness. Then she returned to her house. 5. And the woman conceived and sent and told David and said, I am with child.*

David then compounds his adultery with murder!

2 Samuel 11:6. *And David sent to Joab saying, Send me Uriah the Hittite. And Joab sent Uriah to David. 7. And when Uriah had come to him, David asked of him how Joab did and how the people did and how the war prospered. 8. And David said to Uriah, Go down to your house and wash your feet. And Uriah left the king's house and a present from the king followed him. 9. But Uriah slept at the entrance of the king's house with all the servants of his lord, and did not go down to his house. 10. And when they had told David, saying, Uriah did not go down to his house, David said to Uriah, Haven't you come from your journey? Why did you not go down to your house? 11. And Uriah said to David, The Ark and Israel and Judah are living in tents, and my lord Joab and the servants of my lord are camped in the open fields. Will I then go into my house, to eat and to drink and to lie with my wife? As you live and as your very being lives, I shall not do this thing. 12. And David said to Uriah, Wait here today also and the next day I shall let you leave. So Uriah stayed in Jerusalem that day and the next day. 13. And when David had called him, he ate and drank with him and he made him drink and at evening he went out to lie on his bed with the servants of his lord, but did not go down to his house. 14. And it was in the morning that David wrote a letter to Joab and sent it by the hand of Uriah. 15. And he wrote in the letter saying, Set Uriah in the forefront of the hottest battle and retire from him, so he will be smitten and die. 16. And it happened when Joab observed the city that he assigned Uriah to a place where he knew that valiant men were. 17. And the men of the city went out and fought with Joab and some of the people of the servants of David fell and Uriah the Hittite died also.*

What did the Lord think about all this?

2 Samuel 11:26. *And when the wife of Uriah heard that Uriah her husband wa*
dead, she mourned for her husband. 27. And when the mourning was past, Davi
sent and brought her to his house and she became his wife and bore him a son. ***Bu***
the thing that David had done displeased the LORD*.

There were more problems, caused by David's lack of caring for his sons
detailed in 2 Samuel13:7–14, when his son Amnon raped David's daughter
Tamar. Later in 2 Samuel 15:7, Absalom led a rebellion against David, then
in 1 Kings 2:17–25 Adonijah led another attempt to usurp the throne o
Israel.

Solomon had lapses because of greed and lust. He just had to have more
horses and more wives. Kings were not to multiply horses:

Deuteronomy 17:14. *"When you have come to the land which the LORD* you*
God is giving to you and possess it and live there and say, ***'I shall set a king over***
me, like all the nations that are around me,' *15. and you in any way set*
king over you, whom the LORD* your God will choose from among your brother
you will set a king over you. You may not set a stranger over you, who is not you
brother. 16. ***#1. But he will not multiply horses for himself,*** *#2. nor caus*
the people to return to Egypt, to the end that he should multiply horses since th
LORD* has said to you, You will from here on not return that way. 17. ***#3. Nei***
ther will he multiply wives to himself, so his heart will not turn away, *#4*
nor will he greatly multiply silver and gold for himself. 18. And it will be when
he sits on the throne of his kingdom that #5. he will write for himself a copy o
this Torah in a scroll out of that which is before the priests, the Levites. 19. And i
will be with him and he will read from it all the days of his life, so he can learn to
revere the LORD* his God, to keep all the words of this Torah and these statutes
to do them 20. so his heart will not be lifted up above his brothers and so he doe
not turn aside from the commandment to the right hand, or to the left: to the end
that he may prolong his days in his kingdom, he and his children, in the midst o
Israel."

Solomon multiplied horses, but it was his many wives that really got Solomon
into idolatry.

1 Kings 11:7. *Then* ***Solomon built a high place for Chemosh, the abomi-***
nation of Moab on the hill that is before Jerusalem and for Molekh, the
abomination of the children of Ammon. 8. And he did likewise for all his

foreign wives, who burned incense and sacrificed to their gods. 9. And the **LORD* was angry with Solomon, because his heart was turned from the LORD* God of Israel, Who had appeared to him twice 10. and had commanded him concerning this thing, that he should not go after other gods, but he did not keep that which the LORD* commanded.** *11. Therefore the LORD* said to Solomon, Since you have done this and you have not kept My covenant and My statutes, which I have commanded you,* **I shall surely tear the kingdom from you and will give it to your servant.** *12. Only in your days I shall not do it for David your father's sake, I shall tear it out of the hand of your son. 13. However, I shall not tear away the whole kingdom, but will give one tribe to your son for David My servant's sake, and for the sake of Jerusalem which I have chosen.*

Solomon got off to a good start and had much going for him, but took his eye and his heart off the LORD and went after the pleasures of life.

Rehoboam started right away to consult the elders, but rejected their counsel to go along with his childhood friends.

1 Kings 12:6. And king Rehoboam **consulted with the elders** *who stood before Solomon his father while he was still alive and said, How do you advise me to go back to answer this people? 7. And they spoke to him saying, If you will be a servant to this people this day and will serve them and answer them and speak good words to them, then they will be your servants forever. 8. But he forsook the counsel of the old men, which they had given him and consulted with the young men who had grown up with him, who stood before him. 9. And he said to them, What counsel do you give that we go back to this people, who have spoken to me saying, Make your father's yoke lighter which he put on us? 10. And the young men who had grown up with him spoke to him saying,* **Thus will you speak to this people who spoke to you saying, Your father made our yoke heavy, but you should make it lighter for us. You will say this to them, My little finger will be thicker than my father's loins. 11. And now whereas my father put a heavy yoke on you, I shall add to your yoke. My father has chastised you with whips, but I shall chastise you with scorpions.** *12. So Jeroboam and all the people came to Rehoboam the third day as the king had appointed, when he said, Come to me again the third day. 13. And the king answered the people roughly and forsook the old men's counsel that they gave him 14. and spoke to them after the counsel of the young men saying, My father made your yoke heavy and I shall add to your yoke. My father chastised you with whips, but I shall chas-*

tise you with scorpions. 15. Therefore the king did not listen to the people, for the cause was from the LORD*, so He could perform His saying, which the LORD spoke by Ahijah the Shilonite to Jeroboam the son of Nebat.

Rehoboam's big mistake was not consulting God first, but never called for the Urim and Tummim. The elders gave good advice, but Rehoboam rejected that and gave the arrogant answer suggested by his childhood friends, who should have known better, since they were forty years old when Rehoboam became king.

Asa was off to a good start:

1 Kings 15:11. *And **Asa did that which was right in the eyes of the LORD** like David his father. 12. And he took away the prostitutes, both male and female from the land and removed all the idols that his fathers had made. 13. And also Maacah his mother, he even removed her from being queen because she had made an idol in a grove, and Asa destroyed and burned her idol by the brook Kidron. 14. But the high places were not removed. Nevertheless Asa's heart was faithful with the LORD* all his days. 15. And he brought in the things which his father had dedicated and the things which he himself had dedicated into the House of the LORD*, silver, gold, and vessels.*

Asa drifted in faith, relying on the knowledge of men rather than the counsel of the LORD.

2 Chronicles 16:7. *And at that time **Hanani the seer** came to **Asa king of Judah** and said to him, **Because you have relied on the king of Syria and not relied on the LORD*** your God, therefore the army of the king of Syria has escaped out of your hand. 8. **Were not the Ethiopians and the Lubim a huge army, with very many chariots and horsemen?! Yet, because you relied on the LORD*, He delivered them into your hand.** 9. For the eyes of the LORD run to and fro throughout the whole earth, to show Himself strong on behalf of those who look toward Him with their whole heart. Here you have done foolishly therefore from now on you will have wars. 10. Then Asa was angry with the seer and put him in a prison house, for he was in a rage with him because of this. And Asa oppressed some of the people at the same time. 11. And, behold, the acts of Asa, first and last, lo, they are written in the book of the Kings of Judah and Israel. 12. And **Asa in the thirty-ninth year of his reign was diseased in his feet, until his disease was exceeding great, yet in his disease he did not seek the***

LORD*, but the physicians. 13. And Asa slept with his fathers, and died in the forty-first year of his reign. 14. And they buried him in his own sepulcher, which he had made for himself in the city of David and laid him in the bed, which was filled with sweet odors and different kinds of spices prepared by the perfumers' art and they made a very great burning for him.

Asa blew his good start by not seeking the LORD in different crises. He was like many strong Christians today, often thinking when they should be praying and seeking the LORD's counsel.

Jehoshaphat made the same mistakes his father Asa had made. When he did consult the LORD he had amazing success.

1 Kings 17:1. *And **Jehoshaphat** his son reigned in his stead and strengthened himself against Israel. 2. And he placed forces in all the fortified cities of Judah and set garrisons in the land of Judah and in the cities of Ephraim, which Asa his father had taken. 3. And **the LORD* was with Jehoshaphat, because he walked in the first Ways of his father David and did not seek baalim, 4. but sought the God of his father and walked in His commandments, and not after the doings of Israel.** 5. Therefore the LORD* established the kingdom in his hand and all Judah brought presents to Jehoshaphat and he had riches and honor in abundance. 6. And his heart was lifted up in the Ways of the LORD*. Moreover he took away the high places and groves out of Judah.*

Off to a great start, Jehoshaphat's human nature led him astray.

1 Kings 18:1. *Now **Jehoshaphat had riches and honor in abundance and joined affinity with Ahab.** 2. And after certain years he went down to Ahab in Samaria. And Ahab killed sheep and oxen in abundance for him and for the people with him, and persuaded him to go up with him to Ramoth-Gilead. 3. And **Ahab king of Israel said to Jehoshaphat king of Judah, Will you go with me to Ramoth-Gilead? And he answered him, I am as you are and my people as your people, and we will be with you in the war.***

After this Jehoshaphat again calls on the LORD.

1 Kings 20:1. *It happened after this also, that the children of Moab and the children of Ammon and with them others besides the Ammonites came against **Jehoshaphat** to battle. 2. Then some came who told **Jehoshaphat** saying, A great*

multitude is coming against you from beyond the sea on this side of the Dead Sea and, behold, they are in Hazazon-Tamar, which is En-Gedi. 3. And **Jehoshaphat was awed and set himself to seek the LORD* and proclaimed a fast throughout all Judah.** *4. And Judah gathered themselves together, to ask help from the LORD*, and they came to seek the LORD* out of all the cities of Judah. 5. And* **Jehoshaphat** *stood in the congregation of Judah and Jerusalem, in the House of the LORD*, before the new court 6. and said, LORD*, God of our fathers, are You not God in the Heavens? And You rule over all the kingdoms of the nations? And in Your hand is power and might, so that no one is able to withstand You?! 7. Are You not our God, Who drove out the inhabitants of this land before Your people Israel and gave it forever to the seed of Abraham, who loves You?! 8. And they lived there and have built You a Sanctuary there for Your name, saying 9. If evil comes upon us, like the sword, judgment, or pestilence, or famine, we stand before this House and in Your presence, for Your name is in this House, and cry to You in our affliction, then You will hear and help. 10. And now, behold the children of Ammon and Moab and Mount Seir, whom You would not let Israel invade when they came out of the land of Egypt, but they turned from them and did not destroy them. 11. See, I say, how they reward us, to come to cast us out of Your possession, which You have given us to inherit. 12. O our God, will You not judge them? For we have no power against this great company that comes against us; neither do we know what to do, but our eyes are upon You. 13. And all Judah stood before the LORD*, with their little ones, their wives and their children. 14. Then the Spirit of the LORD* came upon Jahaziel the son of Jeiel, the son of Mattaniah, a Levite of the sons of Asaf, in the midst of the congregation. 15. And he said, Listen, all Judah, and you inhabitants of Jerusalem and you king Jehoshaphat, Thus says the LORD* to you,* **Do not be in awe! Do not be dismayed because of this great multitude!** *For the battle is not yours, but God's. 16. Tomorrow go down against them! Behold, they will come up by the hill of Ziz and you will find them at the end of the brook, before the wilderness of Jeruel. 17.* **You will not fight in this battle: set yourselves! Stand still and see the deliverance/salvation of the LORD* with you, O Judah and Jerusalem. Do not be in awe! Do not be dismayed!** *Tomorrow go out against them, for the LORD* will be with you.*

Fasting and prayer by a nation in unity brought amazing results!

1 Kings 20:24. *And when Judah came toward the watchtower in the wilderness, they looked at the multitude and, behold, there were dead bodies fallen to the earth and no one escaped. 25. And when Jehoshaphat and his people came to take*

away their spoil, they found among them in abundance both riches with the dead bodies and precious jewels, which they stripped off for themselves, more than they could carry away. And they were three days in gathering the spoil, it was so much. 26. And on the fourth day they assembled themselves in the valley of Berachah, for there they blessed the LORD. Therefore the name of the same place was called, The Valley of Berachah, The Valley of Blessing, to this day. 27. Then they returned, every man of Judah and Jerusalem, and **Jehoshaphat** in the forefront of them, to go back to Jerusalem with joy, for the LORD* had made them to rejoice over their enemies. 28. And they came to Jerusalem with psalteries, harps, and trumpets to the House of the LORD*. 29. **And the fear of God was on all the kingdoms of those countries, when they had heard that the LORD* fought against the enemies of Israel.** 30. So the realm of Jehoshaphat was quiet, for his God gave him rest all around.*

Jehoshaphat ended on a very high note because of his leadership in bringing the people of Judah back to God.

Joash did very well while Jehoida mentored him, but back-slid after Jehoida died.

2 Kings 12:19. *And **Joash king of Judah took all the hallowed things that Jehoshaphat, Jehoram, and Ahaziah, his fathers, kings of Judah, had dedicated and his own hallowed things and all the gold that was found in the treasures of the House of the LORD* and in the king's house, and sent it to Hazael king of Syria, and he went away from Jerusalem.** 20. And the rest of the acts of **Joash** and all that he did, are they not written in the Book of the Chronicles of the Kings of Judah?*

Joash did not pray, just sent tribute to Hazael.

Josiah was the most godly king, but even he was not perfect.

2 Kings 23:29. *In his days Pharaoh Necho king of Egypt went up against the king of Assyria to the river Euphrates and king Josiah went against him and when he saw him he slew Josiah at Megiddo. (Revelation 16:16) 30. And his servants carried him dead from Megiddo in a chariot and brought him to Jerusalem and buried him in his own sepulcher. And the people of the land took Jehoahaz the son of Josiah and anointed him, and made him king in his father's stead.*

2 Chronicles includes the warning that Pharaoh Necho had sent to Josiah, but Josiah failed to heed the warning and even failed to pray about it, costing Josiah his life and cutting short a godly reign.

2 Chronicles 35:20. *After all this, when Josiah had prepared the Temple, Necho king of Egypt came up to fight against Charchemish by the Euphrates and Josiah went out against him. 21. But he sent ambassadors to him saying,* **What have I to do with you, king of Judah? I am not coming against you this day, but against the house with which I have war, for God commanded me to make haste. Refrain from meddling with God, Who is with me, so that He would not destroy you.** *22. Nevertheless Josiah would not turn his face from him, but disguised himself, so he could fight with him and did not heed the words of Necho from the mouth of God and came to fight in the valley of Megiddo. 23. And the archers shot at king Josiah, and the king said to his servants, Take me away, for I am severely wounded! 24. His servants therefore took him out of that chariot and put him in the second chariot that he had, and they brought him to Jerusalem and he died and was buried in one of the sepulchers of his fathers. And all Judah and Jerusalem mourned for Josiah.*

Each one of these men was godly, but made mistakes. Often the problem was thinking they could do something without asking God, with disastrous results. All of us have the same problem and each one of us does foolish things when thinking we can say to God, "It is all right, Lord. I can take it from here." Even though we do not utter those words, that is what is in our minds. When will we learn? When will I learn?

CONCLUSION

This task of bringing various teachings to light is one that will never end. The Bible is such a rich source that the Holy Spirit will always have more to say. No matter how long I live, this series will not be completed in my lifetime. Many others have similar assignments, and there is so much depth in Scripture that the sum of all such works will never be reached.

Enjoy these and seek more on your own, knowing that all the books in the world cannot contain all the knowledge of the Living God.

Jeremiah 9:22. *Thus says the LORD*,* **Do not let the wise man boast in his wisdom! Do not let the mighty man boast in his might! Do not let the rich man boast in his riches!** *23. But the one who boasts will boast in this, that he understands and knows Me, that I AM the LORD* Who exercises loving kindness, judgment, and acts of loving kindness in the earth, for in these things I delight, says the LORD*.*

BIBLE WEIGHTS AND MEASURES
These are approximate and can vary by era and location

Lengths

Finger	0.73 inches	1.85 cm	Jeremiah 52:21
Handbreadth	2.92 inches	7.4 cm	Exodus 25:25
Span	9 inches	22.86 cm	Exodus 28:16
Cubit	18 inches	45.72 cm	Matthew 6:27
Long Cubit	20.4 inches	51.9 cm	Ezekiel 40:5
Fathom	6 feet	1.829 meters	Acts 27:28
Reed (6 cubits)	8.75 feet	2.73 meters	Ezekiel 40:5
Furlong	1/8 mi.	201.2 meters	Revelation 14:20
Stadion	697 feet	185.4 meters	Luke 24:13
Sabbath Day's Journey	3/5 mile	0.9656 km	Acts 1:12
Day's Journey	20 miles	32.19 km	1 Kings 19:4

Weights

Gerah	1/50 ounce	0.567 grams	Ezekiel 45:12
Bekah (10 gerahs)	1/5 ounce	5.67 grams	Genesis 24:22
Pim (2/3 shekel)	1/3 ounce	9.45 grams	1 Samuel 13:21
Shekel (2 bekahs)	2/5 ounce	11.34 grams	Exodus 30:23
Mina (50 shekels)	1.25 pounds	0.567 kg.	Ezra 2:69
Talent	75 pounds	34.02 kg.	Ezra 8:26

Liquid Measures

Log	0.65 pints	0.31 liters	Leviticus 14:10
Kav (4 logs)	2.6 pints	1.2 liters	2 Kings 6:25
Hin (12 logs)	0.98 gallon	3.7 liters	Numbers 15:4
Bath (6 hins)	5.9 gallons	22 liters	Isaiah 5:10
Homer (10 baths)	59 gallons	220 liters	Ezekiel 45:11
Kor (10 baths)	59 gallons	220 liters	Ezekiel 45:11
Metretes	10 gallons	37.85 liters	John 2:6

Dry Measures

Kav	2.6 pints	1.2 liters	2 Kings 6:25
Omer	2.3 quarts	2.2 liters	Exodus 16:36
Seah	7.7 quarts	7.3 liters	2 Kings 7:1
Ephah	0.63 bushels	22 liters	Ruth 2:17
Lethech	3.16 bushels	110 liters	Hosea 3:2
Homer	6.33 bushels	220 liters	Leviticus 27:16
Kor	6.33 bushels	220 liters	Ezekiel 45:14

Money

Denarius	Day's wage	Matthew 20:2
Drachma		Luke 15:8
Didrachma		Matthew 17:24
Talent	Approx. 75 lb	Ezra 8:26

Time

Sunrise	6 AM	06:00	Mark 16:2
First hour	7 AM	07:00	
Second hour	8 AM	08:00	
Third hour	9 AM	09:00	Matthew 20:3
Fourth hour	10 AM	10:00	
Fifth hour	11 AM	11:00	
Sixth hour	Noon	12:00	Matthew 27:45
Seventh hour	1 PM	13:00	John 4:52
Eighth hour	2 PM	14:00	
Ninth hour	3 PM	15:00	Acts 3:1
Tenth hour	4 PM	16:00	John 1:39
Eleventh hour	5 PM	17:00	Matthew 20:6–9
Sunset	6 PM	18:00	Luke 4:40

HEBREW MONTHS
From Yashanet.com

Mo. #	Babylonian Calendar	Meaning of Babylonian Months	Theme of Month (Babylonian & Biblical)	Biblical Calendar	Meaning of Biblical Months (Harvesting Schedule)	Biblical Feasts
1	Nisan	Their flight	Redemption, Miracles	Aviv	Ripening of grain Barley	Passover, Unleavened Bread, First-fruits
2	Iyyar	(natural) healing	Introspection, Self improvement	Ziv	Splendor or Radiance [Flowers] (Barley harvest)	
3	Sivan	Bright - their covering	Giving of Torah	3rd	Wheat	Feast of Weeks (Pentecost)
4	Tammuz	Hidden - giver of the vine (A Phoenician deity)	Sin of the Golden Calf, guarding of the eyes	4th		
5	Av	Father	Av the Comforter	5th		
6	Elul	A vain thing - nothingness	Repentance	6th	(Fruit harvest)	
7	Tishri	Beginning (from reishit)	Month of the Strong or Month of the Ancients	Etanim	Ever-flowing streams	Rosh Hashanah, Yom Kippur, Succot
8	Kheshvan	Eighth	The Flood (of Noach)	Bul	Produce (in the sense of rain)	

9	Kislev	Security, trust	(Restful) Sleep	9th		
10	Tevet	Good (from "Tov")	Divine Grace	10th		
11	Shevat	meaning un-known	Tree of Life	11th		
12	Adar	Strength	Good For-tune	12th		
13	* Adar II					

Additional month added during Leap Years. About every 3rd year. There are 7 leap years in a 19 year cycle.

MAP OF UNITED KINGDOM
DAVID AND SOLOMON

INDEX

INDEX

INDEX

Made in the USA
San Bernardino, CA
24 April 2018